MW00564070

SHARING A TABLE

Knowing the Love of God in Community

CANDYCE ROBERTS

Sharing a Table
Knowing the Love of God in Community

Copyright ©2016 Candyce Roberts
ISBN **0997660317**

Published by Candyce Roberts
info@CandyceRoberts.com

Edited by Robert Averbeck
Rob1138@Gmail.com

Cover by Eric Hurtgen
EricHurtgen.com

Except as noted, all citations are from
The New American Standard Bible.

DEDICATION

This book is dedicated to Sarah Brooke Roberts Hart.
A life touched by the hands of evil,
A life returned to the hands of love.

Thank you to the loving people of our community.
I will be forever touched remembering your care for our family, affirming
the significance of living a shared life.

CONTENTS

INTRODUCTION

The need to belong is universal. Emotions stir when lonely people view photos of family meals or hear stories of intimate gatherings. Hearts respond to movies where the love of family is unshaken in the face of adversity or estranged families reunite after pain and trauma has divided them. If we are honest we all want a place where we fit and we want that place to be safe and unconditional in its invitation. Although there are many expressions of belonging, this book suggests spiritual community as the answer for a restless heart searching for meaning and purpose in life. A community of faith can be the place where lonely, isolated, marginalized people find acceptance and experience the love of Jesus.

It is impossible to define community apart from the climate of the present culture. The worldview of Millennials must be considered as we strive to create spiritual communities that bridge the gap between the generations. Young adulthood is the prime time to mature one's life with God or be introduced to Jesus for those who question the Christian faith. There are many ways to approach community but there are constant elements that are relevant to all who unite around a common conviction. Although social norms and habits of culture shift, when people share a Christian commonality hope is released when we feel loved.

It is a challenge to not compromise the standards of an authentic Christian community while still helping people feel loved for who they are and where they are in their journey. It is helpful that spiritual communities are not attached to a place or bound by geography. Jesus is the connector who links spiritual communities together, creating a unity that cannot be separated by time or space. For many years Christian traditionalists (and *their* ancestors) have paved the way for communities of faith, offering wisdom, experience, and establishing sustainable fellowships for succeeding generations.

We all have the same basic physical and psychological needs for safety, esteem, maturity, love and belonging. However, many Millennials approach belonging with a confidence that mimics entitlement. If we are committed to creating multi-generational, multi-cultural, inclusive communities that are pursuing the mission of the gospel, the Millenials' way of thinking must be considered. God and His creation are the value that can harmonize Christian believers, allowing us to overcome the temptation to divide based on age, race, gender, status and messages from our surrounding culture.

Spiritual communities are met with new challenges due to the social and philosophical views of the age. But life with God is available to all who say 'Yes' to Jesus, regardless of the effects of the postmodern mindset. Although choosing Jesus means saying no to other things, life with Jesus sets us in a family with others who also choose to live like Jesus. It provides a sense of belonging. I want to encourage God's people to simplify how we welcome into the church those who are confused by the spirit-of-the-age. I am convinced the best way to demonstrate the gospel is by inviting people into our lives and loving them as family because the gospel lifestyle is social as well as spiritual.

Community is the perfect context for exploring God. When spiritual people extend mercy to those who don't know God and are trying to make sense of the world there is opportunity to introduce them to Jesus. We have been conditioned to think that the most effective way to salvation is through condemnation of sin and intense preaching. Perhaps the better way to display Jesus and develop spiritual community is around a dinner table.

Sadly, Americans rarely sit down and eat meals together because hectic schedules warrant drive-through meals and smartphones are replacing eye contact and dialogue. Since meal times are no longer sacred, hospitality for the purpose of intentional conversation and community building can be a challenge. The writings of the Apostle Paul tell us serving God is best accomplished by serving others. Because watching lives that have been laid down for others reveals the Bible truth that holiness cannot be taught; it must be experienced through relationships. Those seeking spirituality should note the love of Jesus in the lives of spiritually mature people. Paul says it this way, "Now, those who are mature in their faith can easily be recognized for they don't live to please themselves, but have learned to patiently embrace others in their immaturity. Our goal must be to empower others to do what is right and good for them and to bring them into spiritual maturity. For not even the most powerful one of all, the Anointed One, lived to please himself." (The Passion Translation, Romans 15:1-3).

I want to suggest that we develop spiritual communities that focus on building loving relationships that bridge racial, gender, political, socio-economic barriers and teach people to find the love of God in the everyday practice of sharing a table. May we embrace the everyday practices in our lives as sacred and may we lift them to the Lord as an offering as we gather together in His name. A healthy spiritual community can serve as a source of life for the lonely and oppressed who need help and for those who are joyful and ready to celebrate life. The family of God is open to all.

CHAPTER ONE
June 14, 2012

It is unusual for my husband and me to actually spend our mutual Thursdays off together. The busyness of our lives often interrupts our desire for a date, even though it would be nice to put life on pause for at least a few hours.

However, I recognize that my husband's long hours in his chiropractic clinic leave him longing for the outdoors. When Ray comes home from the clinic each evening he magically transforms from starched shirt Ray Roberts: Wellness Doctor into Ray Roberts: Camo-Country Guy in less than five minutes. Then he heads out the back door to connect with the land, walk through the woods or fine-tune his hunting skills.

The reality of our life is that Ray must juggle the hours in his week to accommodate his career, the responsibilities of a spiritual father in our church community, the numerous agricultural needs of growing eight acres of grapes, as well as all the activities of our large family (which includes 13 grandchildren). So I must acknowledge when he dashes out the back door on a Thursday it isn't an attempt to escape my presence, it is usually the call of deprived grapes demanding his attention.

Thursday, June 14, 2012 began with a familiar dialogue concerning the length of our to-do lists and an end of the day goal for a meaningful conversation over a quiet dinner. Our schedules looked promising and I grabbed my computer and headed for my office and Ray jumped onto the tractor to spray our needy grapes. A hot, humid day when Ray has to spray grapes garners no sympathy from me because his tractor has an enclosed glass cabin with air-conditioning, a stereo system, a port for his iPhone, noise-cancelling headphones and a seat that swivels.

My husband couldn't have sprayed more than two rows of grapes, and I had barely cleared a spot on my cluttered desk to plug in my laptop, when he received a call from his brother announcing that our niece Sarah was missing.

"Missing?" I asked myself, "What does 'missing' mean for an adult woman who is one of the most responsible people I know? Sarah has been an independent, self-confident, overachiever since she was two years old." Sarah Hart (née Roberts) was a former high-school athlete in track, a college graduate, a University of Kentucky graduate with a doctorate degree in pharmacy, a leader of women and a loving wife.

I can relate to independent, overachieving women and the way they think. I am not an emotional thinker. I am logical. And I admit my logic is often a contradiction to grace. My husband frequently informs me that not all women think the way I do or function as independently as I do. And I can be guilty of assuming other people think the way I do and often expect them to behave like me. With Sarah, though, this was never an area of incongruity.

My brother-in-law's phone call kicked my logic into gear. My mind began creating a file of various explanations for Sarah's absence. But though my logic was in high gear, I was still also gripped with mixed emotions. My emotions were defeating my logic as I switched between tears-of-compassion and tears-of-fear that did not coordinate with my reasoning. Still, my husband and I assumed there was a rational explanation.

We changed our clothes, ran for the car and headed for the next town to be with our extended family. The short drive to Russell County felt like weeks as my husband and I exchanged different plausible explanations for Sarah's absence. I was convinced she got sick and perhaps passed-out. Ray added that she might have been found injured and taken to the local hospital. Maybe she experienced a runner's stitch in her side, and waved down a friend driving by and asked for a ride home or to the hospital. Even though we were both participating in this reasonable discussion we both confessed we felt like something bad had happened.

We began to pray and ask God to reveal Sarah's whereabouts. We called our daughters and sons-in-law requesting they join us in asking God to show us where Sarah was. A few minutes later our daughter Heather called us back. When she had asked her children to pray about the situation her ten-year old son, River, said he saw pine trees and pine needles and Sarah was there.

God's prophetic voice has no age limit and I love that. Though River's words had no concrete meaning to us, of course, we didn't doubt what River saw; we just doubted our ability to locate the trees.

This moment was a reminder that confusion and fear just multiply pain. We didn't want Sarah's parents, husband and children having to live long with the anxiety of not knowing the truth. So we refined our prayers and began asking God to reveal what was going on with Sarah before the day ended.

Thursday, June 14, 2012 began for my niece Sarah Hart with an early morning run with her sister Elizabeth Roberts. Sarah and Elizabeth had both begun running in high school. Their mutual love of running lingered long past high school. Both were excellent athletes who embraced running as part of their training regiment. And their route on Hwy 127 between Jamestown and Russell Springs Kentucky was familiar for the sisters' daily run.

Sarah and Elizabeth shared a bond that many sisters would envy. Life in a small rural Kentucky town created an environment for people to know everyone. The sisters' Kentucky roots extend deep and wide into their community. Sarah and Elizabeth's father,

Wendell Roberts, is a known, loved and highly-regarded pastor. Cindy, their mother, is a cherished and respected principal.

Wendell has a pastoral heart with many expressions. Whether he is relating to people in camouflage clothing on a hunting pursuit, repairing automotive or household needs for someone, preaching or speaking at a local event, leading a mission trip, or drinking coffee with the locals, his infectious laugh makes you feel good. Wendell has preached at the same church for 30 years. He has invested in the same community and developed friendships that are solid because they were built by transparency and living life together.

People often over-spiritualize the Christian lifestyle believing behaviors should look different inside the church building than they do outside the church building. I'm sure this amuses Jesus. Wendell acts the same behind the pulpit as he does on the ball field. His life has touched many hearts with his organic, spiritual lifestyle. Wendell's devotion to Jesus and the community was evident during this time of confusion and anxiety. We continued to pray and ask God to reveal where Sarah was before the day ended.

When we arrived at Wendell and Cindy's house our logical conversations were overpowered by our emotions and the dread we sensed in our spirits as we cried and hugged each other. I wasn't sure for whom I was crying the hardest - Elizabeth, the sister who might possibly blame herself for her sister's disappearance; Wendell and Cindy, the parents with a missing daughter; Sarah's husband, Ryan Hart, who now had no idea of his wife's current situation; or Sarah and Ryan's three little children, who only knew mommy was somehow just suddenly gone and no one knew when she'd be back. Through the tears and hugs we collectively began asking God to quickly reveal the truth about Sarah's condition and location.

Sarah's father, Wendell, is not only a pastor, but also a friend to many of the local policemen, EMT workers, the sheriff and many others who flooded his house with calls of information and sincere concern. My husband, Ray, and his brother Wendell wanted to assist the search-and-rescue team. So they headed to nearby Lake Cumberland in hopes of uncovering a clue that would lead to Sarah.

The waiting was torturous to everyone sitting in silence in Wendell and Cindy Roberts' living room. But I was overwhelmed by the sense of love and comfort I felt as we silently related to each other in the stillness surrounding us. The momentary locking of our eyes communicated the feelings of our hearts.

A steady stream of people began to parade through Wendell and Cindy's house with boxes of food and drinks. Every person who entered the house seemed to understand the reverence of the silence. Each person quietly cried and hugged Cindy, expressing their love through teary eyes and casseroles placed gently on the dining room table. The volume of southern meals delivered to the Roberts home that day reflected relationships developed over many years. I could sense everyone's honor for Wendell and his family. I witnessed the connectedness they all felt for Wendell, Cindy, Elizabeth and Sarah's husband Ryan. I began to cry again as I realized the tremendous importance of community. And I cried, also, for those who face traumas alone.

The silence of the Roberts' living room was finally interrupted by the ringing of Cindy's cell phone. Her facial expression conveyed the officer's phone message. The atmosphere in the room shifted and felt cold and gray. Sarah's body had been found and Cindy was asked to meet the officer at the site.

The familiar numbness of silence transferred from the living room to the car as we individually attempted to prepare our minds for what might lay ahead. My thoughts were stuck on my repetitive plea to God, "Jesus, please give Cindy the strength she needs; Jesus, please give Cindy the strength she needs; Jesus..." I so wished I had the ability to hug her pain away.

As the car screamed out of the driveway my mind drifted to memories of Sarah as a little girl. I remembered our years of Friday evening visits with Wendell and Cindy and the giggling of our five girls as they played together. I remembered Sarah and Heather, the firstborn child of each, bossing the younger girls. I remembered how the younger girls, Elizabeth, Summer and Kendal, would actually allow them to do it!

Tears streamed down my face as my thoughts returned to the present reality of where the car was headed and the pain Cindy must have been feeling. I cried because I cared. I cried because I knew how much Cindy loved Sarah. I cried because I didn't understand.

Although June 14, 2012 began as routine, it ended in tragedy. Elizabeth shared details from the early hours that helped the police and family members piece together the fatal morning. On their shared morning run, Sarah's unannounced pregnancy did not permit her to partner with Elizabeth's pace. Sarah insisted that Elizabeth continue the full morning regimen while she would return to the car. But an evil, deranged stalker circumvented Sarah's wisdom.

Sarah never made it to her car. Sarah was abducted then brutally murdered on the final mile of her run. Sarah's body had been dragged off the sidewalk and hidden beneath the nearby pine trees and covered by a light layer of pine needles.

When I heard where Sarah's body had been found my eyes filled with tears and my heart filled with awe as I remembered my daughter's ten-year-old son, River, saying when he prayed he saw Sarah laying under a pine tree covered with pine needles. Such terrible tragedy, but in the midst of these awful circumstances I also loved the fact that God's prophetic voice is accessible even to little children.

On the drive back I struggled with feelings of guilt because my husband Ray and I left his brother Wendell's home, a home filled with sorrow, and were returning to our everyday world. An everyday world with our daughters. It didn't seem fair.

I couldn't stop crying. I had no place to put this tragedy in my logical brain. I thought about the times I had ministered to people who'd experienced similar tragedies. Yet this was the first time I could truly empathize. I had a new level of compassion for broken-hearted people and a fresh commitment to comfort grieving people.

I was comforted by the support system that surrounded the Roberts' family. Sarah had graduated from the University of Kentucky College of Pharmacy. Her husband, Ryan, and her sister, Elizabeth, were also UK grads. But even though Sarah's Russell County roots extended 85 miles north to Lexington, KY, where she attended UK, I was astonished that Lexington, Louisville, and Bowling Green news stations all covered the tragedy.

The magnitude of Sarah's memorial service was equally amazing. The memorial service was held in the gymnasium of the church where Wendell is pastor. It is a modest country church. The service was scheduled to begin at 6 p.m. with the family invited to enter at 5 p.m.

As soon as I entered the gym I began to cry. The entire gym was lined with family portraits of Sarah, Ryan and their three beautiful blonde children. I thought their children looked like golden-haired angels. Underneath the gallery of photos were tokens of affection from the community. Stuffed animals, quilts, flowers, and sports memorabilia represented a community's expressions of love and compassion for the loss of Sarah.

The room was also lined with large flat-screen TV's displaying a photographic timeline of Sarah's life. Pictures of her wedding day made me cry the hardest. I remember the day of Sarah's wedding and how she recorded a song to sing to her groom. It was an audible pledge of her love and commitment to the man of her dreams with whom she had chosen to spend her life. I was sad that this marriage was robbed. I was sad that the children would grow up without Sarah's influence. I was struggling to gain control over my emotions.

I headed to the restroom to compose myself and dab my eyes with cold water when someone suggested I look outside. I cracked the back door of the church and any composure I'd gained instantly left and my tears returned. Outside was a pilgrimage of sweaty people waiting their turn in the hot Kentucky weather to embrace some sense of closure. The line began at the back door of the gym and stretched one-fourth of a mile to the main road. At the main road people began to form a double line. The extreme June heat appeared to have no effect on those in line. This procession continued until after midnight.

The message my husband, Ray, shared at his niece's memorial service replayed in my mind for weeks: "God is good and His love endures forever" (Psalm 100:5). I quoted it to myself very often in the days following the service. I was feeling waves of anger when people approached me about Sarah's murder and blamed God for the evil act. I struggled to remain calm as I replied, "You are placing blame in the wrong direction." My angry feelings were connected to thoughts of the widespread dysfunctional theology about the character of our Heavenly Father and how stupid it is to blame God for a man's evil choice to murder someone.

Over time I have refined my ability to tell others that God is not responsible for Sarah's murder, but that without His wanting to shake people, "In all things God works together with those who love him to bring about what is good" (Romans 8:28). I can now actually respond in a peaceful manner without feeling the need to tell them how wrong their belief system is. I still hate bad theology, but I think my heart is beginning to heal and my mind beginning to process the tragedy.

An act of honor

As time passed Elizabeth and a few of Sarah's close friends wanted to set up a run/walk in honor of Sarah. They decided to call the event, 'Run with All Your Hart.' The race's logo was of an angel formed from the footprints of Sarah and Ryan's three children. Their son's footprint forms the body of the angel while the two girl's handprints create the angel's wings. The heart in the middle of the angel symbolized the family's last name, Hart, while the angel's halo signifies Sarah's ten-week-old unborn baby who Ryan named Alexander.

The race event was posted on Facebook and the family anticipated the usual small-town race support. One hundred registered runners is a good turn out for a small town run. The surprising registration of three thousand people represented hearts that were all touched in some way by Sarah's story. The dramatic registration and the numerous emails led to the inclusion of virtual runners in other states wanting to participate in 'Run With All Your Hart' who were unable to travel to Russell County. All fifty states were represented by virtual runners who ran in their hometowns in conjunction with the Kentucky race. The need for closure and the desire to honor Sarah's life touched segments of our entire nation.

The local community continued to find ways to support the race by donating fruit, sport drinks, homemade muffins, handmade medals in the shape of a heart and many other race-related items. Over two hundred people generously shared their time taking care of the event's practical aspects by volunteering before, during and after the race.

Wendell asked Ray if he would lead the runners in a pre-race prayer. Ten minutes before the race was scheduled to begin Ray stood before thousands of athletically-dressed people and led them in a prayer of thanksgiving to God for the gracious support of those gathered together in love. He asked the crowd to join hands as a sign of unity and to lift their faces and hands toward Heaven in reverence as he declared that Sarah was in Heaven with Jesus.

In the name of Jesus Ray invited people to open their hearts to the Lord's presence as he prayed and asked Jesus to teach us to love each other and challenged us to run with all our hearts in our daily lives. It would be unrealistic to think everyone who lifted his or her hands was a Christian. It is fair to conclude that many people sympathized with the Roberts and Hart families and cared enough about Sarah's death to participate in the event and the prayer. It is also appropriate to deduce that most of the gathered people felt the need to engage in the run hoping it would help them process the tragedy.

Sarah's death is a calamity that stains the hearts of many who knew and loved her. But how we respond to disaster reveals our compassion for the broken-hearted. And the love extended toward the Hart and Roberts families during the loss of Sarah's life has affirmed my faith in the significance of community.

A loving and supportive community is vital to processing pain. I have always known that Jesus says to bear each others' burdens (Galatians 6:2), but it became real to me as I watched so many people care for my extended family's burden.

A community model

This book is not about Sarah's death. However, the responses mentioned in this story represent many significant aspects of what 'community' is, which are discussed in the chapters that follow.

This book is not about my family as a model family, but family stories are shared because our family intentionally lives a shared, connected lifestyle and with a commitment to loving people.

This book is about communal principles which are not intended to be seen as exclusive to small-town, rural America.

This book is about Biblical truths concerning a connected, spiritual life. These truths are universally applicable.

Questions to Consider

- Are you connected to a spiritual community?
- Do you have people in your life to help you process pain?

CHAPTER TWO
The Safety of Community

The word 'community' calls up a mental image of groups of people spending time together talking about things they have in common. A visual image of community can be formal or casual, organized or spontaneous, intellectual or simple; it can be composed of a few people or a large number of people. Some feel strongly about the definition of 'community' and argue for the importance of it being an intentional gathering. We might even have a negative reaction to the word because it has been weakened by overuse.

But though a community can be centered on many causes, topics, beliefs or people, the common denominator of every community is always relationships.

I think the reason the word 'community' can be such a hot topic is because we are living in a disconnected culture where people are hungry for connectedness yet still struggle to define it. Whether you are religious and prefer the term 'Koinonia'; trendy and prefer the term 'gathering'; Evangelical and prefer the term 'church'; professional and prefer the term 'meeting'; or relevant and prefer the term 'tribe' for everyone 'community' is still a great word to define the desire within every heart to belong to a group and be unconditionally accepted for who you are.

Belonging

I remember the strong feelings of loneliness that influenced my high school years. I remember the sadness that accompanied my thoughts about being too different to fit in. I was an artist, which created its own set of challenges. I always looked at things differently than my friends. I dressed differently than many of my peers and I overanalyzed everything. I was fixated on color, design and the condition of the world. As I reflect on my teen years, I admit I felt things deeply and over thought everything. These are not adolescent characteristics conducive to acceptance.

I spent great amounts of time daydreaming during the doldrums of algebra or Spanish classes because I viewed them as non-creative expressions of academia. My belief about, and response to, those classes were clearly reflected on my report card. I admit I have always struggled to engage in things that don't hold my interest. Although I had many friends, I learned to keep my thoughts to myself because when I shared them my comments were often met with confused looks and frowns I interpreted as unacceptable.

I concluded that my sense of not fitting in and my belief about myself would change when I went to college. I believed the unity of higher education would be inclusive and maturity would eliminate the rejection of diversity among students. I envisioned a tight-knit group of people sharing their educational goals, intellectual pursuits and future aspirations. I anticipated a place of belonging. I was wrong.

I was seventeen when my closest friends invited me to a revival at their church. The message was boring and the music didn't sound anything like the genre I enjoyed listening to while I painted. I was inspired when I listened to Carole King play the piano and sing. The church songs and the pianist on the church stage annoyed me. However, something was happening in my heart.

The preacher announced that no one could be saved unless they accepted Jesus as their savior and were baptized to wash away their sins. This was a new concept to me because I was baptized as an infant.

I analyzed everything I heard so I thought I should investigate what the preacher was suggesting. I made a plan for that evening, after leaving the church building and going home, to research the pastor's proposal. Somehow my heart and the Holy Spirit overruled my plans and before realizing it I had walked forward to say 'Yes' to the preacher's invitation. My heart overruled my mind and I confessed to the preacher that I believed Jesus is the only way to be saved. Although I didn't understand why I needed to be baptized in front of many unfamiliar onlookers, I did it. At the time it did not make sense, but it seemed right. Today, though, I understand the importance of being baptized into a spiritual family.

I joined the youth group. I added the numerous weekly church services to my social calendar and began reading the Bible. I loved learning about the Bible and attending Bible studies, but I quickly learned my thoughts and my questions were not acceptable.

I wanted to know how Jesus fit into my everyday life. I wanted to know how Scriptural principles related to the Vietnam War. I wanted to know how being a Christian would affect my future. I wanted to know if Jesus was okay with me being an artist and pursuing an art degree. The Bible teachers at the church wanted me to keep things in proper context according to their doctrinal beliefs about life with God. I was confused.

It was wintertime and eleven of the teens I had befriended in the youth group were planning on attending Bible College in the Fall term. Doing so seemed to be an unspoken expectation for all the teens in that church. I began feeling bad that I had fallen in love with Jesus because I still loved art and wanted to be an artist. I began to feel the familiar feelings of not fitting in.

My sense of being different was intensifying. I began thinking that in order to fit in with the Jesus group I needed to change who I was and release my worldly creative goals. I needed to learn to conform to the religious community. In my new church family I was frequently told I was rebellious because I questioned scripture. Some of the older women in the church told me I thought too much for a girl and that it would interfere with me being a submissive wife. I was often told that I was worldly because I designed clothes that looked like something hippies would wear and my eye shadow looked like a hooker's. I needed to change if I wanted to be a proper Jesus girl.

I didn't want to be rebellious. I wanted to learn more about the Bible and how to become the spiritual person I was supposed to be. I also wanted to fit in. I didn't like the rejection I felt about being myself. I wanted to make Jesus happy and the only advice I was getting was that I needed to change. Although my art teacher of 10 years had assured me I had artistic ability, the greeting-card design class I took senior year at a nearby college was my last artistic endeavor before I joined my Christian peers at Bible College in the Fall. I put down my paintbrush and picked up my Bible.

It didn't take long for me to realize that I had a lot of changing to do before I could fit in with the Bible college girls. None of the girls looked like I did. None of the girls thought or talked like I did. They were serious and I was silly. I quickly learned I wore too much make-up, my clothes were too tight, my hair was too trendy, my shoes were too high, my skirts were too short and my attitude was completely inappropriate.

I challenged the rules and I broke many of them. I continued questioning things others seemed to accept as the spiritual norm. In New Testament class I excitedly asked questions about Jesus healing people and shared with the class how I loved reading about miracles. The Bible teachers informed me that miracles were not applicable for the present age and I should understand that the miraculous signs of the Holy Spirit stopped long ago. My 'Why?' questions were shut down along with my enthusiasm. I believed the Bible and I loved Jesus, but I was more confused than ever about my identity and how I could ever comply.

I began believing I wasn't a good fit for the new Christian world I had joined. My demeanor shifted from a creative, carefree girl who loved life to a person consumed with internal turmoil trying to figure out what was wrong inside. The spiritual list of do/do-not behaviors and the weird girls in the dorms made me question my decision to join the Jesus club.

Something didn't feel right to me, but I didn't know what it was. I didn't feel loved; I felt condemned. I didn't feel accepted; I felt judged. Not only did I feel judged, I felt like I was supposed to learn to judge others who didn't follow the do/do-not spiritual list. I was surrounded by an us-vs-them attitude that felt oppressive. And this attitude wasn't restricted to just those outside the Christian community; it included Christians who danced, smoked, drank alcohol or played cards. Somehow, my new Christian family believed Christians who did things on their no-no list were bad and we were good; even though I read in the Bible about David dancing and Jesus turning water into wine. I knew something felt wrong but I didn't know what it was.

Confusion about Jesus

My introduction to Jesus was in a religious community that had a narrow view about life with God. My initiation into the Kingdom of God was restrictive and heavy. The restraints were harsher than those I experienced before I invited Jesus into my heart. I felt like I had to choose between being myself and becoming spiritual in order to be accepted. Yet I believed that Jesus loved me like I was. More confusion.

When we feel disconnected and believe that who we are is unacceptable it can feel heavy and oppressive. We begin to blame ourselves and believe lies about ourselves. We embrace a mantle that Jesus opposes. Jesus says that when we are in this position we should turn to him and he will replace our heaviness with rest (Matthew 11:28).

A healthy spiritual community should be inclusive. A healthy spiritual community should be composed of a vast variety of people who are equally valued: introverts and extroverts; professionals and non-professionals; those with formal educations and those with great life experience; entrepreneurs and employees; those from religious backgrounds and charismatic worshipers; emotionally healthy people and broken people; happy people and depressed people; enjoyable people and difficult people; those who want to give and those who want to be served; wealthy people and those who struggle financially; creative people and literal thinkers; enthusiastic, impulsive youth and older men and women who share wisdom with the younger generation; tattooed and pierced artists and preppies with ironed shirts; leaders and followers; those who have it all together and those in the midst of figuring it out. The list of diversity is endless, but the principles of God's love are consistent.

God loves us with an unconditional love and we should love others with that same degree of love. Honestly, it is easier for me to unconditionally love some people more than others, but I want to learn to enjoy difficult people as well as pleasant people.

And I often struggle with people who won't release their pain to God or ask for help. I find myself thinking it wouldn't take *me* so long to do the right thing. But I know Jesus waits patiently for me to realize these aren't compassionate thoughts. And I admit my willingness to turn to Him has been influenced by the many experiences I've already had in which God has healed my heart.

I recognize that many people don't have any positive influences to encourage them to make good choices. If we want to be like God, we need to love other people like He loves us. (1 John 4:10-12). The primary goals of spiritual communities should be to teach people to love God, love themselves and love each other without exception.

A True Story

Leigha was raised in a traditional, conservative church. Leigha is not traditional or conservative. Leigha is a performing artist. She is a passionate actress with a flair for drama that she likes to express with her clothing. Because Leigha doesn't fit the traditional Christian profile she has received a lot of criticism.

Leigha tells me that many people who have judged her have never had a conversation with her. As she shared this comment with me, I smiled because conversations with Leigha are very theatrical. Those watching our interaction might conclude Leigha was demonstrating a skit from an audition. In our brief chat Leigha laughed loudly, cried dramatically, jumped joyfully and made exaggerated arm gestures resembling a dance all in her attempts to express her thoughts.

Leigha tells me that she never felt accepted by the church in which she grew up. She shared stories of being greeted inside the church doors with frowns. Intense stares are not inviting or affirming. Churches are often slow to embrace people who look and act differently than their church norm.

Many churches react to broken people with broken attitudes. Many Christians miss the opportunity to hear a person's story because they can't move beyond the person's appearance. Tattoos, odd-colored hair shaped in non-traditional styles, multiple piercings or mismatched clothing offend religious people who believe loving Jesus and living a Godly life is defined by what we wear, what we say and how we behave. I am thankful that Jesus is more concerned with the condition of our heart than the condition of our clothes.

When we perceive someone is tainted by how they look we often reject them. I once heard about an adolescent who actually had a teacher tell him he couldn't be a good witness for Jesus in skinny jeans. Yet I know many people who dress conservatively and live like the Devil. When a community practices such exclusivity it loses the opportunity to represent the love of Jesus to hurting people.

Rest for the weary

We need to welcome people who have been rejected, labeled and hurt by judgmental churches. Jesus says that He will give rest to those who are worn out and heavy-hearted (Matthew 11:28). I think it is very important that we develop spiritual communities which embrace people who need to rest and recover from life's painful experiences. We need to depart from the religious spirit of this age which tries to regulate God with man-made rules that are actually personal opinions imposed on others in an attempt to control them.

Leigha felt accepted and peaceful in our church family. Leigha's story now includes a community that values her for who she is. She frequently tells me that since she feels loved by a spiritual family it is easier to feel loved by God.

We really can't experience the complete love of God if we don't feel loved by others. God expresses his love for us through other people. It is poor theology that tells us we only experience God's love when we are alone with Him reading the Bible. It is important to feel loved and accepted by a spiritual community.

It is equally as important to be the person who extends love and acceptance to others who are searching for a safe place to call home.

Questions to Consider

- Do you feel loved by God?
- Do you feel loved by other people?
- Do you love those who are different than you?

CHAPTER THREE
Becoming a Family

My ministry office is outdated and ugly. The walls are a boring shade of white, marked by years of ministry. Chairs that are frequently moved around the room to accommodate group sessions have left permanent scuffs. The antique hutch housing files of peoples' memories is mahogany and unappealing. The once defined flowers on my office couch presently resemble the blurred pallet of a Monet painting. And my burgundy-colored recliner should be restricted to old men over the age of ninety who refuse to embrace modern décor.

However, I love walking into my office because it houses the sweet Spirit of God's peace. When I enter my office I get excited about what Jesus is going to do for those who come for prayer.

My old-man recliner, on which I perch, faces the worn floral couch. A line of family photos is displayed above the couch. It is somewhat ironic that I often enter the paradox of praying for broken families who have come to me for ministry while seeing my family pictures which represent, to me, good memories and a lot of love. But the pictures I am seeing above the couch are small in number compared to the gallery wall behind my dilapidated recliner. My sentimental exhibit there is a timeline of family life capturing my daughters' youths, their weddings and the births of their children. Their framed faces always stir happy emotions as my heart connects my past with my present and future family life.

Once, I was startled by a middle-aged woman who came in to my office and plopped on the couch. She seemed agitated when her eyes landed on the photos behind my chair. She glared at the pictures behind me and then said in a very angry tone, "Ok, now that is too much. I can't do the happy family thing!" She got up, left and didn't return.

I have had many others react to my gallery wall in a similar manner. Some people express their anger, but most people are able to compose themselves after a brief trip to the rest room. I later learned from a relative of the plopping woman that it is common for her to get angry when she sees family pictures, movies about family, or sees kind interactions between families in public. My office was a too painful reminder of her very different family story.

The reminder of family

We cannot deny the fact that our response to the term 'family' is directly related to our biological family. Whether positive or negative, we are imprinted by our family-of-origin or those who cared for us during childhood. If we grew up in a loving, nurturing family our childhood memories are usually warm and happy.

A peaceful childhood experience often makes people smile when the topic of family is discussed. You can almost feel a person's joy as they share memories of meaningful times when their parents affirmed how much they loved them by spending time with them in fun-filled activities or teaching them how to properly process life. They seem to come alive when they share sentimental stories about their nuclear family. You can actually feel the energy bounce off of people as they recap holiday celebrations. It amazes me how happy memories retain emotional intensity, smell, and color as people step back into their past to bring family treasures into the present. The feeling of belonging fills the room when happy people express memories of being unconditionally loved.

On the other hand, many people sit in my office and cry as they lament over years spent in a home of pain and sorrow. They tell me about being ignored in their family, compared to their siblings, punished unfairly, or shamed for how they think and feel. They tell me how they struggled to figure out life on their own as a young child because their parents were entangled in drugs, alcohol or other addictions, or were emotionally disconnected, unavailable, or too busy for them.

It is common for dysfunctional family experiences to rob precious aspects of childhood and oppress people with responsibilities that destroy their youth. It is very common for people to share childhood abuse memories with me that have distorted their perception of life, God and other people. Those with such experiences have no real comprehension of a happy, healthy family. So the word 'family' provokes emotions of sadness, pain, anger, resentment, and hate for many people. I understand how happy family photos make them sad.

I often feel emotional when I hear stories of abuse becoming a person's norm. I think how very sad it would be to be a child who had to grow up without a healthy adult in his or her life. When hearing such stories my mind usually goes to how much I loved raising my daughters or how wonderful it is to watch my daughters care for and love their children. If I imagine one of my grandchildren being traumatized it is overwhelming. Yet an abusive childhood is many people's reality.

Sometimes when my office is filled with the cries of a broken-hearted person expressing childhood pain I think about my grandchildren and find myself struggling to compose myself enough to pray for the person. I often have to fight the temptation to instead just sit beside them and hug them. I want to step out of the role of prayer minister because the mother in me wants to wipe away the person's pain along with their tears.

I think Jesus feels this way when we are hurt. I think Jesus cares about our broken hearts, but his compassion is released through healing. In Psalm 34:18 David shares from personal experience that the Lord is near to the broken-hearted and rescues those who are crushed in spirit. David is an example of a person who kept focused on the Lord and recognized His presence even when he was distressed. He chose to worship God and not allow suffering to distract his praise.

Life has a way of wounding us and there are seasons in our lives where the temptation to turn away from God and community is greater than others. But it is during these times that we most need the love of others to lead us to the presence of the Lord.

It has been my ministry experience over the past twenty years that people are much more familiar with abusive, dysfunctional families than they are with healthy, happy families. Many people survived painful childhoods without having a safe person to hug them and care for their pain. Consequently, there is a tremendous need to provide a safe place for hurting people who need to experience the love of a family.

People raised in dysfunctional homes are usually emotionally and socially challenged. When parents are struggling with their own unresolved life issues, their children are often shortchanged emotionally, psychologically and socially. If a person grows up feeling unwanted, unloved and devalued, they often become adults who do not know how to relate to others in an intimate, meaningful manner. They sometimes act like they are socially and emotionally stuck at the ages when they did not receive what they needed during a specific developmental stage. It is interesting to notice how many adults who have childhood voids talk and behave in childish ways.

I minister to many adult men who act like pre-teen boys. They have a very juvenile approach to life and their decision-making skills mimic a self-centered adolescent. They resist my counsel about the importance of developing relational skills and the importance of taking personal responsibility for their lives. They minimize the role of maturity, arguing it is normal to not work a consistent job, pay bills on time, or develop healthy, meaningful relationships. They seem genuinely unaware that this mindset is only appropriate for a tween.

I also meet with many females for prayer who act like broken little girls in seductive adult clothing or broken little girls who dress and act like boys. This is a reflection of a childhood that was void of the foundational love bonds that a little girl needs from her father. When a girl feels loved by her parents or caregivers, she doesn't need to seek attention in unhealthy ways. A female who was affirmed and loved unconditionally during the developmental stages of her sexuality doesn't seek unholy male or female attention. When a little girl grows up knowing that her daddy thinks she is beautiful, worth listening to and spending quality time with she won't dress like an unloved prostitute.

I am amazed at the number of young women who love Jesus, serve Jesus and are raising their own children to love Jesus yet who wear clothing that reveals insecurity and unmet childhood needs. Many of these young women share a common theme directly related to their relationships with their fathers. Fathers who love the Lord but are emotionally distant from the hearts of their little girls raise insecure women.

Fear of family

Our family-of-origin influences our sexuality and our ability to live from our true identity. Our childhood experience of family determines the degree to which we embrace or reject both relationships and ourselves. It also affects our willingness to connect and trust a spiritual group of people.

I think it is fair to say that most people want to be part of a loving community, but many don't have the ability to relate to others on an interpersonal level. Abraham Maslow's psychological hierarchy of needs teaches us that love and belonging include the ability to develop healthy friendships and relate to family members.

These are foundational requirements for maturity and adult morality.

We should note that it is God's design for the family-of-origin to also be the spiritual family. Though many people do not have a healthy family unit, we are acting foolishly if we do have a healthy natural family and don't acknowledge or utilize it. However, when our needs are not met in the context of our natural family, it leaves people challenged in their ability to give and receive love. This lack results in people who long for the connectedness of family, yet they think and behave like orphans or resist those who attempt to love them.

Jesus says that we always have a place in the family of God. Jesus knows some people are raised by broken parents and grow up feeling disconnected and bruised. The Heavenly Father says when we invite Jesus into our hearts we are spiritually adopted into His family. In the family of God we are all called sons and daughters and are positioned to call the Heavenly Father our dad (Romans 8:13-14).

To some people this is a comforting representation of family, but to others it is painful because even in their new spiritual families there can be dysfunctional members who often remind them of their painful history. It is common for Christian brothers and sisters to trigger painful childhood memories. And it is easy for people to transfer their unresolved daddy issues to the Heavenly Father, beginning their life in a spiritual family with a guarded heart and a skeptical mind. When we are overly defensive, we act as if we dare anyone to like us and accept us. We behave like orphans.

My first spiritual experience

I was welcomed into the family of God by legalistic brothers and sisters with a long do/do-not list. But I eventually learned that many people in God's family are joyful, healthy people who know God intimately and represent his love well. Early in my spiritual-journey I also learned there are many Christians who understand we cannot earn God's love through avoiding things on the no-no list, but that we learn to say 'No' to sin because God loves us regardless of what we do or don't do.

The Bible tells us *nothing* can separate us from the love that God has for us (Romans 8:38-39). I think this includes the no-no list. I don't promote sin or think it's appropriate to excuse poor choices or wrong behavior, but I do believe that far too many Christians do not understand that God is after our hearts and not our religious practices. He actually loves people who are trapped in sin and wants them to know that he is waiting to lift whatever they choose to give to him.

It is a positive step in our life with God to shift from an intellectual knowledge of God's unconditional love to an experiential love. We cannot give to others anything we do not have ourselves, nor can we share the truth about God's love with others until we are living from this truth. If we don't feel accepted by God, it is difficult to love other people. If we don't know who we are, it is a struggle to help others find out who they are.

I began life in a spiritual community with people who viewed God's love as conditional and earned. I presently tell people, "God loves you just because you're you." I can say this because I know in the depths of my heart that God loves me just the way I am.

I entered the Jesus club as a spiritual daughter and I have transitioned to a spiritual parent. My husband and I have many spiritual sons and daughters who we love unconditionally, embrace as our own and have invited into our lives. I want to show the joy of a healthy spiritual family to people who are stuck in the pain of a negative family system. I am not saying my husband or I or our families are perfect spiritual examples. I am saying we make it our intention to simply love and accept those who God puts into our lives.

It is exciting to know that even if our biological family was dysfunctional, or our parents decided to dissolve the family unit through divorce, that in the family of God we have a spiritual inheritance that is secure. There is comfort in the fact that God chose to adopt us and that our adoption isn't based on how good we are.

Paul writes about spiritual adoption in Romans 8:14-16 that when Christ empowers our life we no longer have to be dominated by our past, but we can be lead by the Spirit of God. When we are spiritually adopted as sons and daughters we don't have to be tied to lies from our history telling us we aren't good enough. Because we have been accepted into the family of God. We no longer need to feel orphaned because God's Fatherhood becomes real to us as He whispers into our innermost being that we are His beloved children. Since we are His true children we qualify to receive the good things He has for us. That includes healing the empty places in our hearts.

The Trinity

If we understand that the Trinity includes the unity of God, Jesus and the Holy Spirit, we can look at the Trinity as an example of a spiritual family unity. The relationship of the Godhead is inseparable. The Father, the Son and the Holy Spirit are dependent on each other and work in unison.

I love the fact that within the Trinity each member has a distinct function, yet operate together and are available as one. If we pray to God we are actually reaching Him through His son Jesus. We are able to experience Jesus through the Holy Spirit. And the Holy Spirit personalizes our interaction with a sovereign God and the Savior of the World, providing a way for everyone to come into the family of God.

This Heavenly reality is mirrored in God's design of the spiritual family on Earth. Each person who is part of the Kingdom is unique in what they bring to the community of faith. And each expresses different aspects of Jesus. Diversity is a vital part of a spiritual community.

We should pray as Joshua did and choose Jesus today. Because, as Joshua knew, it is always a good idea to face the adversity in our lives with the Lord by deciding to fear Him and serve Him sincerely - even if our family doesn't acknowledge God or our ancestors served other gods (Joshua 24:14-15).

Joshua encouraged the people of his day to choose God for themselves. It is encouraging to know we can have a life with God that is not restricted by the choices of our natural family and that we don't have to live with historical scars incurred in childhood.

The comfort of God's family is only a choice away.

Questions to Consider

- What does the thought of family evoke in you?
- What family memories bring you joy?
- What family wounds could you release to Jesus?

CHAPTER FOUR
Unconditional Love and Honor

I love Sunday evenings because our family gathers for a weekly dinner. Our house is an open-living floor plan with a fireplace on one end and the kitchen on the opposite end. Sandwiched in-between the fireplace and the kitchen island is a long handmade dining table that comfortably seats eight-to-ten people. Each Sunday eight adults surround the table along with the three youngest grandchildren and the oldest grandson who transitioned to the adult table when he turned thirteen.

In years past our Sunday evening meals were low-key, focused and prayerful. We intentionally took turns sharing what we wanted the family to pray for in the upcoming week. The prayer requests would frequently deviate to joyful memories we shared and clouds of laughter would erupt. Tender smiles would be followed by conversations about future experiences we desired to share as a family. We are a very loud family so I am amazed when I think about our family ever being quiet. But we intentionally did not rush our meal or our conversations.

Sunday dinners are still sweet and cherished, but they are no longer quiet. We now have thirteen grandchildren joining the Sunday gatherings. Although the children have an adjoining dining room to themselves, where they eat and discuss their world of Legos, swords, dress-ups and baby dolls, our meals have entered a new level of energy. Our dinner conversations are now interrupted with shouts of "Whose turn is it to get the babies off of the steps?" or "No sugar until you finish your meal" or "Stop throwing food!" Other favorites I've overheard include "Stop annoying her and she won't scream" and "Do not choke each other; it isn't nice. Love your cousins!"

We still love being together and sharing stories from our week and asking each other for prayer, but we now must submit our requests in much louder volume to compete with the noise of our growing family. We have adjusted the pace of our family meals, rearranged the seating and altered our menu, but our intention to gather as a family remains steadfast.

Life in a small town

I think it is fair to say that a large part of my social life is my family. Campbellsville is a small rural Kentucky town. The bad thing about living in this town is the fact that it is extremely limited in some ways. There are only a few non fast-food dining options for foodies. Art and culture are minimal. Shopping outside of a superstore is sparse. Venues to house large social gatherings are non-existent. And purchasing clothing from the present century for fluffy women is not an option.

Despite the fact that our town is wanting in some areas, the lack is actually an asset. The shortage of social options allows life in this small town to be more about relationships. A person's desire for a fine dining experience and their social needs must be met in homes with family and friends. You might cringe when thinking about living without numerous options, but a dinner table surrounded by friends is a wonderful invitation to create or expand a family. And such opportunities aren't limited or enhanced by geographic location.

My husband and I live in the country on a farm housing our family vineyards. My oldest daughter's house and vineyard abuts our land on one side while my youngest daughter's home merges with our land on the other. Our middle daughter lives in town, a mere ten-minute drive. Our family lives in a very emotionally, socially, spiritually connected fashion. Our thirteen grandchildren are in and out of our daily lives on a regular basis. We live a very connected lifestyle that many people don't understand. I know because I am frequently told how my lifestyle would drive others crazy because they would feel constantly invaded by family.

Although our large family meals compare in loudness to a crowded playground - all the little children talking at the same time or multiple babies all wanting milk or crying or pooing at the same time - it is still a cherished time for our family. The activity around our dinner table seems to give us joy which paves the way for the next week. When I am emotionally exhausted from the demands of my week, the thought of my family gathering makes me smile even though the energy it requires can be tiring.

It makes me sad to think many people have no place to connect with others in such a meaningful way. It is the compassion of Jesus when we care about those who do not have a family and we find ways to include them in ours. I think it is the heart of God to consider the needs of others. I have found that actions are much more helpful than words to people who are lonely. It means more to them to give them your time and include them in your life than to tell them Jesus loves them and then go about your life.

Bridging the generation gap

Our present society tells us the younger generation doesn't need the older generation and the older generation is finished teaching anything when they younger generation completes puberty. Our society stresses independence above relationship. Our culture promotes quick wealth and influence above process and personal journey.

The western mindset values accomplishment more than good character, which is often seen in what people are willing to do to gain promotion. This standard has gripped the present generations referred to as Millennials, Generation Y, or Echo Boomers - those who are followers of Jesus and those who are not.

'Millennials' are defined as those born between 1980 and the year 2000. They are difficult to evaluate and even harder to nurture because they are the generation which has been raised with technology, entertained by electronics, and who are living life with the American values taught by the previous generation.

Millennials frequently say they were raised with more time spent with screens than people and that they received more information from the Internet than their parents. Such circumstances are creating a culture of socially awkward young adults. Replacing eye contact with an iPhone's screen hinders a person's social intelligence, presenting a challenge for those trying to relate to them in a personal manner. It is difficult talking to someone about the need for community if they lack much true face-to-face relational experience.

As I minister to Generation Y, I have observed the fruit of these poor social skills. The fascination with cell-phones and social-media is changing the way they think and act. Such obsession creates an allure to be more concerned with self than others. Very few Millennials see value in serving others or the need to surrender their life to Jesus.

Bombarding Facebook with selfies is indicative of a generation obsessed with its own image and which desperately needs the opinions of other people for affirmation. Have you ever followed a specific person on Facebook or Twitter and noted how many times they invite affirmation for the perfect picture they've posted or phrase they've tweeted?

Generation Y is known for being web savvy and the first generation to be automatically equipped to navigate the technological world. But they are also identified as the most likely to repeatedly change jobs as quickly as their clothes or simply to fund the urgency of their next trip. Their technological dexterity is creating a generation that in many ways sees no need to interact with the older generation. This can create an insularity that ends up being narcissistic and self-serving.

Entitlement is also characteristic of those who have been permitted to endlessly indulge themselves in hours of electronic escape. It has been my experience that Generation Y feels inherently owed certain things that in reality take years to develop or obtain. They think they can bypass the steps needed to grow and mature and many believe that they know more than they actually do.

I have also witnessed many Echo Boomers having their hopes, dreams, and futures anchored in technology, travel, a trendy appearance and ever-new experiences. And they refuse any counsel that contradicts their right to do whatever they choose, whenever they choose to do it. The Echo Boomer generation is convinced they do not need advice from anyone older and many are opposed to spiritual direction.

However, I have also discovered that many Millennials struggle mightily with anxiety and fear underneath their intellectual, digital façade. When Millennials come to me for ministry I frequently ask them what they feel when they consider a fast from electronics. This question doesn't need a verbal response because I see their answer by their reaction to the mere idea of even asking the question.

It must be difficult to lay down something electronic that has been a substitute for intimacy for many years. When adults who have, since childhood, substituted human interaction through electronic-disconnection, there are bound to be withdrawal symptoms.

I wonder how much sadness and loneliness lives behind the screens accumulating Facebook friends rather than authentic relationships. Meanwhile, Baby Boomers and the Silent Generation, who are not as tech savvy as Echo Boomers nor 'interfaced' by them, have spiritually mature life lessons to impart that can only truly be received through actual relationship.

A shared life

A shared spiritual life is familiar to me. My oldest son-in-law and daughter are the pastors of the Vineyard Church in our community. All our other daughters, our sons-in-law and their parents, our grandchildren, and my brother and his family attend services there. Our next-youngest son-in-law is on the worship team and the youngest son-in-law pastors the prophetic team. I love that my family lives life together, but sharing life should not be restricted to just our natural families. We should embrace people who God entrusts to us and invite them into our lives.

I enjoy inviting people to our church, but believe it is just as spiritual to invite them to dinner in my home. I am not suggesting your life should necessarily look like mine. It is impossible to think that all families live in the same town, for one thing. And it would be unfair to think all families express their love the same way mine does or live parallel lives. I am sharing my story merely as an illustration of how it relates to embracing others.

Sharing life with other people often reveals conflicts of values and beliefs. The line between good and bad, right and wrong, appropriate and inappropriate are blurred in our present culture. I have had many conversations with Christian young adults who have the same moral code as the world. Generation Y particularly falls prey to this ambiguousness of moral code, with an unhealthy tolerance for immorality and sexual impurity. The degree of tolerance and acceptance many young adults have for sinful acts amazes me.

We have an opportunity to teach Millennials the ways of God when we adopt them in to our spiritual families. God has designed families to train children and young adults in righteousness and scripture tell us this will make a difference when the person is older (Proverbs 22:6). Demonstrating a healthy spiritual life to young adults is a process requiring us to invest in them and not be in a hurry. Morality requires intentionality and time.

Authenticity

The scriptures tell us that spiritual fathers and elders should be men who have their homes in order before they attempt to instruct others outside their homes. This does not mean spiritual fathers don't have any unresolved issues or that they are without sin. It does mean spiritual fathers should be intentionally seeking God for wisdom and direction, that they should be training those under their authority in righteousness, and that providing for the needs of their natural family should be a priority (1 Tim. 3:1-16; 5:8).

Natural fathers and spiritual fathers should be safe and loving men who are honored and respected by their family for the way they live life, love God and take care of children. I would add that 'children' should not be limited to those who are toddlers or adolescents, but that adult children need their fathers as much as they did when they were younger - they just need them in different ways. Our expression of honor and respect changes with age and time, but the practice of honor should not.

The honor we extend others should be authentic. We have all been around people who are sugary when chatting at church, but we encounter completely different interactions with them at sporting events or during business hours. I appreciate consistent, genuine people. And I have the privilege of watching authentic interactions in much of my life.

My husband is the most consistent person that I know. He wears many hats, but he always relates to people with the same inclusive manner. Whether Ray is talking to a chiropractic patient, interacting with local farmers, mentoring younger men or spending time with grandchildren he finds a way to honor them and encourage them.

My oldest son-in-law, Adam, and my daughter Heather relate the same way to people in their health food store as they do at Sunday morning church services in their positions as pastors. Adam doesn't have a pastoral façade; he delivers the truth in a matter-of-fact manner that is consistent regardless of topic or place. In fact, it is somewhat amusing to me how very real Adam is with people. He speaks truth whether he is preaching, teaching younger people about the value of getting a job, addressing sin in a person's life, or encouraging someone to move forward with their dreams. Adam is consistent. And Heather is one of the happiest people I know and a great example of the joy of the Lord. Whether painting a picture, teaching pre-school or teaching an art class she finds a way to make the atmosphere happy. I love watching her interact with strangers in her health food store because it is the same as her interaction with an intimate friend. Consistent.

My middle daughter, Summer, though a highly-educated and excellent physician, is in now way arrogant. She relates to her patients and talks about Jesus healing them the same way she talks to her sisters or friends. Her husband, Josh, is a very even, constant person, as well. His church manner looks the same as his interactions with people who dine in his restaurant, or those to whom he is teaching guitar.

My daughter, Kendal, is unique in her ability to represent Jesus with humor. She relates spiritual principles during a home group gathering in the same fashion that she converses with her massage clients or coffee shop patrons. Kendal's husband, Justin, is a peaceful, laid-back guy. Justin really demonstrates the peace of Jesus in his approach to life. He delivers a prophetic word from God with the same gentle demeanor he uses to correct his children. His soothing spirit encourages friends and strangers who frequent his coffee shop. He has a way of standing strong in the Lord with kindness.

I share these family observations because I have watched each of these people develop over many years and I know their behaviors and styles to be authentic. When we live a shared life we have the privilege of watching our natural and spiritual families mature.

Spiritual mentors

Many people react negatively to immature Christians who try to act 'spiritual.' You know the person who can't relax and enjoy a gathering because they feel the need to preach to everyone around them or answer all questions with Bible verses. Most people appreciate authenticity. And it is difficult to trust people who don't know who they are or who Jesus really is.

There should be no separation between our normal daily routine and what we define as spiritual. Our lives with God need to include Him in our everydayness and show people that Jesus loves daily life. When we belong to God, living our ordinary lives is spiritual. We are lying to people when we lead them to believe God loves us more if they become a missionary or live in poverty. The truth is that work is spiritual and family life is sacred and releasing the love and character of Jesus into the community where you live pleases God as much as foreign missions.

But many people have been disillusioned by such immature, 'religious' Christians yet are still in search of genuine spirituality. When we present a judgmental, harsh, unapproachable picture of Jesus to those who have already been hurt or rejected by the church we limit our chance of developing relationships or building trust. We need to redefine community and create opportunities to restore disillusioned men and women who have had negative religious experiences. Unconditionally loving people and teaching them the truth about the Kingdom of God can restore past hurts.

Christians have the ability to transfer God's peace to others just by their presence - because internal peace is released when we interact with people in a genuine way. Our spiritual communities should be places of rest that resemble a safe family. Jesus is the one who can give a person complete rest because he can lift the heaviness we carry and replace it with peace (Matthew 11:28). A great way to show skeptical people the truth about Jesus is to provide a space that is restful and introduce them to God's supernatural peace. This need not be limited to the inside of a church building. Christians can also provide peace for others in their homes or at various gatherings because the authority we have in the name of Jesus can change any atmosphere. These are positive ways genuine relationship and community can restore a person's distorted view of family and church.

The Kingdom of God is not a perfect group of people. The Kingdom of God is often a group of misfits, but it should be a group of misfits who unconditionally love each other and encourage one another to become who God created them to be. It is easy to honor those who are honorable, but it is challenging to honor those we see as unworthy. It is even harder to honor those who we know are living a life of Christian leadership but are not true to what they represent.

Opportunity to honor

God's plan for us is simple. God intends for His church to function as a family. God intends for a family unit to begin with healthy marriages that produce healthy children who are taught to love and trust Him. God blesses the marriage of a man and a woman but does not say that they have to know how to act like Him before they can become husband and wife. God promises to always be with us as He works in our lives to transform us into the image of Jesus if we will allow Him. God had a plan for marriage and family from the beginning and it has not changed (Mark 10:6-9). The world continues to distort and try to re-define marriage and family, but God's plan does not change. The government does not have the ability to change what the creator of the universe designed, but it does have the ability to deceive people.

God defines a Christian marriage for men and women and even tells us how we should treat each other. I love that the scriptures are so specific in telling women how to honor and respect their husbands and instructs men to love and cherish their wives as much as Jesus loves the church (Colossians.3:18-19; Eph. 5:22-23). This is important because men and women need different things within a relationship and feel loved in very different ways.

We often confuse the roles of a husband and wife and try to help people by encouraging them to act in ways that God did not design them to act. I do not have the same emotional needs as my husband. I don't even have the same social needs as Ray. My journey with God is unique to how He designed me. And I know my story reflects Jesus in a way that is different than any other person's. We can't learn to honor others if we don't accept their differences.

Everybody has their individual and unique story and it doesn't take long after you meet someone to hear their family history. It amazes me how many times I meet new people who voluntarily spew their family scars. Sometimes I think our greeting to church newcomers should be "What is your name, what is your story, and how do you feel about God?" instead of "Good morning, how are you?" However, we have to be prepared to listen if we ask honest questions.

My daughter and I were standing in a checkout line in a grocery store in Maui when the cashier looked at me, smiled, then continued bagging a few items. Suddenly she was asking about our relationship and passionately began to tell me how sad she was that her daughter doesn't pay much attention to her since moving to her own apartment. This total stranger continued on, telling me when she calls her daughter to check on her and chat the conversations end abruptly with her daughter saying, "If you don't want anything else, I need to go now."

Clearly, the cashier's story contains painful chapters of family dynamics and a daughter who didn't know how to honor her mother. I told the sad mother I was sorry and suggested that perhaps her daughter was trying to figure life out and would connect with her in a more positive way as she matures.

The context of family is the perfect place to learn how to honor others. The Bible tells us to honor our parents and says honoring our parents is connected to living a good life (Ephesians 6:1-3). Many fathers are not aware of their important role in their children's lives of affirming their identity and teaching them to honor others.

I believe a father's intentional blessing over his sons or daughters is closely related to a person's self esteem. Fathers are positioned to affirm the manhood of sons by speaking words of truth over them about becoming Godly men; likewise to their daughters about becoming Godly women. In reality, most of us did not receive our father's intentional blessing over our lives or our sexuality. The church has a wonderful opportunity to heal father-wounds through spiritual fathers and mothers blessing young men and women and affirming who God says they are.

Spiritual fathers should be older men who have matured in their relationship with Jesus and are living a life lead by the Holy Spirit. This positions spiritual fathers to teach younger men about following the promptings and whispers of the Spirit. Spiritual mothers should understand the ever-changing dynamics of family and share wisdom with those who are raising young families. A mature spiritual mother can teach young adults the nurturing nature of God if it is missing from their lives.

Those who have the greatest need for spiritual parents often reject them because they are reminders of painful family experiences. It is common for people to transfer their dad wounds to men who resemble their father and to God. When spiritual fathers embrace younger men and women as sons and daughters and love them unconditionally negative mindsets begin to shift and hearts begin to open to God's love for them. As a result, the fatherless who once had no framework in their lives for honor see value in those around them (Psalm 68:5-6).

We need spiritual parents, brothers and sisters in Jesus to rebuild familial bonds pain has broken. We need to welcome people into our spiritual communities just like we welcome our family during holiday celebrations. Most of us can reflect on a time when we visited a church and felt loved and accepted. I cherish memories of the gatherings that resembled a family reunion. You know the ones where your quirky cousins embarrass you and your crazy aunt is loud and obnoxious and your distant cousins are spoiled and throw fits and patronize you, but you still walk away with a strong sense of connectedness in spite of the differences? Our spiritual communities should be such places.

Meeting the unmet

Ted is one of our spiritual sons. Ted physically stands heads above others and has an amazing smile. I love to watch Ted worship. His stature and arm span brings a sense of spiritual authority when he raises his hands to praise Jesus. I love when he feels led by God to move to the front of our church to worship. I envision this is what Moses would look like if he visited our worship service. I can see Ted's outstretched arms representing Moses' staff leading people forward in pursuit of God.

Ted's height would suggest that he is confident about who he is and where he is going. However Ted will tell you that he often feels insecure about his identity.

My husband and I embraced Ted into our lives and hearts several years ago. Ted's childhood would likely be thought of as 'normal' - he didn't encounter overt trauma during his childhood. He does not have scars from physical, sexual, or spiritual abuse. Ted's parents provided for his physical needs. He grew up in a nice neighborhood in a nice house. His parents both love Jesus and raised him in the church.

However, Ted is very different from his parents. Ted was very tender and spiritually sensitive. Ted was joyful and laughed a lot. Ted realized at a young age that his personality didn't match the family profile, so he began to feel like something was wrong with him. We love Ted and our family thinks Ted's sensitivity and laughter is a wonderful expression of his heart and that he is a great fit for our family. As we grow in relationship with Ted we hope we can meet some of his unmet needs.

God has designed our spiritual-journeys to intersect with those who need us and those we need. This is because we need more than God in our quest to be like Jesus. We need each other. We need a family.

My family is not a perfect family, but we are committed to loving people for who they are and where they are in their journey. I am far from a perfect mother, but I do love my family unconditionally. I would likely not be voted wife-of-the-year, but I adore my husband and try to honor him. There is nothing any of my family members could do to change my love for them. I love them because they are who they are.

I enjoy watching how love for each other is expressed in very different ways in our family. There are some family members who are more open with me than others. They talk to me about life decisions without any hesitation because I am the mom. There are some family members who hug me more easily than others and some I wouldn't dare kiss. Some family members are comfortable letting me know they are upset with me and will gently tell me and others who don't.

I realize every one of my family members have different spiritual designs and unique personalities influencing how they relate to each other and to me. Differences are not negative. Differences are God's intentional design. Natural and spiritual families must embrace the uniqueness of each family member and love each for who he or she is.

Family is a great opportunity to experience unconditional love that can transfer to the world around us. Sometimes learning to love and be available to others can seem overwhelming, but God will provide everything we need to meet the needs of those we embrace. When Paul wrote to the Philippians about God's provision and how God will supply all of our needs, I think it includes more than our personal spiritual needs. I think it includes spiritual, physical, emotion and social needs. I believe it includes having whatever is necessary for those who we have adopted as family and community.

Let's become healthy, healed spiritual families who love each other with the kindness of God. Let's not reject or neglect those who are different than us. May our communities of faith develop a culture that knows how to honor.

"Love is patient, love is kind, and is not jealous; love does not brag and is not arrogant, does not act unbecomingly; it does not seek its own, is not provoked, does not take into account wrongs suffered, does not rejoice in unrighteousness, but rejoices with the truth; bears all things, believes all things, hopes all things, endures all things. Love never fails." (1 Corinthians 13:4-13).

Questions to Consider

- Do you have a spiritual family?
- Are you a spiritual family to others?
- Do you recognize daily life as spiritual?

CHAPTER FIVE
Learning to Trust

There are many reasons why people stop trusting. When we are neglected or repeatedly disappointed in life, we lose hope and stop trusting others. Unattended distrust from childhood deepens turning to skepticism in adulthood. This creates men and women who enter our communities of faith with their boxing gloves on daring us to like and accept them.

Why am I talking about trust when this book is about the shared life of community? Because those saying they've lost trust in mankind, God or both actually desire for us to see them, accept them and love them. The church has a great opportunity to rebuild trust with cynics who have been disillusioned by the world around them.

It is common to lose trust in people and life whether we had a traumatic childhood or an enchanted one. When we do not see our parents handle broken relationships in a positive manner or teach us how to trust people who hurt us, we are left with uncertainties about how to be joyful when life is painful. During childhood we are not emotionally mature enough to understand complex life issues without the wisdom and instruction of loving adults. Initially we learn to trust by watching the adults in our lives and the repeated messages we receive through safe life experiences. These life experiences follow us in to adulthood and influence our emotional and social intelligence.

Broken hearts are fertile soil for deception and lies. Broken hearts often create elaborate narratives to reinforce pain or create scenarios of fear. Every disappointment has a story of its own, revealing the condition of our heart through our actions.

Unresolved disappointment can make us sick emotionally, spiritually and physically. The Bible says it this way, "Hope deferred makes the heart sick, but dreams fulfilled are a tree of life" (Psalm 13:12). I pray we will be agents of grace who help discouraged people find their dreams. Let's be the ones who restore trust for skeptics.

The need for defenses

Long-term disappointment can create elaborate defenses that keep us separated from others. We have all experienced times when we were transparent with our pain only to become a target for a person's prejudices to be expressed. We have all had vulnerable moments when we shared a secret and had that person use it against us. If we are not careful this can lead us to put everyone in the 'can't trust them' box, encouraging us to keep secrets hidden, pain denied and our masks refined.

A 'mask' is another way of saying we are hiding behind false selves we have created. It is a defense. Somehow we think masks can protect us from hurtful people and additional disappointment by convincing ourselves to pretend. Perhaps we feel it isn't safe to take off our mask and be real. Perhaps we were taught to act as if everything is okay even when we are hurting. Religious people are quite refined in the art of pretending they are always happy even when they are in the midst of sorrow. Fear is a liar. And fear has the ability to tell us to stay hidden. Satan loves when we use our defenses to stay hidden.

It is true that judgmental people cannot be trusted with broken hearts. However, it is equally true that not all people are judgmental. Behind every mask is a person afraid of rejection who probably creates scenarios and projects personal insecurities onto other people.

When we are hiding and don't feel safe we often automatically think people will reject us - before we even interact with them. It is important for us to create communities where people feel safe enough to take off their mask and let us get to know them even if they have things they feel they must hide. This must begin with love. When we feel unconditionally loved we usually feel safe enough to stop hiding.

Confession

Most people need to feel safe before they are willing to confess their struggles to another person. So it's a good idea to choose a safe person with whom to share your pain. The Bible tells us that when we confess to God we are forgiven, but when we confess to each other we are healed (1 John 1:9). This is a wonderful spiritual practice but not everyone is mature enough to handle our confessions. It is immature to think everyone in a spiritual community can be trusted with our hearts, but it is equally immature to think there are no safe, trustworthy people in a church community. Confession is a Biblical principle that can unlock and heal broken hearts and save us years of therapy. When we allow ourselves to develop relationships we create opportunities for God to teach us how to give and receive love. We are building trust.

I have on occasion shared my feelings with a friend only to regret my decision afterwards. And I admit when I share a sensitive matter with someone and they discount it, shame me for it or defend the person who hurt me I struggle with remaining in a transparent friendship with them. I retain relationships with people who offend me, but I am quick to learn who is trustworthy and worthy of my confession. There is a tension in learning how to relate to people who you cannot trust in this way while still remaining friends with them.

It is important to not shame people for their confessions. Hurting people already struggle with shame and shame keeps secret pains buried. We should know how to help people release shame, not reinforce it. I like the fact that Jesus made it possible for us to resolve the effects of shame. The scripture tells us that Jesus died for us and that he is sitting beside the Father praying for us and making our ability to run the race of life possible without shame (Heb. 12:2).

Relationships are an important part of our spiritual-journey and the foundation of authentic Christian community. The journey of life is marked by many experiences where friendship with Jesus and other people are the only viable means of navigation. Without trustworthy relationships our lives lose momentum. We can steer life more easily when we have other people praying for us and helping us process life's struggles.

Many Christians believe time alone with God reading the Bible or listening to worship music will resolve heart issues. Although quiet meditation with God is a vital aspect of spirituality, it is not all that we need. Many of our needs can only be met in the context of relationship and most of the things that keep us trapped in darkness require intentionally talking to another person about them.

Psychology and psychiatry strive to quantify the health of a relationship and spend great amounts of time studying how needs are met within the context of relationships. I enjoy reading such books and believe they contain valuable information. However, I think we can simplify the process by asking people if their relationships meet their needs.

It is common for people to discount their needs. And often religious people deny their needs completely. Vulnerability is threatening for those who have developed a self-sufficient lifestyle and spent many years refining their defenses. Frequently people create sophisticated defenses internally and externally to convince people they are okay. I, however, am not very skilled at hiding what is bothering me; my facial expressions and my attitude let everyone around me know how I feel.

A religious spirit hinders our story

Emotional needs are universal. We all need to feel unconditionally loved, valued, respected, trusted, accepted, desired, appreciated; and that we belong to some group – that there are people like us with whom we can share life.

People cannot feel emotionally secure in a relationship if they are not valued for who they are. Everyone reacts negatively to relationships where others expect change. Intelligence, age, status, or accomplishments cannot fulfill the innate desire within the human heart to be unconditionally loved by another person.

Most people have numerous one-sided relationships in which they do all of the giving and they receive nothing in return. Deep friendships contain mutuality. In an intimate friendship both parties are devoted to developing the friendship.

Religion tells us that we should never expect anything in return for our kindness. We should only give and never expect to receive. This is an unhealthy view of relationships. Healthy relationships should give and receive. Jesus gives and likes to receive. Jesus loves us and wants us to love Him. A one-sided relationship with Jesus may be 'religious' – but it is also anemic. And it isn't relational!

The Pharisees were religious. They were not intimate friends with Jesus. They valued rules more than relationship. They wanted to impress Jesus more than love Him or be loved by him. We need to acknowledge this reality because many people enter our churches with pharisaical, 'religious' masks and, in order to love them unconditionally, we need to recognize this as a defense mechanism.

I have relationships in my life that meet my emotional needs. And I am very aware of the relationships that cannot meet my needs. I have several relationships where people only talk at me and not with me. They tell me who I should have as friends and how I should feel about them. They tell me what they think I should do with my life and what they think God wants me to do. They don't empathize with me when I need it; they only advise me. In these relationships I am never asked questions or included in conversations unless I insert my comments. There is no context for mutuality. They never have issues, need prayer or have needs. I love the people to whom I am referring, but my reality is we do not, in fact, have healthy emotional connections. I often leave conversations with them feeling disappointed the person doesn't have the ability to relate to me on an emotional level.

I also have relationships that are life-giving and I cherish the fact that I am loved for who I am, my opinion is valued and I am free to be myself in every situation. Sandie is one of those friends in my life. Sandie is someone I can call when I am rejoicing and want to share my joy because she celebrates with me. She is also the person I call when I want help processing a painful situation and she cares enough about me to create time and space to listen to me and pray with me. Sandie never shames me or judges me. She always relates to me in the same manner. She definitely speaks the truth in love when I need it the most. Since I trust Sandie with the deep issues of my heart I give her permission to talk directly to me when my thoughts are toxic. She opens her heart to me in the same manner and calls me to listen and pray for her. This is how a mature, loving, healthy relationship with mutuality should look. And if we hope to share God's love and foster authentic relationships built on the love of Jesus this open, honest, empathetic mutuality must be a vital, necessary part of our spiritual communities.

We all have stories and we all need people in our lives who will help us sort through the emotional details of our lives. Emotional support is a key component to intimacy. When we invite Jesus to tell us the truth about any chapter of our story it often changes direction and we can be sure that it will be what is best for us. We can expect Jesus to speak directly to the root issues of our hearts.

When God transforms our story it also encourages other people. When we tell other people how Jesus changed our lives we are actually releasing hope for the listener's life direction. This is a practical way to overcome evil because Satan wants to destroy our lives by convincing us our stories are both unique and hopeless. When we talk about our redeemed stories we can overcome the destruction that Satan intends for us (Rev. 12:11). We should discuss the confusing parts of our story with someone we trust and allow him or her to help us process it with God's truth. We cannot rewrite our histories, but we can redirect our lives and decide how we want our stories to end and ask God to lead us in that direction.

Liz and I spent several years together as I helped her process her traumatic history. Liz often told me she was able to engage in the difficult work of healing her painful memories and history because I helped her feel safe during our times of prayer and ministry. She repeatedly told me if I had been judgmental or harsh when she told me about her abuse she would not have continued on her healing journey.

Safety is vital to people who feel insecure in sharing their life stories. It was vital for Liz. She experienced several counseling sessions, home group settings, and religious pastors who shamed her for having unresolved pain and emotional needs because she was a Christian. The religious leaders who talked to Liz believed the cross resolves all traumas from the past and that she should not be affected by her history any longer.

I have always been confused by this doctrine because it leads people to believe baptism washes away all of life's hurts. In truth, baptism and the resurrection power of Jesus we encounter when we invite Jesus into our hearts makes it possible to deal with painful life experiences, but it doesn't resolve a painful history or guarantee a painless future.

Religious doctrines lead people to create un-Godly checklists of how we should respond to pain. Religious leaders frequently judge people who are weak and shame them into thinking they don't really belong to Jesus because they aren't stronger. Liz was the recipient of such religious judgment. Liz spent many years guarding her heart and hiding her pain because of the response she encountered from immature Christian leadership.

I must admit that 'religious' people are difficult for me. It is strange; the sinful things people feel they need to hide from me don't influence me this way, but the religious spirit that controls many Christians is a struggle for me. I think it is fair to say that Jesus did not agree with the beliefs and double standards of the Pharisees and that he probably didn't enjoy interactions with them.

The Pharisees made up religious laws for people to follow which they themselves did not obey (Matthew. 23:1-3). Considering the pastors, elders, and Christian counselors who were judgmental toward Liz, I wonder how many of them would prefer kindness if they were honest enough to share their secrets. Jesus was and is very familiar with judgmental religious leaders. The religious leaders Jesus encountered wore the appropriate ceremonial garments and quoted the law but were harsh with weak, hurting people. The Pharisees made people's burdens worse by judging them and not helping them. They were more concerned with tithing the proper herbs than with the condition of person's heart (Mt. 23:1-39). Although clothing and culture has changed, the religious spirit is the same. Many spiritual leaders today are still more concerned with a person's appearance or behavior than the condition of their heart.

Jesus also responded to how the religious leaders treated people in need. Jesus reacted to the fact that the religious leaders were more concerned with ceremonies and rituals than they were with the emotional and spiritual needs of the people. The Pharisees had the opportunity to introduce people to God by granting them access to Him just like Liz's pastors had a chance to bless her and connect her with God but chose instead to shame her.

Mercy is better than judgment

Safe people care about the needs of hurting people and will take time to extend mercy. Jesus is mercy. Jesus corrected religious leaders when they honored God with insincere words while their hearts were far from God's heart. He did this specifically by exposing their disrespect for their parents.

Jesus addressed their approach to God by saying, "Why do you use your rules to play fast and loose with God's commands? God clearly says, 'Respect your father and mother,' and 'Anyone denouncing father or mother should be killed.' But you weasel around that by saying, "Whoever wants to can say to father and mother 'What I owed to you I've given to God.'" That can hardly be called respecting a parent. You cancel God's command by your rules. Frauds! Isaiah's prophecy of you hit the bull's-eye: 'These people make a big show of saying the right thing, but their heart isn't in it. They act like they're worshiping me, but they don't mean it. They just use me as a cover for teaching whatever suits their fancy.'" (The Message, Matthew 15:3-9).

Jesus was serious about not letting the religious leaders misrepresent or confuse people about life with God. If we want to create safe communities of faith of which Jesus approves we must not give more attention to a person's behavior than to caring for their needs or teaching them the truth about God. We cannot do this if we are intimidated by a person's sin or feel personally responsible to correct their sin.

I encouraged Liz to forgive those who gave her harsh counsel and to give herself permission to be honest about how the judgments hurt her. I explained to Liz the principle of talking about her pain and being healed (James 5:16). She later told me that she could feel the results of her confession. I encouraged Liz to make this a regular part of her life because I believe that confession should be a natural part of our daily lives. It shouldn't be something awkward that is only done in a counseling session or a confessional booth in a church. It should become a natural regular practice.

My conversation with Liz also gave me an opportunity to explain to her that there is a difference between Godly people and religious people. Godly people can be trusted. Jesus is not religious. Jesus is spiritual. Jesus is God.

Liz now recognizes appropriate emotional, social, spiritual needs that can only be met in the context of relationships. Liz acknowledges she must be connected to a spiritual group of people in order to move forward in her life with God and her journey to wholeness. When Liz and I talk about this reality she lets me know that developing relationships is still not easy for her. Relationships for Liz are hard work. She has to continually remind herself that the people she is presently living life with are not abusive.

Liz is currently involved in a healthy spiritual community that knows her story and accepts her for who she is. Liz's church family does not define her by her history; they love her unconditionally and embrace the gifts and talents that she has to offer the body of Christ. Liz could still be trapped in the pain of her childhood and writing a dysfunctional life story if she hadn't shared her broken heart with other people.

She now has the opportunity to lead other people to freedom and teach them the value of communal living. Liz is an example of the power of a transformed life which has energy that is transferable to others through hearing the encouragement of her story. I desire to see our spiritual communities equipped to transform lives and position people to live healthy, productive lives that are centered on

Jesus. I want the church to become less religious and more spiritual so we can help people stop searching for God and realize that Jesus lives in those who choose Him.

Questions to Consider

- Do you trust yourself?
- Do you trust other people?
- Do you trust Jesus?

CHAPTER SIX
Pursuing God with an
Uninterrupted Life

We pursue things about which we are passionate. And we travel the path leading to our dreams when we have done the inner work that releases the desires of our heart.

One of the ways God communicates with us is through dreams. Perhaps God can speak to us when we are unconscious because we can't make our own plans or talk constantly at those times. Sleeping lets us go deeper into ourselves than the barrier of consciousness, which restrict us, allows when we're awake. It is hard to listen to God in the midst of the busyness of our lives. Sleep is a time in which we are not distracted and can receive God's direction. So He frequently speaks to us when we are asleep.

God knows the desires of our heart even when we don't and He knows what we need long before we realize it. He even knows when we are moving toward destruction in our lives and He can choose to warn us. Job refers to God directing our lives through dreams by writing, "God always answers, one way or another, even when people don't recognize his presence. In a dream, for instance, a vision at night, when men and women are deep in sleep, fast asleep in their beds—God opens their ears and impresses them with warnings to turn them back from something bad they're planning, from some reckless choice, and keep them from an early grave, from the river of no return" (The Message, Job 33:14-18).

Joseph dreamed about marrying Mary, escaping to Egypt, then returning home. He also dreamed about wise men who were told not to return to Herod (Matthew 1-2; 27:19). These dreams were very helpful to a man trying to pursue God in the midst of life circumstances he did not plan.

Joseph did not consider a pregnant fiancée when he envisioned his future with Mary. But God spoke to him in dreams and visions. God even sent him an angel in a dream to deliver a message about the birth of Jesus. So Joseph then did not have to consider ordinary explanations for what was truly a supernatural event. God used a dream to speak truth and direct a chapter in Joseph's life that could have otherwise derailed his story.

It should be noted that not all dreams are from God. Some dreams are just random, some are self-indulgence, some are influenced by lies or exaggerated by demonic spirits. I am referencing here not all types of dreams, but rather those where God steps past the obstacles our intellect can build and speaks directly to us through dreams.

A life surrendered to Jesus

When we are living a life committed to Jesus we have the ability to fulfill the desires of our heart, contribute to the needs of people in our lives, and simultaneously pursue God without interruption. Jesus makes it possible for us to maintain momentum in our lives and live life in a rhythm that is fluid, not static. This does not contradict the need to be still and listen to God. Rather, it emphasizes the power and authority dwelling in the righteous spirit of a follower of Jesus when they've surrendered their life story to God and are led by the Holy Spirit.

We can all recall times when we have experienced pain or disappointment in our lives that we allowed to put us on pause, derail us or even fully stop us. During those stuck times of not moving forward we often assign the wrong meaning to our loss of momentum. Sometimes we get religious and frame our inability to process pain as a spiritual move on God's part and call it a 'desert season' divinely orchestrated to teach us a lesson. God does use immobile times when we feel like we are stranded in the wilderness to work things out. But I am referring to specific times when our choices impair our ability to move forward.

At such times we often grab a drug of choice to distance our minds from our hearts to more easily justify our present status. I've talked with many people with so many disappointments and such lack of direction in their past they have decided to exit daily life and spend all of their time praying. We have even created schools designed to disconnect us from the world in order to pray. Believe it not, prayer can be used to distract us from what we need to address in our lives in order to regain movement.

It isn't God's plan for us to hide from everyday life in our prayer closet. It is His plan that we integrate our prayer life into our daily life. I am not discounting divinely inspired seasons of life during which God call us to slow down and seek Him. I am highlighting the unhealthiness of only praying and never contributing. I believe God's plan is for us to help others, serve others, and partner with Him to change the world. This cannot be accomplished if we spend all our days alone praying.

An exceptional model

The Gospels give us the story of Jesus' life. Through the four separate narratives of Matthew, Mark, Luke and John we are shown the incidents of Jesus' life and His character. We see Him acting and reacting to many different kinds of situations.

Many times throughout the Gospels we read that Jesus went off alone to pray. However, Jesus was never isolated, He was focused. This is a crucial distinction to make, understanding the difference between time alone with God and isolating yourself away from daily life.

Jesus is our perfect example of this balance. Jesus never lost sight of where He was headed. And Jesus was not self-centered (Hebrews 12:2). He began and finished the race we are in. He didn't hide himself away from life and its daily interactions, nor did He allow life to distract him. It is fair to say Jesus lived an uninterrupted life.

The busyness of our lives often pulls us away from the course of our lives. We are part of a society which is easily distracted. We set goals and dream dreams, but we don't want to exert the time and energy required to achieve our goals. We often opt for shortcuts and settle for less than God's best for our lives because we can have it sooner.

We are witnessing a culture that is losing touch with the ability to work for its dreams. It is presently very popular with Millennials to want other people to pay for their dreams both physically and financially. You can browse the Internet and find numerous 'go fund me' pages where people encourage others to finance their dreams. I believe this is a result of losing touch with the cost of living a focused life and working for the desires of our heart.

The 'go-fund-me' attitude can also interfere with the realities necessary for a full, authentic spiritual-journey. This happens because many people think there are shortcuts to spiritual maturity. So they miss many aspects of Jesus because they are in a hurry and want to bypass the time and energy required to develop a genuine, relational friendship with Jesus and a sustainable life of faith.

Healthy people have the ability to process overwhelming life experiences, regroup and move forward. Healthy people's lives have momentum. Positive life experiences can derail a person's spiritual-journey as easily as painful experiences, but the ability to grow and mature after an interruption exposes the condition of a heart and its level of emotional and spiritual maturity.

I can honestly say I have processed many painful life experiences well. And I can honestly say there have been times in my life when I allowed trials to become bigger than Jesus. I often feel a great sense of satisfaction remembering my response to a cancer threat. I was in the midst of writing my doctoral dissertation and had to extend my completion date to deal with a fifteen-pound tumor. I remained peaceful because I trusted Jesus to heal my body. Though I approached surgery not knowing if the tumor was cancerous or not, I remember the confidence I felt when praying about post-surgery life and how I knew Jesus would take care of me regardless of the outcome. I retained a sense of humor and I even named the tumor Tina and delivered many jokes about Jesus defeating 'Tina the Tumor' when the surgeon announced the tumor was benign.

Although I was disappointed that my academic endeavor was delayed nearly one year, my relationship with the Lord was secure. Even in the early days of every doctor involved telling me the specific location of the tumor made cancer probable, I trusted Jesus to take care of my body and my heart. I cherished the sweet hours of recovery that I spent with Jesus. The trauma of a tumor affected my health, but it did not bruise my heart or interrupt my life with the Lord.

I regret the times when I allowed agonizing experiences to distract me. I distinctly remember my reaction to two different incidents when emotionally wounded people decided to tell lies about me. Although these particular people, out of their own traumatic pasts, had already falsely accused others, lacked healthy relationships, lacked social skills, manipulated, deceived, and were trapped in their own internal worlds, when they verbally attacked me... I plummeted. The disappointment, sadness and discouragement I felt was disproportionate to the true situation. My awareness of their dysfunctional mindsets did not diffuse the ache I felt in my heart.

My pain began to lie to me and I decided I was not fit for ministry. I began to embrace the thought, "I have no place in prayer ministry because I cannot lead dysfunctional people to truth." I took my eyes off Jesus and focused on the offenses in my heart. I allowed heartbreaking experiences to divert me. Unresolved pain simply has the ability to derail us - even if momentum is the usual rhythm of our lives.

And we all know people whose life seems to be standing still rather than flowing. There are many people with whom I have been acquainted for years, but I do not know them in any greater depth today than when I met them. We all have individuals in our lives who remain seemingly unaffected by time spent together sharing life.

'Suzi' is fictitious, but I use her to represent some common behaviors I have observed for years in numerous and diverse people. Suzi is middle-aged, yet she communicates like a young child. People like Suzi often speak in a childlike manner indicative of the age at which they got stuck. She cannot engage in a serious conversation, diverts all questions about herself to random topics, and becomes anxious when group conversations move in the direction of personal content, depth, or intimacy. Suzi is a Christian believer who loves Jesus, but spiritual conversations with her are limited to a cycle of quoting scriptures or preaching. She is uncomfortable with disagreement or any resemblance of honest opinion and her physical fidgeting turns into nervous chatter redirecting conversation to people who are unfamiliar to the group.

Suzi's lack of social skills and inability to move forward in life are directly related to something in her life that still has not been properly processed. Her life does not have momentum. She has not changed or matured since meeting her years ago. She never talks about new goals or dreams. When others introduce their goals to the group she responds with confused expression as to their need for change. Suzi doesn't appear interested in learning anything new. She is perfectly content with life as it has always been.

The people in Suzi's life recognize her social, emotional and spiritual maturation does not match her chronological age. However, she remains unaware of her immature stage of development and the lack of progression in her life.

We can deduce that 'Suzi' is in denial about something still unprocessed from her history and her behavior reflects her departure from reality. Someone similar to 'Suzi' has created a world of their own they do not want touched.

Denial is one of the biggest ways we lie to ourselves. Denial enables us to remain in dysfunctional behaviors and it can easily interrupt our lives. I tell people who seem to have little or no self-awareness or no healthy relationships that there is a strong probability their perception of God is skewed and inaccurate. If we can't authentically relate to people, we usually can't relate honestly with God.

Anxious ways

Intimacy makes unhealthy people anxious and uncomfortable which in turn causes them to interact awkwardly with others. An anxious heart is frequently indicative of an unhealed experience. Living life at an accelerated pace often means finding ourselves in a constant state of anxiety. Anxiety is frequently indicative of a busy, distracted life that doesn't have time to listen to the small, still voice of the Lord - because being quiet often surfaces internal pain and brings us to places that are off-limits to Jesus.

I know many people who love Jesus and don't know how to be comfortable with the Lord and stop talking and moving because they are more comfortable ranting. Sometimes people call their nervous chatter prayer because eye contact is intimidating and unfamiliar to them. But their version of 'prayer' allows them a place to hide away even though the Bible says an important way we can get to know God is to, "Be still, and know that I am God" (Psalm 46:10).

We are living in an age of electronic communication. Time that was once spent reading novels is being replaced with hours devoted to screens. It is becoming normal for a person to watch TV, work on their laptop, check their iPad, or text or instant message others on their smart phones while spending little time developing relationships with God or other people.

Social media allows people to remain in denial and avoid developing relational skills. It allows people to avoid eye contact. It allows us to lie about who we are and what we are truly dealing with in our lives. We are conditioning our brains to be on alert, over-stimulated and over-excited. It makes stillness a challenge.

We can assume our brain focus and social skills are compromised because of the overuse of screen time. Many Millennials with whom I pray tell me they don't understand how slowing down could be a good practice. Their brains began their cognitive development with over-stimulation by video gaming as young children and it has sped up with technological advancement. This creates a pattern of hyper-movement and short-segmented communication. It is understandable that it is challenging for an electronic culture to sit still, be quiet and communicate with God.

The challenge

Creating new habits requires intentionality. Developing a sustainable spiritual life also requires intention. Slowing down necessitates an awareness of the importance of quiet time with God and an honest evaluation of how much time is spent escaping human interaction. Learning your exit strategies is worth your attention.

Young mothers in the throes of raising children would agree it is one of the most rewarding, precious times in life. However, it can feel overwhelming. The daily demands of motherhood, household tasks, extra-curricular activities, marriage, finances, health, friendships, and career can easily combine to create a daily schedule that is stressed to find time to slow down and talk to God.

It is challenging to juggle daily life with time to meditate and focus on Jesus. Family life is a positive life experience, but if we allow it to consume us it can interrupt pursuing God and developing meaningful relationships. Raising a family or maintaining relationships with adult children is wonderful. But it can also become bigger than our life with God and derail our spiritual-journeys if we are not intentional about time devoted to God. The proper conclusion is not either family-and-friends or God. The correct answer is both. And the challenge is finding a way to simultaneously implement them both in our busy lives.

Many people try to process the busyness of life without God or other people and get trapped. This often results in emotional, psychological, or physical breakdowns. Anti-depressants are swallowed along with the person's pain in an attempt to function and maintain an overextended lifestyle. Life moves into survival mode and God is set aside until life slows down.

The problem is that we don't know how to slow down; we are becoming comfortable responding to God in an instant message manner. One of my ministry goals is to teach people the importance of disconnecting from electronics and waiting on the Lord. Psalm 27:14 is a great verse to encourage us to intentionally slow down and learn to wait on the Lord because stillness allows us to move to higher ground as we learn to trust what God speaks to us when we pause.

Stillness is a skill that can be developed and a perfect opportunity to expand the fabric of our stories, but we must recognize the resistance to this practice. Satan is not the only obstacle vying for our attention. Most of the time our distractions are good things such as social gatherings, family activities, laundry, dishes, children, or mates and our distractions will continue as long as we excuse them.

It is part of the human condition to be easily distracted from God, but it is comforting to know when we stop and connect with the Lord He will direct our paths. When we are silent it creates an opportunity for us to learn how God speaks to us and this awareness opens our eyes to how the Lord is working in our story. Discerning the voice of God should take priority over distractions. This will only transpire if we intentionally schedule times of daily retreat.

It is easy to miss divine direction if we don't recognize the voice of the Lord in our life. It gives us permission to remain stuck in the past rather than take responsibility for our life and commit to the work required for freedom.

The human condition contains many common themes and one of them is that pain and hopelessness lead to loss of direction. And a person's pain can often stay part of their identity because they fear who they will be without it. So it is easier for some people to remain in denial than move forward in God's healing.

People need community in their healing journeys because psychological pain can cripple people who do not have the skill to process it. And isolation is not conducive to transformation. When a person's pain is greater than his or her hope, doubts that God can help surface and heal the pain become bigger than Jesus. When pain is directing a person's life, lies become their guiding force and derailment is probable.

The truth sets us free

God's truth is the key that will unlock a life frozen in denial. I often remind unhealthy people that listening to the voice of God will bring them out of denial and into reality. I reference John 8:32 by sharing the principle that truth is what sets us free.

I realize many people have no framework for God speaking to them. They only understand reading the Bible and learning about Him. When people only have an intellectual awareness of Jesus, they need faithful communities to teach them how God speaks. The Bible tells us that God is not limited to communicating with us through scripture, but that God literally speaks to us.

John 10 compares us to sheep and tells us Jesus is the shepherd leading us through life. I love the image of Jesus as our shepherd. I envision scattered, stubborn sheep - representing many of us - calmly gathered by the loving guidance of the shepherd's staff and His voice calling the sheep to order. The text stresses the importance of knowing and following the voice of our shepherd and clearly says followers of Jesus can know His voice.

In John 10:27 Jesus says, "My sheep hear my voice, and I know them, and they follow Me." This verse tells me our relationship with Jesus is intended to be a friendship. Close friends don't restrict their communication to notes, or texts, or learning facts about each other; they talk to each other. Their affection for each other deepens and they build an intimate relationship.

When we decide to deal with the denial in our lives it is important for us to understand reality. Reality does not always feel good. I think it is fair to say that reality is more often unpleasant than pleasant. For some reason people have the misconception that reality means that everything should be happy and feel good. This is rarely true.

A testimony of trusting Jesus

I watched Nora process the pain in her life. Nora has been a Christian for many years, but her faith was visible when she found out that her husband had been living a double life. When Nora found out her husband had been unfaithful to her during their entire marriage, her response amazed me. Nora kept her eyes on

Jesus and trusted He would help her process her new world. She cried, got angry, yelled and grieved the loss of a marriage, but she did not lose the momentum in her life. She did not get stuck in the pain of her new reality. Nora turned to the people in our church who she trusted and gave them permission to tell her the truth as she tried to make sense of her husband's choices.

It is well with our soul when we choose to live by truth and not be persuaded by circumstances or emotions. Nora could have easily blamed herself or believed the lies her husband threw at her. But she did not take the blame for her husband's behavior, nor did she buy into untruths about herself. She knew Jesus was the answer to peace and truth. So Nora was intentional about protecting daily time devoted to listening to the Lord. Nora's focus was on Jesus and listening carefully to His direction.

In her pain, Nora pursued God and did not disconnect from the spiritual community she knew as family. Nora knew the shepherd's voice and the peace that comes when we turn to Jesus in times of trial. To me, Nora's response to her husband's betrayal is an example of the biblical principle that through Jesus we can overcome the power of our stories and the trials in our lives (Revelation 12:11).

When we listen, the shepherd's voice can lead us to peace in the midst of a painful reality. Broken people often confuse numbness for peace. Numbness is rooted in lies. Peace is rooted in truth. Reality helps us develop Godly character and sustainable faith, stimulating a desire to fall deeper in love with God.

When we love God with our hearts and our minds, and our desire for Him is stronger than our pain, we can begin to develop an uninterrupted life (Mark 12:30). When we learn to seek God and His ways first and live a surrendered life we no longer need to worry when the waves of life crash over us. We can then react like the psalmist David and say, "I've thrown myself headlong into your arms - I'm celebrating your rescue. I'm singing at the top of my lungs, I'm so full of answered prayers" (The Message, Psalm 13:5-6). Pain and suffering will always exist, but how we respond to it can change.

Living surrendered lives gives God permission to help us become more like Jesus. It grants Jesus access to chapters of our stories we are trying to write without him. It closes the gap between our thoughts and behaviors that we try to deny.

Great amounts of energy are spent trying to convince ourselves that our struggles have nothing to do with how we think. The Apostle Paul says that we are changed when our minds are renewed; this confirms that cognitive changes are expressed through our actions (Romans 12:2). The relationship between thoughts, behaviors and emotions cannot be ignored. I often tell people that how they feel about a situation is always connected to what they believe about the situation. Negative emotions usually correlate with specific lies. Anxiety, fear, depression are always by-products of the beliefs that empower them.

And it sometimes appears as if negative emotions are contagious. It is interesting to me that most people who view everything from a dismal perspective are also very unhappy people who frequently struggle with depression and don't have peace or joy in their lives. Their response to any given situation is critical and judgmental. And they can strongly defend their point-of-view with illogical thinking. Have you ever walked away from such a conversation feeling negative? Time has proven to me that negative people often transfer their thoughts and feelings to God and blame Him for their emotional condition and their state-of-affairs.

The Bible tells me so

The Gospel of Luke says we should love God with our whole selves. This confirms that although our minds are an integral part of loving

God, we love Him completely when we love Him with our hearts, emotions, souls, spirits, and minds.

Many Christians love God more with their mind than their heart. Luke was a physician and he understood the importance of loving God with every part of our being. I think all good physicians understand that people are complex and cannot be treated by only considering the physical condition of their body. When we compartmentalize ourselves, we risk separating our spirituality from our humanness, ending up with a disrespect for wholeness and a fragmented approach to helping people.

Since how we live is influenced by what we think, it is beneficial to examine our thoughts. When we acknowledge and accept Jesus as our savior and invite Him to direct our life everything we do should be thought of, and is, 'spiritual.' When we separate 'daily-life' and 'life-with-God' we relate to God in a very disjointed, uneven fashion. Our daily life becomes secular and our church lives are defined as spiritual and thus the two shall never meet.

Life with God should be constant and mobile. Loving God must be comprehensive, not restrictive. Loving God completely means giving Him access to our thoughts, our feelings, our behaviors, and every area of our life. When we choose to love God with every part of ourselves we create a solid relationship that is stable and less likely to derail. When we are fully connected to Jesus we can pursue God and continue moving forward even when life circumstances are unsure.

Obedience and devotion

It is obvious Hosea knew how to slow down and listen to God for direction. Hosea is a great biblical example of an uninterrupted life. Hosea's story is a spiritual picture of life with God and how his love for God enabled him to unconditionally love a dysfunctional wife. The divine messages Hosea spoke to Israel as a prophet shows us

God's heart for people. And Hosea's obedience in marrying his wife reflects a life devoted to love, justice and trusting God's direction (Hosea 12:6).

But reading Hosea's story is also comparable to watching a movie that has several intertwined X-rated plots. Israel had been seduced by pagan gods and turned away from God. The climate of Israel had become idolatrous and unfaithful. The culture was enticed by lusts displayed through sex with temple prostitutes. Yet God told Hosea to marry Gomer, just such a prostitute. Hosea's life with Gomer paralleled Israel's life with the Lord. Hosea obeyed the Lord and embraced Gomer, being faithful to her though she continued in her promiscuous ways. There were many obstacles in Hosea's life, yet Hosea was not distracted from God. He lived an uninterrupted spiritual life.

What we read about Hosea exemplifies a person loving God with his body, soul and spirit. Though Hosea is considered a last-chance prophet in the urgency to warn Israel to return to the Lord, he delivered God's message to the people with intense emotional appeal. It is fair to say Hosea was confident in who God designed him to be - a tender, emotional man able to speak God's truth and implement God's truth in an unyielding manner. He wasn't distracted by dreary situations. Hosea knew the reality of Israel's condition and the condition of his wife's heart, yet he remained faithful to God.

"What are you waiting for? Return to your God! Commit yourself in love, in justice! Wait for your God and don't give up on Him – ever!" (The Message, Hosea 12:6).

We have to make many of the same choices Hosea made to live an uninterrupted life. The climate of our nation can seduce us, distract us and become the loudest voice in our hearts whether we are Echo Boomers, Baby Boomers, or senior citizens. We must choose to develop a sustainable life with God and commit to it.

If we become distracted we should repent, regroup and return to the Lord and His people. We are best able to do this when we are in a community of genuine, authentic people with open hearts truly hearing our story. This allows us to maintain the momentum God intends for our lives in Jesus and not become stuck in the pain of our story. Community is necessary in maintaining an uninterrupted spiritual life.

Questions to Consider

- Does your life have momentum?
- Are you living an uninterrupted life?
- What has interrupted your life?

CHAPTER SEVEN
A Safe Place to Heal

Hopelessness leaves us feeling like we are disconnected from God. It dulls our senses, grips our mind and impairs our health. We lose our desire for life. Our passion slips into oblivion when we doubt God's omnipotent ability to alter our circumstances. Hopelessness robs the present and clouds the future. When we lose hope, we lose heart (Proverbs 13:12).

When we are hurting and feel disconnected from the Lord we often need another person to help us return to God's presence in order to heal our broken hearts. Understanding God is the healer of our wounds and that we need other people to help us process our pain are important keys to healing.

Sadly, it is much more common for hurting people to turn to broken people for help rather than healthy people or God. Trauma-bonding can form powerful connections which delay a person's healing through a sense of empathy from those trapped in the same struggles. Trauma-bonds tether people to unhealthiness, risking the danger of developing co-dependent relationships held together by emotionally-dependent attachments.

Deception often disguises pain and sin as comfort. I often meet people for prayer who have allowed poor choices or addictions to destroy their families. These people need wise counsel, the love of a caring family and spiritual direction. Yet they often listen only to poor advice from immature Christians or the reassurances of other addicts. Pain and disappointment can lead to separation. But, comforting as they may appear, health is never found in isolation or resolved by the counsel of others struggling with the same unhealthiness.

Living socially is a very significant piece of the fabric that needs to be woven into our stories. In order to break the power dark spots in our stories have in our lives we must share these parts of our story with others. Such sharing, especially with those who have traveled the same dark roads and are on the other side of a mutual bondage, can serve as encouragement to those afraid to move forward into healing. The path to healing cannot be traveled alone and the steps to freedom require relationship. We can change our lives through connectedness.

Hurting people need help forging new paths for their lives. This is the perfect opportunity for a community of faith to introduce the love of Jesus and show people love extends beyond the barriers of trauma. I realize people trapped in addictions have vulnerable infrastructures drawing them to other struggling people. I also know that expressing love often takes the form of intervention. John Donne spoke a spiritual truth that I love when he poetically stated, "No man is an island, entire of itself." We cannot heal or be made whole outside the context of relationships.

Whether a person's pain is the result of repeated disappointments, the effects of a broken home, extensive sexual, physical, emotional, or spiritual abuse, or an inability to handle the stress of a hectic lifestyle the path to healing is the same. The path to freedom must lead to God and it must be traveled with other people. We must look to others who have turned to God in times of trouble or people who live a Godly life.

Hurtful experiences tell us our pain must be hidden from ourselves and others. Lies keep the doors of shame closed and secrets trapped behind them. Such untruths start as tiny seeds buried under years of disappointment or shame which eventually poison us by growing out of proportion. When Christian people are under the authority of shame they lose touch with their internal spiritual radar system. They disregard the fact that the Holy Spirit living in them, prompting them to turn to Jesus for help, has everything they need for freedom.

Most people do not understand that personal choice is the key which unlocks the dark doors to their internal prison. Wise choices lead to liberty. And such freedom awakens us to many needed truths. Liberty stirs us to the reality of our life's condition and highlights how God is presently working with us.

Freedom releases an awareness of Satan's involvement in our lives. Secrets, sin and addictions blind us to Satan's activity. When we are unaware of demonic activity we tell ourselves we are doing well and don't need anything or anyone. It doesn't take long to create an isolated world open to Satan and closed to God.

Satan has a great opportunity to distract us from God when we partner with him in allowing darkness into our lives. This is the time when some people begin changing the gospel, reframing sin and justifying their secrets.

Addictions of any form do not start grandly. Addictions begin with one poor choice at a time, growing into obstacles which feel bigger than God's ability to resolve them. When addictions are justified and downplayed, they become the loudest voice in a person's mind. When they are nourished, addictions have the ability to create lives of their own within the human heart, just as sin has the power to manipulate people with lies.

I believe lies are as diverse as the demons attached to them, but there are common lies that always seem to accompany addictions: "I can stop this behavior by myself at any time." "I am not hurting anyone other than myself." "This isn't that big of a deal." "No one will ever find out." "It is easier maintaining a life of addiction or sin than to living with the consequences of exposing sin." These are a few lies that I have heard repeatedly over the past 20 years from people too afraid to take responsibility for their actions.

People trapped in addiction are usually afraid to confess the things controlling them because they fear rejection. But recovery must include family, natural or spiritual. I know sin is strong and can blind very wonderful, intelligent, gifted people, but I also believe no one truly wants to be trapped in darkness. So when someone feels safe enough in our family to acknowledge what has been controlling them, this is a perfect time to show people how much we love them by supporting them.

There is no fear in love, so when we believe in someone and love them unconditionally we help them overcome the things that have dominated them. John says this very simply: "Perfect love casts out fear" (1 John 4:18). We could rephrase this to say when we feel loved, we aren't afraid. When a person makes the choice to stop hiding his or her sin our love can actually help transform that person. Love has a face seen through people and received through relationships.

The human condition is universal and individual so is therefore closely related to each person's story. Every scar a person bears holds a piece of his or her story and has the power to propel or hinder their journey. It is easy to gain insight into someone else's life when we listen to them.

It is sometimes more difficult to evaluate our own story. When we consider our personal story we tend to reframe the chapters we don't want to own. If we are honest with ourselves, most of us have edited the parts of our stories that remind us of our poor choices and the seasons in our lives produced by these choices. When we are afraid we usually remain trapped because we lie to ourselves.

When darkness overcomes a person to such a degree that it becomes the norm, change is met with resistance even though change is a perfect catalyst for growth and transformation. Dark times are often examples of seasons we edit and try to reframe for many reasons.

Although many people work hard to control their pain with various drugs of choice, we must remember God is the only one who can turn our pain into something beautiful. We can deny our reality, disconnect from our pain and create an internal word of denial, but we cannot produce divine peace for ourselves.

Satan loves when we think we know more than God and can change ourselves. It gives him an opportunity to reinforce our self-reliance and increase our introspection. The Devil delights when our plans for recovery don't include a spiritual community or dependence on Jesus. It is a demonic scheme to keep people believing they are too damaged for God or that they don't have a place to turn for help.

Practical application

A very practical way to help people choosing to step away from addictions is to teach them the truth about the power of demonic spirits' ability to pull them back into deception. We must go beyond quoting scriptures about demonic spirits. We need to teach people how to stand against demonic agendas.

Paul gives us distinct truth about the spirit-realm in Ephesians 6 when he uses military language to instruct us about spiritual struggles. Paul uses the term armor as an analogy for Christians learning to stand firm against the things that demonic spirits throw at us. Take note that Satan throws specific arrows at us personally related to our weaknesses or the addictions we are trying to overcome. Because he knows how to deceive people who aren't aware of his schemes.

Though it appears as such, it is profound to understand that most of our life struggles are not against people. Paul says most of our struggles are spiritual and related to demonic spirits doing what demonic spirits do. Demonic spirits deceive us with lies keeping us trapped when we make choices based on such lies.

It is comforting to read Paul's instruction to us to stand against the Devil rather than fight. I have seen many people exhaust themselves by engaging in unnecessary battles with demonic spirits. These battles are usually fought with loud voices and dramatic behaviors. I often envisions demonic spirits laughing when people act foolishly instead of knowing darkness is only defeated with the name of Jesus. We can actually win demonic struggles by quietly saying the name of Jesus. The power is in the name of Jesus, not how loudly and dramatically we say it.

Paul gives detailed instruction in standing firm when he explains that we defeat the works of the Devil with God's truth and that in order to do this we must be familiar with the Word of God. Paul also tells us to be alert and pray all the time. These principles should be part of our daily lives and are definitely principles people who want to overcome addictions need. We should be in tune and recognize when Satan tries to influence us and simply pray calmly against it. Followers of Jesus can do this because our spirits are connected to the Holy Spirit who empowers our authority over darkness.

When we understand the dynamics of the spirit-realm and learn to stand against Satan, scripture says God's grace will give us the utterances we need to pray. This is important because many people get hung up on trying to craft appropriate prayers. Our words can be very simple. I think some of my most powerfully crafted prayers are "Help Jesus!" and "Go away in the name of Jesus!"

We can condense all that Ephesians 6 teaches by systematically understanding the importance of choice, the power that is in the name of Jesus, the unchanging truth of the scriptures, and the intentional life of prayer. Jesus must be bigger in our lives than Satan if we want to be equipped to stand against demonic attacks. Remember that the attacks will be something that hits the spots in your heart that you have not opened up to Jesus. That means that if we don't give God complete access to constantly search our hearts we are in danger of having Satan pull us into sin. David prayed a powerful prayer when he asked the Lord to "Search me, O God, and know my heart; Try me and know my anxious thoughts" (Psalm 139:23).

The power of personal choice

In our present culture there is great emphasis placed on natural health care and self-diagnosis. It is becoming acceptable to determine our health status from an online medical checklist and create a personal treatment plan independent of a human health care professional. We are constantly bombarded with advertisements for life changing, anti-aging supplements and protocols. Health drinks are replacing meals and vitamins are replacing the discipline of a nutritionally balanced diet.

Don't misunderstand me; my belief in integrative healthcare is strong. I have a Magic Bullet sitting beside my Pro-Juicer which are worn from regular use. Both appliances share space with a basket full of supplements I ingest on a daily basis. However, there is a tension between our willingness to do the hard work required to say no to junk food and yes to nutritious food and the quick results we want from supplements.

We frequently extend this quick fix mindset to our spiritual life. We want to swallow a capsule that will transform our physical, emotional and spiritual wounds. We want someone to lay hands on us and pray a prayer to supernaturally replace the hard work required to overcome poor choices or traumatic histories.

I am not saying God is not capable and doesn't instantly heal people. I am not suggesting God doesn't perform miracles in this present age. I am familiar with the supernatural power of Jesus and I love miracles. I have prayed for people who have been instantly healed from life-threatening illnesses and physical infirmities.

However, God has never supernaturally healed my health issues apart from surgery and intentional healthy pursuits in my daily life. God has not supernaturally released an anointing for weight loss although I believe He could do so. I have had to alter my diet and work out on a semi-regular basis. (Yes, I am aware that it should be a regular basis.)

God often leaves our daily choices up to us concerning diet, exercise and healthy lifestyle practices as well as our spiritual lives. We have a role in determining our level of health that is in addition to prayer. I think that it is fair to say we have more control over our lives than God does because He has lovingly given us the freedom of personal choice.

There is a tension in our pursuit of freedom because God often releases our healing in many ways and through many different people. Our faith should not be challenged if God heals us differently than we request. Let us develop safe places for people to heal that are diverse enough to include every person and every need. Let us not be narrow and religious when it comes to life with God and what we believe it should look like.

The Lord knows what we need much more than we know what we need. In fact, scripture says God will meet our needs according to the riches of His glory (Philippians 4:19). God not only meets our needs, He usually surpasses what we need with blessings that we did not consider.

We often restrict God because we can't comprehend how much He loves us, and how He delights in taking care of us. When we experience God's love we learn to trust Him and live with an unmovable confidence that He will never leave us. This as opposed to thinking God doesn't love us if He doesn't supernaturally heal us. When we trust God, and not the outcome of our circumstances, we create expectation for God that allows us to mature in our approaches to healing.

A woman of faith

I think of the woman in the Bible who had bleeding issues and knew if she pressed into the crowd and touched Jesus she would be healed. The story doesn't say anything about her thoughts, but we can imagine she believed in the supernatural powers of Jesus. We can assume since her bleeding is defined as an issue that it was prolonged. I am suggesting that the woman probably dealt with disappointment because her bleeding was chronic. I wonder if people knew about her condition and openly talked about her. I wonder if they taunted her, adding emotional pain to her physical pain (Matthew 10:1-6). I wonder if she expected her healing to come in the manner she received it.

Consider being the blind man at the pool of Siloam standing before Jesus, the healer, as He puts mud on your eyes to restore your sight (John 9:7). How would you have reacted? The story leaves us wondering about the man's exact response to how Jesus approached his healing. I wonder if the man thought Jesus' methodology was unorthodox and turned and ran. I have many questions about this healing story that are not directly addressed in the text.

The story, however, does reveal an unspoken reality. The story tells us the man trusted Jesus to heal him - because he allowed Jesus to touch him. The man spent many years without sight and could have developed an isolated life and a bad attitude that kept him away from the public place where Jesus restored his sight. Fruitless years spent hoping for healing might have discouraged many of us, but the text says the man was persistent and went to the pool for healing many times (John 9:7). I think this is another silent sign of a person who trusted Jesus.

We can surmise that the blind man by the pool, in addition to the challenge of his blindness, probably also experienced many times of emotional disappointment and discouragement. I would certainly be disheartened if I had to beg because I could not work and my repeated attempts at being healed had not yielded the result I'd hoped for. Yet this man chose to continue his pursuit of healing despite multiple incidents of discouragement.

The blind man's story is a Biblical example that healing affects every part of us. We cannot receive a physical healing that does not affect our emotions. And an emotional healing often releases ailments in our body - both of which will be visible in our behaviors. When Jesus restored the blind man's eyesight, the Bible says that he felt differently and acted differently. The man felt so differently that he acted differently. The story tells us that after Jesus restored his eyesight he was so changed that people who knew him didn't recognize him.

I can imagine people talking about the blind, begging pool guy who looked and acted completely different. I wonder if they made comments like, "We saw Jesus put mud on his eyes, send him to the pool to rinse and he came out of the water with his sight restored, but why is he looking and acting so differently?" But I think both Bible stories are examples of people who trusted Jesus to heal them and ended up experiencing more than they anticipated.

When Jesus binds up our physical wounds, he also heals our emotional and spiritual wounds. When Jesus speaks peace to our hearts, it often also heals our bodies. When Jesus heals our bodies it changes our thoughts and feelings. Trusting Jesus is the answer to all of our wounds, of any kind. When we trust – which we do when we feel safe - we can allow ourselves to heal.

Stops along the way

The path that leads to healing is straight and requires intentionality. We know healing and deliverance take place in the presence of God. And most people understand that when we are in need we should run directly to the Lord. However, our choices often lead us down side-roads that cost us unnecessary time, energy and movement in our journeys to freedom. When we are alone, we can easily derail our momentum. It is easy to talk yourself out of needing God when you are alone with your thoughts.

But God will even use our poor choices and dark seasons to equip us for the next leg of our journeys if we will allow Him. God is so kind that He promises to use everything in our lives for good, but He will not force it upon us (Romans 8:28). It is comforting to know even the ugly chapters of our lives can be used in a transformative way or to encourage others. Hindsight confirms that nothing is lost or wasted when we are on spiritual-journeys with Jesus.

Our emotional capacity determines how quickly we travel the path to healing and wholeness. Capacity is measured by the amount of energy we have to deal with stressful situations or stressful people. It also controls our willingness to open our wounds to God and other people. Fear, doubt, shame, sin, or addiction influence our capacity and weaken our ability to trust God to heal us.

God knows the length of stride we need at every step in life. He knows there is a strengthening that must take place before we are comfortable allowing Him to expose the roots of our pain.

Trust is the first rock God uses in expanding our capacity for healing. Safety cannot be separated from trust in the context of building the capacity required to heal. Don't discount your capacity, and allow God to restore it.

A guarded heart

It is a common pattern for people to guard their hearts if they feel threatened. If I think a person is going to judge me when I share my pain with them I am not going to engage in deep conversations. I will keep our interaction on a safe, surface level. I will most likely direct our dialogue to the most recent humorous activities of my adorable grandchildren. I can fill all kinds of time with that since I have thirteen of them. I will not voluntarily discuss sensitive personal issues. I know who feels safe and who doesn't. I know when I need to guard my heart and I can discern when trust is appropriate. When I have doubts about a person's motive I ask the Holy Spirit.

Although discernment prompts us to protect ourselves we also need people to speak into our lives. I value relationships that contribute to my life and the transparency available with intimate friends. There have been many times in my life God has used other people to heal my broken heart. I needed what they had to offer. If we will allow Him, God will bring people into our lives to rebuild our shattered trust. Or He will bring people into our lives so we can help restore them.

Many people are products of divorce. It is common for people to tell me that after their parents divorced one or the other parent rejected him or her. It makes me sad thinking about a young child feeling abandoned and what the effects of rejection can do to a vulnerable life.

I watch my four-year old granddaughter's face light up when her dad walks into a room. She runs for his arms and begins chirping about her daily accomplishments and then pauses for his words of affirmation. I listen as she confidently responds to her hero's compliments. She flips her hair, swirls, smiles and says, "I know," as she embraces her dad's compliments. I can't imagine what it would be like being four-years-old and watching my father or mother leave home and trying to understand what that meant.

To a parent, children can be a reminder of a failed marriage and a broken family. Meanwhile, children often blame themselves for poor parental communication. Many little boys and little girls grew up without the influence of their fathers, leaving voids in their hearts and in their lives. It is hard for people to trust the Heavenly

Father when they couldn't trust their dad. Because we often transfer our experiences with our dad to God.

Children of divorced parents often develop a sense of independence which extends beyond the normal confidence of young child; they are independent to a fault. This is reasonable because divorced women are forced to work long hours to meet the financial demands often leaving children alone for long periods of time.

When children are left alone to process painful life experiences without the wisdom of a healthy adult, he or she must develop strategies to help them deal with their unresolved pain and inability to make sense out of their life. Because a child's brain does not have the developmental ability to independently reason or resolve pain, he or she must create an acceptable presentation that people around them will accept.

Little children are smart enough to understand the raw expression of emotional pain and anger will result in further rejection, so they learn to hide what they feel. An unnaturally sweet disposition is frequently a child's behavior of choice. I have witnessed great pain hiding behind constantly smiling faces.

If we are raised in a divorced or dysfunctional home we are left with emotional, social, and spiritual voids. These vacancies can only be filled with the love of Jesus and the unconditional love of other people. When we give or receive unconditional love, we experience Jesus in a way that can unlock the restraints of years of rejection.

Divorce is not the only way that children lose trust in people and create defensive behaviors. There are many ways our hearts lose hope. We can help those who have suffered in silence overcome the need to live in a defensive mode.

A guarded heart is the antithesis of trust. So it is fair to say that if we are always on guard we are full of mistrust. Rebuilding trust requires risk and does not come with any guarantee of protection from future hurt. But it does prepare our hearts for Jesus to be our protector, allowing us to relax and observe the beauty of our lives.

Questions to Consider

- Do you feel unconditionally loved by your spiritual community?
- Is your community of faith a safe place to heal?

CHAPTER EIGHT
God is Good All the Time

We love the American story of the good life where we are the stars of the narrative who have climbed the ladder of success. We begin planning for our future before we can actually spell it correctly.

The right preschool lays the foundation for a successful experience in elementary school where we learn the skills to become the number one scholar. Nothing less than an 'A' will please our perfectionist parents who often value our report cards more than our hearts. Then it's off to middle school and high school to create an impressive transcript to open the door to the most prestigious college. All of which will lead to an Ivy League Doctoral Degree, the perfect job and an impressive salary.

Now it is time for the beautiful mate. Then the beautiful children who will attend all of the right schools, play with the appropriate friends, reside in the perfect house and be driven in the newest energy efficient car to the ever-so carefully selected - and scheduled - children's activities. This is how we rate success in America.

When life is positive and moving in the planned direction we run with the energy of our youth. Our excitement seems to create a life of its own that we generously share with everyone with whom we come in contact. We are sure of our position in God and feel like nothing could challenge our faith in a good God who loves and blesses his children (Psalm 21:3, Psalm 24:5, Ephesians 1:3).

We begin to convince ourselves we are blessed because we are special and because we do certain things and don't do other things. We consider ourselves worthy because we are wise and that God only blesses and provides for the good people who do it right.

We create philosophies, doctrines and worldviews to support the belief that things go well in our lives when we behave properly. We accept a gospel saying if you live by things on the 'good' list your life will be good. We begin to define 'good' by the absence of anything negative because good Christian people have good, happy lives. And people who don't are not truly living for God.

We think people who struggle in life are doing something wrong because when Jesus is leading a person's life it isn't plagued with problems. I think Job's friends shared this theology as they suggested that the suffering in his life was most likely due to sin.

Prosperity doctrine is popular. The name-it, claim-it, feel good gospel is contagious. Who doesn't want to believe there is a Christian formula for activating God's blessing and warding off evil? Many thriving churches teach people that since God is good only positive things in life are connected with Him. All negative things in life are from Satan.

It feels pleasant to tell ourselves if we say 'yes' to Jesus and His ways all our present struggles will be resolved and we can escape harm in the future. But over time this enticing gospel begins taking on the characteristics of wrapping paper in which we hide ourselves underneath a shiny, spiritual covering. Our struggles are reframed and justified. To acknowledge them would contradict the popular doctrine we want to embrace. Hope is no longer deferred; it is ignored. Who needs hope if nothing can ever be (admitted to be) wrong?

This mindset is problematic because it allows people to live in denial and avoid reality. And if good people only get showered with good things by God, the logical extension of such doctrine is bad things must only happen to bad people who aren't 'good' enough for God to bless. Although it is true that God is not the author of trauma in our lives, bad things do happen to good people. So this 'prosperity' mindset leaves us the options to live in denial of anything going wrong or make good Christian people feel inferior who are struggling with or have survived persecution, pain and suffering.

I notice that this doctrine has become very popular with many young adult Christians. I know many immature Christians who will not accept the truth about the Christian life. Such Christians frame everything in their lives with an unrealistic, religious spin. They don't have any struggles in their lives because they love Jesus and He loves them. They tell me Jesus wants them to be happy so they deny any reality that appears negative.

Young Christians wrapped up in this type of thinking spend most of their energy developing their pseudo-spiritual identities - their false selves - and avoiding any particle of pain. They spend hours in worship, prayer and planning their next spiritual experience. Their ability to relate to other people is anemic because they restrict friendships to people who reinforce their façades. To them, living in God's presence means always smiling, laughing, speaking prophetic words that are often compliments, and trying to convince everyone around them how good their lives are. When older, wiser Christians try to lovingly speak to them about their dysfunctional worldview, they depart from that fellowship to look for people who will speak the words they want to hear.

These Christians don't seem to value the local church or the significance of living a consistent, shared life. They are drawn to lives that are constantly moving from one spiritual location to the next, downplay the spirituality of daily life and believe in a separation of the spiritual and natural life.

They create standards for worship and warfare based on personal expression and dramatics. I have spoken with many Christian believers who believe you are not truly free and worshiping Jesus during a worship service unless you are jumping, swirling, shouting. This attitude is offensive and works against creating a safe place where people can get to know Jesus. Worship is expressed in many ways. Some people are dramatic, intense, and physically expressive in their approach to worship and communication and others are more introverted and prefer to worship God in a less demonstrative manner and have less need for themselves to be heard or noticed. Both should be accepted in a church trying to present the gospel in a way that is inviting and inclusive.

Shemittah

Ancient Jewish culture counted and observed patterns in life by recognizing seven-year cycles. Every seventh year they would release the land and themselves and others to rest. The word Shemittah literally means 'to release.' This timeless principle is a powerful way to restore our souls, our lives and our relationships.

I recently listened to a podcast and the speaker presented a wonderfully practical application of the principle of Shemittah by suggesting we apply a day of rest one day per week by unplugging from the electronic world and spending time in rest and meditation. It was both a challenge and an encouragement to me. Because I have a wonderfully busy schedule I enjoy, but I recognize the value of restoration from its many demands.

Time devoted to self-care if priceless. And ministry schools serving just such a purpose have a great role in the body of Christ. I often bless the taking of a short sabbatical from life to gain information and experience about God. But ministry schools can also be used as an escape from learning to live in reality and contributing to the society in which you live. They can reinforce the message that local community life isn't as valuable or spiritual as ministry school life. While continuing to serve the great individual purposes they already serve, it is key that ministry schools also make sure to equip people to live good, satisfying lives shared by people in community.

Many young Christians sit in my office and argue with me about the importance of developing social skills, planning for their future, earning a living, investing in a community, embracing the hard work required to build relationships or investing in the lives of others because it doesn't make them happy. They don't think it is exciting or glamorous. They don't believe these are spiritual.

They define supernatural as 'somewhere' else. I often wonder where the Christian world embraced the lie that working a regular job, raising a family, or helping those around them who are in need are not spiritual. This belief system contradicts the message of the Kingdom of God and its application to living a sustainable life. We can't share lives or develop intimate relationship or disciple people if we aren't with them. We can't engage in communal life if we believe God is not present to the local church.

I love traveling and going to different places where God is experienced in different ways and I love worship services where God is celebrated with dramatic expression. I also love quiet, contemplative gatherings where God is worshiped very calmly and I think it unfair to promote one expression as superior to the other. I love mission trips and conferences, but I don't believe I have to travel somewhere to experience God. I love supernatural manifestations of the Holy Spirit, but I do not feel that God doesn't love me if I don't speak in tongues or jump up and down during worship. I believe God is omnipresent and that His goodness is available to all who gather in His name.

Jesus tells us when we embrace reality we will be free (John 8:32). So why do people choose false realities? Why do people restrict the goodness of God? The answer has many elements, but the most significant aspect is that reality isn't always warm and fuzzy. Reality is often real, normal, daily and also Kingdom. Until we acknowledge the coexistence of pain, pleasure and normalcy in the Christian life, we restrict our ability to mature in our lives with God. Unless we acknowledge the reality that God is present to us wherever we are and that spirituality is not defined by manifestation we will miss God in the normal rhythms of life.

I think we frequently miss God in the quiet moments of the day because we have been desensitized by the chaos of the culture around us. Perhaps this is why the scripture encourages us to get to know God by putting our life on pause (Psalm 46:10). A hectic life doesn't have to be a contradiction to a contemplative life if we apply the Shemittah principle on a regular basis. Perhaps we should give ourselves permission, even at this moment, to schedule a regular weekly time to press the pause button and rest.

We will never reach a mature place in God if we do not understand that the Kingdom of God includes pain, suffering, loss, and hard work as well as blessings. In order to live in the fullness of God, we must understand that saying 'yes' to Jesus expands into every area of our lives. And that every area is spiritual. In order to live in the fullness of God, we must understand Jesus does not promise a life of only good things, but He does promise that He will always be with us (Ps. 23:4, Joshua 1:9). If He is always with us, perhaps we should begin practicing stillness at the end of each day by applying Psalm 4:4, "When you are on your beds, search your hearts and be silent."

Healthy people

Healthy people understand that life includes pain. Healthy people live in reality and healthy people know how to process the trials in their lives. Healthy people live productive lives and take time to rest and care for themselves. They neither get stuck in pain nor do they deny pain. Mature Christians acknowledge pain and suffering do not contradict God. Wisdom realizes that during times of distress God is present and allows us to see His beauty in the midst.

Life with God includes trials. Knowing how to return to joy in the midst of suffering is a gift from God. James, the brother of Jesus, tells us to be happy when trials enter our lives because if we embrace them, allowing God to tell us the truth about them, trials can actually transform us (James 1:5). Testing can reveal to us how God is good to us even when life is bad.

Learning to be present in the midst of suffering is a discipline worthy of teaching our disciples. A sustainable spiritual life requires spiritual disciplines. And a disciplined life does not mean God is not with us and caring for us. It means we need self-control to sustain what God gives us.

Teaching people how to be present to God in daily life is an even greater challenge. Teaching children how to be present to their current circumstance and process it with Jesus is worthy of our attention and should begin at early ages. It is human nature to run from adversity by denying or numbing our pain, but the best way to learn about the goodness of God is to submit to the pain in your life and give Jesus access. This is a practical way to experience the reality that God is good all the time and not just when life is pleasant.

Philosophy or theology

A danger exists of getting trapped between waves of a turbulent ocean of theology wars when intellectuals try to reconcile the tension between life with God and suffering. If we embrace a doctrine defining life with God as free from pain, we miss the truth. If we join the camp convinced suffering is the only way to relate to Jesus, we also miss the truth.

An appropriate approach to life with God is understanding there are seasons when life is good and pain free and there are times when we will experience great degrees of despair. The gospel includes both. The Bible actually says it rains on the people of God and also on those who don't know Him. So bad things happen to good people.

Kingdom life also includes the many blessings of God. And they are not exclusive to good people. We struggle with this truth, saying, "Wow, you mean God cares and provides for people who reject him?" Indeed He does! God loves mankind. All of mankind.

At this point religious people might want to misrepresent me, saying I've said God is okay with sin. This is not at all what I am saying. But Jesus does love sinful people. You know – people like you and me.

When our hope is rooted in Jesus, and not the outcome of our experiences, we will be better prepared for everything that life presents. When we begin to live in the fullness of Jesus and develop a friendship with Him, suffering loses its ability to lie to us.

The American story is not a true picture of God's love. Nor is the Christian utopia story in which bad things don't happen to good, kind, beautiful people. So how do we reconcile that God is good all the time and His love for us is unconditional with the reality that He doesn't promise us a painless journey?

It is good to consider fatherhood when we explore this question. Good fathers love their children unconditionally. But good fathers never promise them they will never experience any pain in life simply because they are good children. Telling a child nothing bad will ever happen to them is a lie. A good father tells his children that he will always take care of them and never leave them. But he is also straightforward with them. Just like we should honestly tell a small child headed to the doctor for a shot that it will hurt, we should tell young Christians life with God can also often be painful. There will always be cycles of joy and sorrow in the Christian life.

When painful things happen to children, good fathers use the opportunity to teach them how to process the hurt and what to do the next time something painful happens. A good father tells his child the truth about what happened and assures him or her it doesn't change how he loves them. In fact, wise fathers teach their children to worship God during times of pain and suffering. Wise fathers use the pains and trials in the lives of their children to teach them how to deal with it. Yet it would be inappropriate to place blame on the father, saying he wanted something bad to happen so he could train his son or daughter.

Children who feel safe don't always have to ask their father if he is going to take care of them. They know their dad will not leave them when they are afraid or unsure what to do. Secure children trust their fathers even when they don't have answers or understand.

The good and evil tension

Like many of us, David, the psalmist, had questions about good and evil. Throughout the Psalms David asked God the same questions we do about suffering. David repeatedly asked the Lord why innocent people suffer and wicked people prosper and directly asked God why bad things happen to good people who are living for Him (Psalm 73:28).

This ancient question is not simple to answer or easy to digest. The unanswered question keeps many people from choosing to live life with God. I am not attempting to give a concise answer to the reason for evil in the lives of God's people. However, I want to suggest that we redirect our focus away from the question and onto the fact that God is good all the time and that He promises He will never leave us.

We must consider the reality that even though we are children of God, the world is presently under the influence of Satan. Part of the answer to the ancient question is in the tension between Jesus having overcome the world while at the same time Satan still having access to us because we are in the world (1 John 5:19; John 16:33).

This tension has the ability to disrupt our spiritual life if we focus on a definitive answer to the pending question. Getting stuck on the question can derail us, while our momentum can actually be enhanced if we can rest in the fact that God promises to use all of the suffering, pain, trauma, or poor choices in our lives for good (Romans 8:28). I propose we not focus on the contrast between the life of the wicked and the life of the righteous. Instead, find a place of peace in the reality of God's truth that allows us to deal with the good and bad in our lives with complete confidence that Jesus will be with us.

David decided to allow the nearness of God to be his comfort and make the Lord God his refuge at all times, even in the midst of his unanswered questions (Psalm 73:28). Let us learn from David and choose God as our refuge during times of pain and note that suffering can enhance our prayer lives. May we understand suffering is not a sign God has left us and rest assured that suffering is an opportunity to grow closer to Him as we learn to identify His presence at all times.

I find the insight, prayers and spiritual exercises from Ignatius Loyola to be helpful tools in identifying God's presence in daily life as well as times of distress. And we don't have to keep this prayer in an untouchable, historical box. The 'Daily Examen' prayer of Ignatius Loyola is applicable today to us all.

The 'Examen' exercise is a simple, profound activity which refines our ability to locate God within each day. It encourages a nightly, contemplative approach to looking at your day, examining how your actions and responses to the day's experiences drew you closer to God or pulled you away from Him. Every time I slow down, connect with His presence and evaluate my day I find it awakens me to how God expressed His love for me. What better way to realize God is good all the time than to have the ability to find God in all things, big and small, pleasant and painful and proclaim his beauty as worship?

Reflection is revealing. And adding this spiritual practice to the rhythm of your day is easy. Simply follow these few steps to help guide you in the process until it becomes a normal part of your day:

1. Become aware of God's presence.
2. Review your day and thank God for things that come to mind.
3. Pay attention to your emotions; they are linked to how you view your day.
4. Pray from a place of thankfulness for the things of the day that connected you with God.
5. Look forward to tomorrow knowing you will take time to be still and repeat the practice.

This and many other spiritual practices are only possible when we take time to sit still, quiet our minds and meditate on God's goodness.

Questions to Consider

- Do you believe God is good all the time?
- Do you believe God is present during suffering?
- Do you create times of reflection in your day?

CHAPTER NINE
The Path to Spiritual Maturity

A white-haired, elderly man in a worn chair reading from tattered Bible while all who enter his presence are graced with the words of wisdom dripping from his tongue is a great mental image of wisdom. An older man imparting rich conversation to the younger generation seasoned with his memories of life's successes and failures portrays feelings of spiritual maturity. The lines in the man's face tell as many stories as his words and there is an unspoken respect for every wrinkle that reflects a life lesson.

Many people seem fond of the image of seeking out such a person. It seems very common to long for direction from those who have already carved their way, making righteous paths for us to follow. We are drawn to those who have already lived life well, who can save us unnecessary heartaches, but where do we find such mentors with such wisdom?

Spiritual maturity is believed to automatically develop as we age. But though we are intended during our senior years to have the ability to share spiritual and emotional wisdom with others, many people never reach this stage of development regardless of age.

American society is producing underdeveloped adults. Our current culture devalues those who are older and wiser and is embracing a one-generation-at-a-time mindset where youth is viewed as invincible and able to charge through life independently. This can lead to the danger of losing respect for wisdom and the maturity of those who can share it.

Maturity is found in a multi-dimensional life that includes men and women with emotional and spiritual wisdom helping younger generations avoid their father's or grandfather's mistakes. The fullness of community is present when people know how to celebrate and grieve life in multi-generational relationships. We grow by sharing life experiences with others. And we develop wisdom by pursuing God and His ways, including sharing with other people what we have personally learned or learned from others.

Ecclesiastes tells us that as wisdom increases so does grief (1:18). This verse is relevant because it is helpful to have a realistic view of the maturation process and all that it entails. It is about more than just facts or amounts of time spent walking this earth. I am no fan of conversing with know-it-alls of any age, even if they have high IQs. People who have knowledge without the character to sustain it are often foolish.

A price to pay

A significant step in the maturation process is being able to realize your own level of maturity and insight. We all have blind spots hindering our ability to be self-aware. When blinded, you need others to help you discern your stage of development in order to progress to your next stage in life. This sounds like a simple endeavor, but it often presents tension because we can not see what we ourselves are blind to. When we are unaware we are oblivious to our personal needs.

As we mature our elders should have conversations with us about the value of growing socially, emotionally and spiritually and stress the importance of wholeness in our approach to God. Many Christian believers are myopic in their approach to becoming like Jesus. When you are young or new to the Christian faith, it is common for your vision of Jesus to be narrow and your expectation for the future to be restrictive. When our view of the Christian life is anemic, we can become imbalanced in our lives with God by thinking that all we need for spiritual maturity is time spent reading the Bible or attending church.

This is problematic because there are many aspects of God that are found outside of a building or even the scriptures. God is also present in our relationships and in every circumstance. The beauty of the Lord is visible in the world around us and in the creative expression of every person we encounter. Restricting our definition of an omnipotent, omniscient, omnipresent creator just to Bible verses can create a one-dimensional God we can never know intimately. If our development is only based on our Bible knowledge and personal experience, our faith will most likely be presented to others through opinion rather than experiential victory. This is usually only able to help those who have traveled the same path as us.

We all know people who act younger than they are. We probably also know many people who live in denial and enjoy creating their own realities. It amazes me how blinded people are to their own behaviors. Many people only surround themselves with people of the same age. This limits their relationships to one generation, creating groups of people who think, talk, act and dress alike. Without the challenge of younger and older generations interacting, communities never reach the level that God intends for the church.

Approaching life with a single-generational worldview is a restricting, underdeveloped one. Younger generations have a vibrancy to bring to the church many seniors have lost. Seniors have life lessons and guidance that younger generations don't yet have. A healthy spiritual community must be built with a multi-generational foundation.

When communities are focused on all positions of authority being occupied by 20-30 year olds, it becomes an energetic, creative pursuit of spirituality. But I often wonder to what age group Paul was referring when he said to not be persuaded by crafty preachers with poor doctrine who can deceive you (Ephesians 4:14).

Wisdom warns us to check with God's truth for ourselves the messages of charismatic, seductive preachers (2 Timothy 2:15). Communities focused totally on the young and being energetic can lack experiential wisdom and the ability to implement the hard lessons of life to the weak or broken who need direction, authority, and wisdom. It can become a community uncomfortable with input from the older generation if they view the older generation as insignificant or irrelevant.

When wisdom is ignored in a spiritual community and the senior generation not honored, it becomes more easily vulnerable to unnecessarily remaking a previous generation's mistakes.

The value of a mentor

The Apostle Paul instructed, invested and blessed Timothy in his life with God. scripture tells us Paul and Timothy were in relationship that positioned Paul to share with Timothy his wisdom on how to interact with people both in the church and outside of the church. Paul knew Timothy so well that he recognized Timothy's gifts and abilities. The scripture says Paul blessed Timothy and sent him to teach others about Jesus (Acts 13:1-3). This is a beautiful example of the older generation investing in the younger generation. Have you had such a senior person in your life?

We all benefit from intentional confirmation and direction from a wise elder. Whether we are simply ready to move forward to the next leg of our spiritual-journey or are in the process of sorting through our hopes and dreams, there is a type of spiritual covering that comes from being blessed by an older generation who believes in you. There is satisfaction in being affirmed by a spiritual father and there is comfort in knowing that your own father blesses you.

Knowing someone has faith in our pursuits and is willing to guide our steps is great preparation when the advice comes from one who understands what we are about to encounter because they have already traveled the paths of life we are approaching. Paul knew Timothy would meet false teachers who opposed the message of Jesus and warned him about this. Paul clearly had encountered such teachers himself. He speaks from a place of familiarity rather than hearsay. Once again Paul uses military imagery in describing to Timothy what he would need when interacting with antagonistic, anti-Christian teachers of the time. Paul compared Timothy to a soldier and a soldier's need to be prepared for battle. Paul told Timothy to fight the fight with the truth of the gospel and not to engage in debate with the heresies (2 Timothy 2:23-25).

I wish I had this wisdom shared with me in my younger years. I spent many years believing I needed to debate and defend God with people who were confused about the Christian faith. As I reflect on my younger years I think I believed the Holy Spirit needed my help.

Paul also instructed Timothy in the bigger picture of life by informing him of the intent of heretical interactions. He exposed the hidden motives of heretics. Heretics meant to turn people away from God through argument, causing them to question life with God. Paul gave Timothy a strategy to deal with this based on his own experiences. Paul told Timothy to speak the truth he studied in the scriptures, have concern for his opponents, protect the faith of the followers of Jesus, and win back the people who were deceived by false teachers. That is quite an assignment! Know the scriptures and refer to them when talking with argumentative people, but care about the arguers at the same time while also leading people back to Jesus who were influenced by the person's arguments. Before we think, "Poor Timothy..." we need to know we have the same assignment and this same godly wisdom will defeat the false teachers of our present culture.

We all seem to wish we had an older, wiser sage warning us what we will face as we step away from our secure places – be it the security of our youth or other – into a larger world. Yet we all also seem resistant to not doing everything on our own, proving we already know everything that is important enough to know. I wonder how many poor choices or opposition we could avoid if we would submit to wisdom from an older generation.

It is a treasure when we are given spiritual wisdom from our parents and holy guidance is within our family of origin. But such wisdom need not be limited to only our natural families. This treasure can also come within the context of spiritual families which celebrate a multi-generational approach to community.

Paul was able to warn Timothy because he had already paved the way with his life. He knew the reality of the Kingdom of God and how there will always be opposition when we choose to follow Jesus. Paul lived in reality and taught Timothy the reality of the combative nature of the world toward the Kingdom. Paul warned his spiritual son of the dangers of debating God with those who are deceived. Paul told Timothy, and us, we risk suffering a blow to our faith when we engage in arguments that God doesn't approve because divisive words attached to false doctrine can lead us into deception.

Within our spiritual families we must teach immature Christians the importance of knowing the scriptures so they will not be easily deceived, but we must include the importance of a wise mentor and the reality of the snares of the world. I wonder what Timothy's story would have looked like if he only took advice from his peers.

Naiveté

I remember my naiveté when I first became a Christian. I thought everyone who decided to follow Jesus loved each other and only spoke to each other with kindness and sincerity. I had a fantastic image of what it meant to worship God. I believed people both young and old who love Jesus would never be jealous of each other or argue about their faith. I thought all Christians only wanted the best for each other. I needed a Paul at that time in my life to tell me about the reality of those who delight in division and judgment and that sometimes those people are in the church.

I am very connected to my church family and I have a deep love for the local church and the people within it. Because I am involved in inner-healing prayer ministry I interact with many people below surface-level, knowing their secrets and struggles.

I also have the privilege of living life with those for whom I pray. Consistently, those who seek wise counsel, submit to a mentor and invest in the lives of others continue growing and maturing in their life with God. They are teachable and the fruit in their lives is obvious. It is equally visible to watch the fruit in the lives of those who resist guidance from others and only receive advice from peers in their same stage in life.

It makes me sad watching people compromise their faith and embracing poor theology because they refuse to be accountable to anyone or study the scriptures. Those without mentors who believe they know best are usually very defensive, guarded and proud of their intellect and opinions. They value philosophy over sound theology and focus more on the social climate than the constants found in the Bible.

Frequently, those in the church falling into these traps are in their mid-thirties, but present a façade of being elders. They speak with authority about raising Godly teens when they only have a toddler. They speak with authority about the second-half of life when they are in the beginning stages of adulthood. These young adults love Jesus, but they are stuck.

I watch immature worldviews shape spiritual-journeys when God is approached with an independent attitude. Insecurity and unresolved issues combine to create defenses that keep healthy people out and broken people in. The wisdom of others is discounted and themselves elevated, giving way for entitlement to direct their lives. This deserving attitude interferes with a person becoming a mature disciple of Jesus because it clouds self-awareness.

There will always be people like this in our lives who are difficult and need our help; even if they don't know it. There will always be a need for mentors.

There was a middle-aged woman who spent several years in our church family. She wasn't a know-it-all, nor was she teachable, but she was definitely stuck. This woman repeatedly sought counsel, prayer and inner-healing ministry from the transformation team. Every ministry session would end with the same conclusion from those who prayed for her, "You have a very religious, restrictive view of the Heavenly Father."

The resistant woman did not believe the counsel she received so she continued to seek spiritual direction, life advice and marriage counsel to no avail. She attended home groups and never missed church activities. However, this desperate woman never progressed in the years that I knew her because she resisted truthful counsel. In frustration, and in the same condition she entered our community, the woman finally moved to another state.

If we only do what we see wise people do and don't change inside ourselves we risk stalling or losing our own identities in attempts to just imitate someone we respect. Replication is not personal insight or maturation or growth. It is duplication. It is, in fact, a façade delaying truth and self-awareness.

Mentors are only as valuable as our willingness to embrace them and what role they can appropriately offer into our lives. Duplication is sameness and not the goal of mentorship. Wise counsel from an elder is only valuable if we apply it into our daily lives. We should not just seek wise counsel. We must apply the advice received to our own lives. If we only listen to words of wisdom, but do not implement them in our daily life, we become smarter - but not wiser.

The wisdom of Proverbs

The book of Proverbs has much to say about wisdom and wise counsel. Proverbs defines wisdom as receiving guidance and instruction from mature advisors within a community. It says we are considered wise when we listen to life-giving rebukes and we devalue ourselves when we don't (Proverbs 15:31-32).

We can only receive correction if we are secure in knowing who we are and choose to trust those who speak into our lives. I am a big believer in being selective and cautious with the mentors that we allow to speak in to our lives.

The kingdom of God is intended to function as a multi-generational family. There were many things in my youth I needed to hear from my grandmother that would not have carried the same message if they came from my mother. And there were many lessons I could receive only from my mother.

This family dynamic applies to spiritual families as well. There are things we need to hear from our friends, but also words of correction and direction which must come from natural or spiritual mothers or fathers. The older generation has been positioned in spiritual communities to instruct the younger generation in the ancient paths of God. I want to be honest about the tension in choosing a mentor because not all seniors are mature, spiritual people capable of mentoring others.

Jim has been a spiritual grandfather from the first hour he entered our church family. He's an inner-healer with a compassionate heart that represents the love of God in a visible manner. Jim displays God's heart of mercy toward the broken-hearted. I watch Jim care for people and teach them to find rest for their souls as he prays for trauma to be released from people's lives.

Jim's ministry and counsel remind me of Jeremiah 6:16, a text telling us about the value of choice. This scripture verse says when a decision is at hand we should ask where the good way is and walk in it because we will find rest. We could paraphrase this and encourage people to look for the wise counsel in their life and listen to it. Jim is part of the fabric of our spiritual community that weaves generations together by teaching people how to connect with God and find rest.

A spiritual family is not complete if it only recognizes one generation. God is establishing spiritual families on the earth that mirror the heavens. God is relational. God, as father, is in relationship with his son, Jesus. And Jesus is in relationship with all who are part of the family of God, calling them brothers and sisters.

Our family of origin is the perfect context for finding out who we are and developing our ability to receive instruction and wise counsel. If you have wise, spiritual parents and grandparents this is where your counsel should begin. But if we do not have Godly parents or grandparents in our natural family, we can turn to a spiritual family. Spiritual fathers, mothers, grandfathers, and grandmothers can help us grow, mature and learn how to navigate the difficult waters of life. It is my prayer that our communities of faith be rich with the influence of a multi-generational approach to the Kingdom of God.

Questions to Consider

- Do you feel entitled?
- Are you teachable?
- Do you have a spiritual mentor?

CHAPTER TEN
The Fatherless Generation

I remember the day when a confused woman walked into my office dripping with seduction. Her eye makeup partnered with her clothing to tell the world she had sexual issues. The length of her dress could easily have been mistaken for a shirt. I was certain she could not bend more than a few inches before those around her would blush. The shape and size of her lips were exaggerated by the color red and her streaked hair was intentionally placed over one eye to create some sort of mystery. Her stiletto heals enhanced her long legs by providing additional height and her low voice tone finalized the goal of a seductress. She spoke to me in a slow, deep, fake voice.

It was fascinating to watch this woman's demeanor shift as she began to tell her life story. It was difficult for her to stay present to her story. She kept drifting back to earlier chapters of her life. Her voice changed pitch as she pushed her hair away from her face and she slumped into the couch with a blanket. Her story was one of childhood sexual abuse.

The woman's story made me sad, but she had embraced it as normal. It took her years to tell her divorced parents about the abuse. Her parents added to her confusion when they both downplayed the significance of the violation.

Many internal messages where received the day her father discounted his daughter's trauma. Any hope of comfort was swallowed along with the lies that the abuse was her fault. The woman's eyes were filled with tears as she told me lies have dominated her sexuality ever since her confession. The lack of sympathy combined with lies to create a seductive presentation of a traumatized little girl who was showing the world how she believed her father viewed her as well as how she thinks about herself.

As the woman grasped for words to express her pain, I was reminded of the importance of a healthy father-daughter relationship and how daddies are positioned to protect, defend and shape the sexuality of their daughters. I believe God intends for parents to be His voice in blessing their children and helping them understand their sexual identity, especially when abuse lies to them. I wonder what the woman's story would have been if her father validated her pain and affirmed her identity in spite of what the abuse took from her.

I felt compassion for the young, hurting woman. She had lost years to agony and untruth so I welcomed the opportunity to validate her pain and help her release it to the Lord.

Ancient paths

The ancient Hebrew culture understood the relationship between blessing and cursing and how our choice of words is the avenue leading to life or death. They understood that words can either bless children or curse them. The Hebrew culture embraced speaking words of blessing over their children and teaching them to love God (Deuteronomy 30:19-20).

What a wonderful way to position children for a life of blessing, to teach them to love the Lord. It is common for young men and women who had disconnected, unhealthy relationships with their fathers to view God the same way. They transfer the messages they received from their fathers to their relationships with God. This often leaves them with a Heavenly Father they see as uninterested in the details of their lives and not concerned about their welfare. More specifically, it results in a God who is seen as okay with abuse and neglect.

The importance of honor

I often minister to young adults who are trapped in a cycle of dishonor because they were dishonored by their parents. They dishonor their parents and all of the authority figures in their lives. They do not understand the concept of honor and their behaviors reflect this blind spot.

When honor is a foreign concept the ability to give and receive love is compromised. Those operating from a position of dishonor create rough and tough exteriors to protect empty hearts that never received a parents blessing. I listen to young adults angrily tell me God never blesses them. I listen as they blame God for all of the bad and painful events in their lives. They remember being blamed for the bad things in their parents' lives, so they believe the Lord does the same.

When broken people enter our spiritual communities we need to understand that many people do not respect authority not because they are bad or rebellious people, but because they don't know how. They struggle to receive positive words, corrective words, words of encouragement or direction.

It is important to help such people identify the ways they disrespect themselves and others. This teaches them the importance of learning to love and honor themselves. This is critical, because it is impossible to authentically honor another person if we don't know how to honor ourselves.

Extending honor is confusing to those who had a painful childhood or non-nurturing parents because 'honoring' is not exclusive to those we consider to be honorable. Many people are confused about loving and honoring parents who did not meet their needs and even more so if they were abusive. The Bible says if we honor our parents our life will be longer than if we do not. The same verse also says our lives will be better if we honor our parents.

This isn't the only Biblical principle that contributes to a good life, but it is an important one.

The best way we can teach people how to honor others is to demonstrate the gospel with our lives. We need to teach honor by example and we need to acknowledge that it is more challenging to learn how to honor dishonoring, abusive people.

We can gain insight about honor when we study Hebrew culture. There exists a mutual respect between Hebraic children and their parents that is often marked outwardly by such things as ceremonies, celebrations, or family gatherings. Here the grandparents and parents extend a formal benediction over children of all ages.

This form of parental blessing expresses to the world that their most valuable heritage is their children. A sentiment of this culture seems to be one of expectation; they expect their children to succeed. And the intent of the crafted prayers reveals expectation of a good life for their children and grandchildren. This beautiful custom of blessing is rooted in mutual respect. The children respect their elders, but the grandparents and parents also respect their children. Obviously, the Hebrew culture believed more in each other than in each other's behaviors.

We don't have to be Jewish to engage in a life of honor and respect. Although it is more difficult to understand honor and respect if you were raised without it, we can nonetheless always choose to love, honor and respect. It is easier to honor broken, abrasive people if we look beyond their dysfunctional behaviors and love and honor them as a person; a person created in the image of God.

I realize this view is in opposition to the western mindset because Americans tend to have a standard of honor that polarizes the honoring ways of Jesus. Americans, even many American Christians, tend to restrict their respect and honor to those who are financially successful, have achieved high career credentials, built productive businesses and agree with their personal philosophies. But the Bible says to honor your father and mother (Ephesians 6:2), honor the elders of the church (1 Timothy 5:17), honor God (Joshua 24:15), honor your husband or wife (Ephesians 5:22-25), and honor your children (Psalm 127:3-5). These scriptures tell us to honor people because of who they are. We should honor based God's standards not American standards. What would honor look like if we removed our opinions, our prejudices, and our lack of forgiveness?

We frequently misunderstand the meaning of honor. Our definition of honor can become entangled with dysfunctional relationships with parents or caregivers or apprehension of what it will cost us. Somehow many people believe honoring another person requires sacrificing who we are. Honor does not mean that we stop protecting ourselves, compromise ourselves, or dismiss the reality of wrong behaviors. Extending honor doesn't mean we have to like or enjoy the people we honor.

Overly religious people have taught us that in order to esteem another person higher than ourselves we must sacrifice our opinions, dull our intellect, deny our true identity, not guard our hearts, mimic the person we are honoring or dismiss rude, abusive behavior. Religious people often define honor in terms that actually resemble further abuse.

I say this because many people have been traumatized by family members and are trying to process the pain. Oblivious religious leaders tell them they need to overlook the pain and act as if everything is okay. This is not only poor advice; it is abusive.

It is true that as followers of Jesus we must always forgive those who hurt us, but it does not mean we have to have lunch with them. Many people don't know how to honor and respect a person without letting the other person take advantage of them. This, in turn, can create unhealthy religious principles - doctrines distorted to fit our broken histories.

For everyone, even for those who have no framework in their lives of what 'honoring' really means, an understanding of this principle can be developed at any time. A great step in the direction of honor can be applied in your family - the natural family, the family you married into, or your spiritual family - by asking God to show you how He wants you to honor them. This is the best way to initiate honor because Jesus already knows how to best honor every relationship. Taking time to step away from the activities of your day, meditate in the presence of the Lord, asking Him who He wants you to honor and specifically how He wants you to honor them, will begin building the foundations of honoring between others.

Kim was raised without the wisdom of a father. Kim's parents divorced when she was young. Her father was not a regular part of her life. Kim's story is void of many positive daddy memories. She didn't receive a father's blessing and wasn't taught the biblical principle of honoring your father and mother. However, Kim is one of the most respectful young women I know. She submits to counsel from older, wiser people and faithfully applies the advice given to her. She has high regard for those in authority and a deep love for Jesus. She is what I call a delightful person.

Kim is not the exception. There are many people who were raised without their father's guidance. Children do not have to have divorced parents to be raised without their father's direction. Many children were raised with their father in the home and in their lives, yet they still did not receive his emotional or spiritual support.

There is a big difference in knowing you will always have a place to live, food to eat and clothes to wear, even the toys you want, but no attention given to matters of your heart. Many parents take their children to church and even engage in fun activities as a family, but emotions are disregarded.

When children are not taught how to handle their emotions, which includes being able to put off or deny their wants of the moment, being told no, and how to process life's struggles, it leaves them socially and emotionally immature and constantly searching for answers. It leaves a void that God intended fathers to fill and it often creates entitlement.

I have noticed that people who were raised without paternal guidance are often confused about their identity. This is one of the major contributors to people creating false selves. This creates prime opportunities for people to create a fantasy world or turn to addictions trying to fill their heart's empty places and resolve the confusion about who they are.

Fatherless young adults often do not receive counsel very graciously from elders in their lives who disagree with them. Or they avoid them because they refuse to heed their counsel. Such young adults often develop chameleon personalities which change in imitation of those in their environment. This is to cover up the fact that they do not trust male authority figures. This often leads to lives marked by disrespect and young adults who believe they know more than any adult in their life.

It is common for the fatherless generation to gain knowledge but not maturity. They frequently surround themselves with people who tell them only what they want to hear. I want to see the fatherless generation succeed in life and discover the truth about themselves, but I am concerned that without guidance they will be unable to prosper. "Without good direction, people lose their way; the more wise counsel you follow, the better your chances. (The Message, Proverbs 11:14).

Paul warns us it is possible to always be learning, but never gain truth when he writes, "All scripture is inspired by God and profitable for teaching, for reproof, for correction, for training in righteousness; so that the man of God may be adequate, equipped for every good work" (2 Timothy 3:17). I like how the Message Bible phrases this scripture, "But don't let it faze you. Stick with what you learned and believed, sure of the integrity of your teachers - why, you took in the sacred scriptures with your mother's milk! There's nothing like the written Word of God for showing you the way to salvation through faith in Christ Jesus. Every part of scripture is God-breathed and useful one way or another - showing us truth, exposing our rebellion, correcting our mistakes, training us to live God's way. Through the Word we are put together and shaped up for the tasks God has for us."

The sentiments in this passage are encouraging for those who are trying to fill the fatherless voids in their lives with religion because it tells us scripture should do more than increase our knowledge. It has the power to expose the things in our life that we need to deal with and has the ability to direct our paths. Life with God has the power to satisfy the empty places in our hearts. In fact, Jesus is the only one who can satiate an empty, hungry heart.

Lessons from a wise man

Intentionality is a key factor for transformation. Solomon asked God for wisdom and became a wise man. Solomon tells us we need to seek wisdom from other people, gaining it by learning to honor, to receive guidance from wise people, and being willing to submit to correction. "Refuse good advice and watch your plans fail; take good counsel and watch them succeed" (The Message, Proverbs 15:22). This is a powerful proverb for all, but it has special significance to those who didn't have fathers engaged in their lives. It should encourage us to know it is never too late to receive what we didn't receive from our natural fathers.

It is true that those who devalue the wisdom of elders risk remaining immature, but those who fear God learn wisdom and how to humble themselves. Humility teaches us how to honor. This is important because honor and wisdom merge when hearts are open to hearing the experiences of the older generations and the power of the Holy Spirit. This is a great reminder for a culture that thinks life struggles are unique to the present generation.

Solomon tells us there is nothing new under the sun that hasn't been sought in the past. We all know history repeats itself and we have all experienced cycles in our lives that are reoccurrences of our pasts. Solomon compares the history of human behavior and its pleasure seeking strategies to the operation of the earth's seasons: consistent and constant. Yet Solomon understood earthy pursuits apart from God are pointless: Pursuing life apart from God is like chasing the wind.

Solomon also tells us God can give meaning to a life that has been void of a father, which includes lacking an emotional connection with one's father. Oftentimes those raised without a father spend years pursuing knowledge or pleasure or ways to make them feel better when God is the only one who can fill the voids. Even those from the fatherless generation who do turn to Jesus also spend great amounts of time trying to earn God's love because they never knew unconditional love. Some are known to become perfectionist, obsessing about their behavior to avoid messing up and disappointing God.

Solomon tells us we should take the focus off trying to please God through behaviors or knowledge because we can't ever figure God out; we're just humans, He is the maker of all things (Ecclesiastes 11:5). This message that God honors you, loves you unconditionally, and blesses you toward healing, growth and wisdom needs to be a key part of our spiritual communities, especially in terms of ministering to the fatherless generation.

Solomon ends the book of Ecclesiastes by stating that when we are devoted to God everything is beautiful and has meaning. This is a reality that Solomon includes in the maxim that there is nothing new under the sun. He poetically compares the faithful constancy of the wind blowing with the routines of daily life. When we decide to follow God, our daily activities of working a job, eating good food and drinking good wine become rewarding and are gifts from God. Solomon says, "Go, eat your food with gladness and drink your wine with joyful hearts, for it is now that God favors what you do. Always be clothed in white and always anoint your head with oil. Enjoy life with your wife, whom you love..." (Ecclesiastes 9:7-9).

When we belong to Jesus our daily routines are spiritual and an offering to the Lord. As we grow in wisdom we realize the normalcy of daily life is spiritual and that we don't have to be sitting in church, reading scripture or preparing for the mission field to please God.

When we consider the rhythm of our days as devotion to the Lord we are able to see the beauty of the Lord around us in a new way. God is no longer far away and unattainable. He is around our tables and in our conversations. Jesus can then be experienced in our natural and spiritual families in a practical way.

We can best enjoy the fruit of a shared life when we recognize it as a spiritual practice. This realization lends itself to great degrees of peace, allowing us to relax, to stop trying to perform for God and enjoy our lives.

"A father to the fatherless, a defender of widows, is God in his holy dwelling. God sets the lonely in families, he leads for the prisoners with singing; but the rebellious live in a sun-scorched land." (Psalm 68:5-6)

Questions to Consider

- Do you struggle with God as your Heavenly Father?
- Does your story include a healthy father figure?
- Is your community creating a culture of honor?

CHAPTER ELEVEN
Adopting Orphans

I wonder how many of you think of the movie 'Annie' or similar motion pictures about adoption agencies when you hear the word 'orphan.' Most people have a tender spot for children who were abandoned by the death of their parents. And many childless couples are eager to adopt stray children, but the Bible speaks of waifs in a broader context. The scriptures have much to say about people who are considered orphans both in the literal sense and the spiritual sense. Spiritual adoption is God's answer for those who need acceptance and life direction.

It is sad to consider that the fatherless generation has produced many spiritual orphans, but it is comforting to know God has a heart for all lost souls. The Lord has designed the Kingdom of God to function as a family. This is good news for orphans. God says our spiritual communities should represent a family and tells us we should adopt those who are considered orphans.

Spiritual fathers

Charlie was considered an orphan and needed a family to love him. Charlie heard about our spiritual community from friends who moved to our town looking for a church family who embraced inner-healing and transformation. They needed a place to plant roots, process life and engage in a healthy environment. They suggested Charlie join them so they invited him to live with them.

Charlie's father was not a part of Charlie's life. Charlie's dad was in and out of jail and struggled with addictions that kept him distracted from parenting. Charlie's mother was also a prisoner of substance abuse. That situation robbed Charlie from the guidance of a nurturing mother and forced him into many inappropriate situations. Charlie viewed life through the eyes of addiction. Charlie had to learn to navigate life on his own. Life spewed heaviness on Charlie's childhood, creating a much older version of who he was intended to be.

You would expect Charlie to be angry, rude and rebellious, but Charlie is kind, funny, and loves Jesus. I love seeing little children climb and hang on Charlie because he is so attentive to them. They want to be around him because he affirms them and encourages them. It is common to hear Charlie tell the little children stuck to him that they are awesome. They smile and keep pulling his arms yelling new challenges for Charlie to perform. "Play with us," "Show us how to ride a skateboard," and, "Swing me around" are often heard from the little children tugging at Charlie for attention.

Charlie will tell you there have been seasons in his life when he approached life like his parents by numbing his pain with drugs, but Charlie is beginning to believe more in God and less in narcotics. Charlie is now part of a community encouraging him to allow Jesus to heal his broken heart and release his true identity. Charlie wants to be free from the lies that encourage him to deny his internal world, but it is hard to break old patterns when you don't have parents to guide you.

Charlie is learning to listen to advice and slowly receive love from the spiritual family God has provided for him. The spiritual fathers in Charlie's life are beginning to meet needs Charlie has denied for many years. Charlie is receiving blessings from the godly men in his life who are speaking direction and correction over him. Spiritually speaking, Charlie has been adopted.

Words that bless

One night several of the older men in our community planned a dinner for Charlie in order to lay hands on him, pray for him and bless who Jesus says he is. The goal of the night was for Charlie to receive a father's blessing. The men shared a meal together then headed to the barn to pray. Charlie didn't tell me the specific words spoken over him in the barn, but he wore the effects of them on his face for days.

I think the barn has a lot of symbolic meaning to it. That the men chose to pray over Charlie in a barn says that when we gather to honor someone it can be casual and still be spiritually significant. After all, Jesus was born in a barn and the spiritual authority of his humble birth will last for eternity.

I get emotional thinking how much love was extended that night to a young man who needed a father's embrace. Charlie now has several loving father figures in his life who believe in him and have welcomed him into their lives.

Charlie has moved away from our community and I no longer hear from him. I pray that the words of blessing that Charlie's spiritual fathers spoke over him have taken root and released Charlie from the chains once holding him captive. I pray Charlie is making wise choices and continues to believe he is part of a spiritual family that will last forever and always love him unconditionally. I pray Charlie is beginning to believe in himself and a good future. Distance cannot stop the effects of godly men over the lives of literal or spiritual orphans.

The transformation of fatherhood

God's path for family life is centered on fathers training their children in the ways of God (Deuteronomy 6:6-9). This is a spiritual principle. The Bible says if parents train their children in the right course it will direct their older years (Proverbs 22: 6). We must know that there is not a specific timeframe built into the promise. But we need to trust that the timing of God is perfect in the releasing of His promises.

Many Christian parents limit their spiritual training to church attendance and Bible knowledge when they are raising their families. More attention is often given to memorization than to application of the principles of scripture. We often believe if children can recite a passage of scripture they will be able to relate it to their lives. However, the Bible encourages parents to love and train their children like God loves and trains us.

God's teaching is intended to prepare us for life. The wisdom of God is practical and applicable, teaching us how to process the hardships of life (Hebrews 12:7). God is treating us as his children when He teaches us how to endure difficult times and process the pain resulting from trials. And He tells us how to identify appropriate thoughts that will sustain us from toxic thoughts which tear us down.

When children grow up without the ability to process pain, they often find ways to deny or avoid pain. Internal confusion leads many people to reject God and embrace destructive behaviors. Charlie's parents modeled a caustic method of pain management. They did not teach him about God or how to deal with a difficult life.

Though it is good that the face of fatherhood is extremely diverse, the imprint of a father on a child is intended to create security in the child's heart, preparing the way for their future.

Fatherhood has changed expression over the years, shifting from a stern financial provider responsible for harsh discipline at the end of the day to the post-modern nurturing father who is often the stay-at-home parent. The "Leave it to Beaver" era portrayed a father as proper, emotionally distant, unapproachable - in a starched white dress shirt with a perfectly knotted tie and stuck in a very precise male role. The 1950's father instructed his sons in skills specific to boys, such as mowing the lawn, repairing equipment, properly throwing and catching a baseball and respecting the weaker female species. Training included a dose of how to protect women in a man's world and educating little boys about a woman's household duties. Although cleaning, entertaining and child rearing were promoted as female tasks, culinary skills were the ultimate proof of a successful housewife and fathers instructed their sons to seek such a woman for their wives.

Post-modern fathers approach fatherhood without gender specific roles. Modern fathers wear their children in stylish baby wraps, change diapers, hug, cry, comfort, and affirm their children by teaching them how to properly express their emotions, while cleaning the house and doing the dishes. They are often better cooks than their wives. Modern fathers are often who the children run to for comfort and affirmation. Many toddlers want their dad to dry their tears and mom to fix their bikes.

Parenting roles are often interchangeable with the Millennials. More and more mothers work outside the home to share financial responsibilities with their husbands. And more and more fathers understand the importance of time at home with their children. I personally believe this is a positive transition and that the cultural change is producing emotionally healthy men who are becoming in-tune fathers who will produce emotionally healthy sons and daughters. It is the heart of Jesus that little boys are learning the value of emotions and little girls are learning that being a good mother means more than a clean house and a perfect soufflé.

The expression of fatherhood has changed, but the intent of a father is consistent. Fathers are intended to be the representation of manhood in a little boy's life. Boys learn how to be a man from watching their fathers or male role models. And little girls learn the importance of being respected, loved and cherished by watching men who know how to honor women by treating them with kindness and not restricting them to the kitchen. The father-son bond is designed to create stability in the vulnerable time of childhood. The relationship a boy has with his father is connected to how he views God. A girl's interaction with her dad influences her relationship with her husband. The daddy-daughter connection also affects how girls view the Lord and her freedom to, or restriction from, worship. We usually approach the Heavenly Father in the same way we approached our dad. We learn how to interact with the Lord from the way our fathers related to us.

A powerful proverb says when fathers walk in integrity their children will be happy (Proverbs 20:7). Note that this ancient proverb does not say when fathers talk about integrity their children will be happy; it says when they demonstrate good character it will affect their children's happiness. This is an example of the gospel being demonstrated more effectively through actions than words.

This cannot be accomplished in a family where men are still operating from a dysfunctional norm created from a generation driven by fears of violating gender roles. There is a strong possibility that girls raised in sexist homes will struggle with leadership roles in the church because they heard or watched their fathers promote men above women.

Many young men enter our churches with empty hearts and confused minds because a masculine role model was missing in their childhoods. They don't feel like men because they were told that they didn't fit the male stereotype. This confusion is intensified if a little boy is artistic, emotional or expressive and his family believed that boys should be stoic and non-creative.

It is common in rural Christian churches for a man to be defined by hunting, fishing and camouflaged clothing and judgment to rest on those who aren't outdoorsmen. Satan is opportunistic and sexuality is prime opportunity for Satan to lie to us about who God says we are and what we have to offer the kingdom of God. Orphans like this usually struggle with identity and need people who love and accept them for who they are.

Many people love God but hate themselves. They hate themselves because they are confused. Confusion is a liar that always hides the truth. Passion is always hindered when we don't know who we are. This is significant because passion is the force that drives us to our dreams.

Satan loves when we are apathetic about life because he can keep us trapped in a false identity. Confused people want someone to rescue them, but they do not know how to ask for help. They don't have the essential discipline taught by parents to develop the skills required for their futures.

They were not taught the truth about hard work or the fact that most things in life require a process. They want quick fixes and instant gratification because time and patience often include being still. And stillness allows space for thoughts and feelings to surface that are usually associated with a painful past, hurts from lives without parents or with wounded, distracted parents. Reflection and stillness also expose any self-hatred hiding behind an identity facade.

Discouraged people like to keep busy. Many hurting people drink too much, talk too much, move too much, smoke too much, and work too much in order to avoid what they feel. They don't stop long enough for instruction from the people in their lives who have the answers they need. Perhaps broken people feel disconnected from God because they don't know how to be still and connect with Him either (Psalm 46:10). Perhaps hurting people are still hurting because they have not been embraced by a spiritual family and are still living life like an orphan.

It is also possible for young men and women who have spiritually-healthy biological families to reject them and so act like orphans. I meet with many young adults who have godly, successful, wise parents, but they refuse to give them a voice in their lives because they have been told that wisdom is better found outside of the natural family.

Maturity allows us to embrace the fruit of wise parents. When we apply the wisdom of generational counsel it can release us from unnecessary mistakes. It is a wonderful gift when wisdom and guidance comes from our natural parents and grandparents. The goodness of biological and spiritual families should not be mutually exclusive.

Discipline is a loving act

Wise fathers discipline their sons. Mature fathers are not manipulated by their sons' rebellious behaviors or emotional outbursts. Proverbs 19:18-19 states that if a father disciplines his son and doesn't spare his soul because he cries, he will learn a lesson. Many fathers parent from the lie that discipline is not a loving act.

I watch many young adults allow their children to control their family with their bad behavior. They would rather spoil their children than discipline them. They embrace poor psychology that encourages child-centric parenting where the child's freedom to express herself and be creative is more important than a well-disciplined, polite, yet still creative child. This philosophy contradicts the wisdom of the scriptures because discipline is needed in every area of our lives in order to succeed. "Listen to advice and accept instruction and in the end you will be wise" (Proverbs 19:20) is great advice from the scriptures for young men and women who lack self-control.

I recently read three encouraging books about the importance of defeating our internal resistance in order to be successful in life and reach our desired dreams. Each book shared the theme of developing a disciplined life and emphasized that the discipline process begins in our mind.

We must become aware of our internal excuses and move in the opposite direction of the lies that resist discipline in order to be productive and successful. This is a vital skill the church needs to address because we have embraced many lies about being successful. It seems many Christians believe that it is more spiritual to live a hidden, mediocre life and deny their abilities than to excel in what God has gifted them to do in their lives. Some counsel actually reinforces an undisciplined lifestyle if it discloses that it is prideful to excel in life.

A disciplined life

Healthy communities teach young people how to live disciplined lives, slow down and listen to God for instruction and make plans for their lives. It is as spiritual to help a person plan their future as it is to pray with him or her. Actually, spiritual direction is very prayerful.

Little boys who grow up watching a strong father passionately pursue Jesus and trust God with his hardships learn about God easier than a little boy raised in a non-Christian home or in a home without the guidance of a righteous father. This is the context where boys learn how to be a good, loving father.

You don't have to be fatherless to end up with daddy wounds. Many young men had fathers who loved God, worked hard and provided for their physical needs and took them to church, but didn't know how to communicate with them. When fathers don't know how to take care of their son's hearts it often leaves sons with the same wounds as those who didn't have a father. These young men act as much like orphans as a person who suffered the physical loss of his parents.

When a child is imprinted with the right spiritual messages, it is easier for him or her to trust God when confused by life. The opposite is true as well, and the challenges of life can easily derail a young adult who didn't have a spiritual role model. Orphans need adults to help them overcome the scars of their pasts and develop a hunger for God.

No one has trouble understanding malnutrition in the physical sense, but we need to help each other learn to pay attention to our spiritual appetites. It is a fair assumption that many of us are spiritually undernourished and that our physical appetites receive more attention than our spirits. Orphans are not the only people who can suffer from malnutrition. We can all benefit from an honest exam of the condition of our spiritual health.

It is obvious our country has turned away from the truth about the physical requirements to have a healthy, fit body. The obesity rate correlates with our poor food choices. High calorie malnutrition is a result of the American diet. We eat large amounts of empty foods that have no nutritional value and even hinder our health. We have convinced ourselves that the quality of food we ingest does not matter. We have also embraced sedentary lifestyles in which we disregard the importance of regular exercise. We neglect our need to care for our souls and we rarely take time to meditate. We work jobs, earn money, pay bills, have nice possessions and continue to grow more unhealthy and unhappy. Most people are not willing to change what they eat to improve their physical health because they are in denial about the importance of nutrition. I believe we have the same approach to our spiritual life.

We should agree that neglect or empty spiritual practices yield a malnourished spirit and an anemic spiritual condition. Healthy people are disciplined and aware of the nutrition needed to sustain their physical bodies. Spiritually mature Christians feed their spirits with wholesome practices on a regular basis because they know the importance of caring for their body, soul and spirit. Spiritually fit people are disciplined and their consistency is visible in their lives. We have opportunity to share the importance of disciplined lives with those who come to us for help by teaching them that strategy and discipline for their lives are spiritual.

God loves orphans

Family is God's answer for orphans and lonely people. It is God's design for the church to embrace the fatherless and those who are considered orphans. There are many childhood wounds that can only be filled by God, but there are other needs that can only be met in the context of relationships within a loving community and received in the smaller context of a family. God places the lonely in families to be loved and encouraged. Satan draws lonely people into isolation. The Devil wants us to believe family isn't a big deal. But God intends for us to live a shared lives with our biological families, our spiritual families, or both.

Teaching young men to hear the voice of God when they haven't heard their father's voice is a difficult task, but the church must accept this challenge in order to help young men overcome the wounds of their pasts. It is equally challenging to help young women hear the voice of God and learn to trust him when they had a dysfunctional or abusive earthly father. Many young women transfer their dad wounds to God and believe that He will treat them the same way their father treated them.

When little boys grow up in a family without a father, or a broken father, they are often insecure in developing healthy male friendships. They are confused about God as a loving father who cares about their needs and desires. They are quite often confused about how to think and act like a man. They are confused about appropriately relating to the same sex and the opposite sex and this confusion is obvious when people try to love them.

Have you ever tried to hug a man who wasn't hugged by his dad? I often compare it to hugging a tree because they stiffen their bodies, look away and don't respond. Their relationships have been distorted by their self-perceptions, their relationships with their parents and the intentions of other people. They are discouraged about becoming Godly men and they don't have a grid for families who could love them and help them recover.

Our spiritual communities provide opportunities to embrace those who are orphans, or feel like orphans, and help them renew their perceptions of family. Through generosity and unconditional love we can demonstrate the gospel in practical ways by sharing our lives with those who need us.

It is a considerable task shifting a person's concept of family from preconceived ideas, icons on a screen, or words on a page to reality. But it can be done simply by sharing your life with them. God uses our everyday lives, our homes, our time and our conversations to create family and to reveal His love for all of mankind.

Let's not complicate the gospel. Let's be the gospel to the world around us.

Questions to Consider

- Do you feel like an orphan?
- Are the spiritual fathers in your community mentoring young men?

CHAPTER TWELVE
Your True Self

I have always been contemplative. I haven't always known who I am. So several years ago God began talking to me about how I viewed myself. The Holy Spirit was asking me to how I define myself.

Something I do know about myself is that my internal dialogue often creates 'idea boards' in my mind which can interfere with me hearing God's voice. This is problematic because the Lord always knows the truth I need. So at this time, I felt led to purposely respond quickly and to neither dissect nor defend my answers to myself. Just answer, rather than get caught up in logic and the need for things to make sense - according to my definition. So this prompting for immediate responses was an insightful exercise.

I felt secure in my initial responses: I am confident in who I am. I don't care what other people think of me. I am not a scholar, but God loves me how I am. I love art, but I am not an artist. I love children. I am good with children. God will never use me for anything significant because I am not a theologian. I love beauty and color. I am not a fearful person. I love Jesus and want to be like Him, but have a long way to go. Most people like me. I don't fit in where I should fit in because there is something wrong with me. I care about the underdog. I can't sing. I am not musical. I don't look like my beautiful mother so I am not very attractive. I hate drama. I'm not very feminine. I love my daughters unconditionally, but I was too harsh in my parenting... The list continued until the still, small voice of the Lord interrupted me.

The Lord began to reveal how my self-perception was composed of a combination of truth and lies. It still amazes me how strongly attached I was to lies about myself. My identity was influenced by lies I embraced from the world around me. I created a standard of measurement for myself when I was a little girl that I was still using to evaluate myself as an adult.

Take note of the fact that I created this standard for myself; it was not the Lord. I didn't think like my friends when I was young, look like my glamorous mother, or respond to people the same way others did so I decided there was something wrong with me. Many people who didn't understand me reinforced the lies I believed about myself. I allowed unhealthy, broken people to shape my identity by listening to their lies which I then welcomed as my truth.

There is a place within every person that knows the truth about himself or herself and this truth is worthy of exposure. But it wasn't until I belonged to a safe, healthy community that I felt comfortable enough to invite people to tell me how they perceived me. It was the combination of loving people and Jesus that spoke to the deep places in my heart about who I really am.

God began to tell me the truth about myself. He began to show me how I compared myself to other people in several areas. Not everything I believed was a lie. I really am not a natural musician or singer. I didn't like drama when I was an adolescent and I dislike it still as a middle-aged woman. I love God's word, but I am not a theologian. I do care about the broken-hearted. I love art. I love children. And I love Jesus and want to be like Him.

We must remember we have an enemy who wants to destroy us. He wants to rob our lives from all good things God has for us and he wants us to hold onto lies about ourselves. I vividly remember the day the Holy Spirit highlighted my ungodly thoughts and my deceptive self-perception. And I remember how the power of the lies began losing their grip on me. To this day God continues showing me how the Devil uses lies to help ourselves distort our identities, but how Jesus tells us the truth about who we are. And that truth is what always sets us free (John 8:32).

We need to know Satan participates with us in distorting our identities in very subtle, very unhurried ways. The Devil usually begins lying to us when we are children. If our parents are not aware to tell us the truth, the lies that began as whispers eventually turn to shouts which we gradually embrace as normal. Once we partner with lies, they only need reinforcement for Satan to have the opportunity to continually oppress us.

Many people don't believe in the Devil or any form of evil in the world. They don't know that Satan is the father-of-lies and that lies are what he uses to control us (John 8:44). In fact, most of us are oblivious to the lies we believe, especially those about ourselves, because we believe them. Why question something you take for granted is an established truth?

The guidance of the Good Shepherd

The book of John says Jesus is the Good Shepherd who leads us through the gate into His presence by talking to us. When we learn to listen to His voice we won't be confused or go the wrong way (John 10). It is important to recognize the voice of God and listen to what He says because the Devil likes to talk to us also.

Our enemy communicates with lies because he hates us, wants to steal from us, and wants to kill us. The Bible calls Satan a thief (John 10:10). Satan doesn't always have to physically kill a person to end their lives. He can lie to them about who they are and what they can and can't do, restricting their abilities to live full lives. He can lie to them about how to handle their problems and suggest that they turn to drugs, alcohol, pornography, work or anything else to quiet the lies in their heads and the pain in their hearts. It is easier to be demonically influenced when we aren't aware of the power of lies or how darkness can affect Christian believers. Deception is easy when we don't recognize Satan or the voice of God.

Deliverance prayers

There are many doctrines about how to defeat the Devil. Many of them involve very dramatic methods. I have been in many gatherings where people shouted prayers and screamed the name of Jesus. There was an unspoken expectation for drama. It appeared that the thinking was the more emotionally and physically extreme the person receiving prayer acted, the more effective was the person's level of deliverance.

Years ago I was new to this manner of prayer. I remember thinking drama couldn't be God's standard for measuring the freedom He gives us. Where would that leave reserved introverts who also wanted to be free from the Devil's influence? And I have never read anywhere in the Bible that demonic spirits are deaf, so it amuses me to hear this noisy approach.

I have also watched as praying people conclude that evil spirits are released from people based on behavioral responses. Throwing up seems to always earn the most attention. I confess, when I see these approaches I want to roll my eyes and ask those in charge of deliverance prayer, "Seriously?" I am suggesting here that God's truth is what defeats Satan's schemes and releases trapped identities, not drama.

The father-of-lies loses his grip on people when they realize the truth about who they are. I encourage people to give God permission to tell them the truth about their identities and give the Holy Spirit access to their hearts because love is the best deliverance tool. Truthful words can even be whispered yet unlock years of deception.

Lies have power that can only be broken when we choose truth. I have prayed with many abuse survivors. Some have experienced years of trauma, fragmenting their minds and dividing their hearts. Yet most of them believe in Jesus and know that He is the answer to freedom. Many remain in bondage, though, because they believe lies that abusive people told them. But lies, and the demonic spirits who tell them, lose their right to oppress us when we choose Jesus over them. Choice is the key that begins the steps to freedom.

Possessed or oppressed

Many hurting people come to me for help because demonic spirits frequently harass them. I never debate how demonic spirits oppress a follower of Jesus. I personally don't believe Christian believers can be possessed or completely controlled by demonic spirits because Christians are filled with the Holy Spirit (1 John 4:4, 1 Corinthians 3:16). Logic tells me two things cannot reside in the same space at the same time, so if a person is filled with the Holy Spirit, he or she cannot be filled with a demonic spirit. But I have witnessed many people crippled by demonic oppression.

We know from reading the Bible, and some times through personal experience, that Satan's influence begins with our thoughts and translates to our behaviors. Those who are under the influence of demonic spirits are often trapped in deception held in place by lies and cloaked in shame. Demonic oppression can cause people to think and act in ways that contradict their true selves and how they really want to act.

Most of the people who come to me for prayer love Jesus and believe God is powerful. But the people who abused them told them, either directly or through their actions, that Satan was more powerful than God and they believed the lie. And you don't have to be an abuse survivor to have someone tell you Satan is stronger than God. Many people, and many Christians, remain ignorant of the Devil's tricks. Many people are often paralyzed with fear, believing Satan is going to get them at any moment. Others hear voices in their minds constantly telling them to hurt themselves or they have night terrors and feel the need to hide, so they isolate.

Demonic oppression sounds theatrical and some demonized people do, indeed, act extreme. But not all people experience the same level of demonic oppression. Lies can produce subtle behaviors as well as dramatic ones. Both are equally crippling.

At this point you might be thinking that demonic oppression is rare and that a demonic spirit has never influenced you. If you have ever had thoughts that you are not good enough for the opportunities that come into your life or that you are not as good the people you admire, then you believe lies. When you judge other people, you believe lies about them and probably about yourself in comparison to them. If you have ever been struck with a panic attack, trapped in depression or afraid to leave your house, you were most likely believing lies. And those lies were manipulating your emotions.

A life of trauma leads to lies. Trauma and pain lie to people about who they are and who God is. It is common for trauma survivors to react when I begin to pray for them. They often became agitated and tell me that they are hearing scary voices telling them to run out of the room or they begin having destructive thoughts about hurting themselves. It is common for fearful people to tell me that when I begin praying for them they feel internal threats. These threats are always an attempt to stop prayer and God's truth from reaching the person's heart because Satan knows that God's truth will lead them to freedom (John 8:32). It doesn't take a special gift of discernment to realize when demonic spirits are influencing the mind of a hurting person that you are praying for, but we are often blind to the ways that demonic spirits are influencing us.

Sometimes when a person in my office gives me permission to pray for them and deal with the demonic spirits that are holding them captive I kneel down in front of them and ask permission to hold their hands. I also ask them to look into my eyes. Many respond by telling me they are hearing internal voices. "They won't let me look into your eyes," is the most common message people share. I encourage them to listen to me and not to the internal threats.

As people hold my hands and look into my eyes, I feel great compassion for their bondage. I pray and declare they belong to Jesus and that God loves them and claims them as His son or daughter (2 Corinthians 6:18). Then I calmly command the demonic spirit to let go of the person in the name of Jesus (Philippians 2:10).

To be honest, at this point it is common for people to snarl at me and yell derogatory statements they are hearing about me in their mind. My response to this level of demonization is that I remind the person, and the demonic spirit, what the resurrection of Jesus means to the Christian believer against the works of the Devil. (Hebrews2:14-15, 1 John 3:8). I often proclaim out loud specific scriptures that the Holy Spirit brings to my mind as I continue to audibly repeat how much God loves the person. I also state out loud that the person is choosing freedom and choosing to submit to prayer because personal choice truly is a key that unlocks prisoners. Satan knows when we choose truth deliverance will follow.

Other times, I sit across the room and in a normal tone of voice I tell demonic spirits to leave in the name of Jesus.

I share these scenarios about oppression because many people enter our spiritual communities weighed down by the darkness of demonic spirits and need us to help them. They need the support of loving people who will not judge them and who care enough about them to teach them the truth about the Devil. They need spiritual communities that know the truth about evil. They also need friends of Jesus who know how to pray for deliverance. I think it is fair to say most people appreciate people praying for them who pray with confidence that comes from the authority they have in the name of Jesus; not dramatics.

Nothing can separate us from God's love

Most demonized people believe they don't have any power over the oppression in their lives because of the bad things that happened to them or the poor choices they have made. It makes me sad to hear all the different ways Satan has lied to people and convinced them they will be trapped in darkness forever because of trauma, pain or sin. Pain is often the perfect opportunity for people to experience the love of God. I always tell people that nothing that has happened to them, or anything they have done, changes God's love for them.

It is encouraging to be reminded that Jesus is not intimidated by sin. However, I believe many Christians are intimidated by sin. I also believe immature Christians don't know how to separate a person's sinful lifestyle from the person, so they reject the person.

The human heart apart from God is very selective about whom it will accept; most of the time we will only accept those who are like us. A quick, but insightful, test is to consider the sin or lifestyle you find most repulsive then ask yourself if you would prepare a meal and spend an evening with the person who offends you.

We are so afraid of what people will think if we associate with specific people. When we are not confident about whom we are or our spiritual positions, we fear that our morality will be compromised if we associate with people who are struggling in ways different from our struggles.

Yet the apostle Paul said nothing can separate us from God's love, "For I am convinced that neither death, nor life, nor angels, nor principalities, nor things present, nor things to come, nor powers, nor height, nor depth, nor any created thing, will be able to separate us from the love of God, which is in Christ Jesus our Lord" (Romans 8:38). This ancient verse conveys many excuses we still use today. But nothing that happens in our lives, positive or negative, or any demonic entity past, present, or future can separate us from God's unconditional love.

The carrying out of this promise falls to the shoulders of those who have experienced the honesty of Jesus, His freedom, and His unconditional love; especially to those lacking a grid for understanding this truth. Spiritual families which can extend the love of God in this manner can embrace diverse sheep while not compromising the standard of the Gospel. The exhibition of this reality is absolutely key for spiritual communities wishing to speak the truth of Jesus and have it be heard over the father-of-lies. To help break the power lies hold over people, my hope is that we grow in our ability to embrace sinful people - those whose sins look like ours and those whose sins look different from ours.

Deception is sly

We need to teach people the truth about deception and what it can looks like in our lives. People have created an image of deception that is more connected to Hollywood than the Bible. Deception is sly in its presentation. Deception is pretentious in how it shows up in our daily lives. People think evil has an ugly color and a bad taste. But darkness is rarely black and sour. Rather, it is often a color that we like and the taste which we believe best satisfies our appetites.

Addictions may be the best example to illustrate this point. Addictions are often appealing in the way they present themselves during painful times. Satan whispers suggestions of various ways to numb pain and he does it in such a way that Christians embrace his fraudulent ways. It actually becomes an option that entices us more than the beauty of God. This is deception.

Deception is seldom people in black capes circling a fire in the woods forcing their ways upon us. No, it is a subtle invitation, a mere suggestion at our precise moments of weakness and confusion. Delusion proposes that numbing our pain is better than God. When we agree, when we play along, we step into the world of deception even though our intent was merely to stop the pain.

There is such a need to teach people the truth about the chronology and lifespan of a deception. When we are influenced by and partner with evil trickery and refuse to take a stand against the Devil's schemes we are also saying "No" to God. This is the birthing of deception into our lives. When I ask trapped people what they consider to be the beginning of their oppression by evil and lies they are often naïve because they equate demonic access as occult practices or dramatic experiences - not the choices they make daily that say "Yes" to lies and "No" to reality.

Since personal choice is an important key to freedom during deliverance prayers, I ask people if they want the demonic spirits that are oppressing them to leave. This sounds like a question that would always have a resounding 'yes,' but it often does not. Many people become so familiar with lies and dysfunction that they resist letting go of them.

Dysfunction, deception, and denial have a way of becoming normal. I believe this is mostly due to people being afraid to connect with their true selves. When a person's identity has been defined for many years by lies the thought of freedom can be unsettling. Change and the unfamiliar are, by definition, a disturbance to the status quo. The changing of your conception of your self... what could be more of an all-encompassing change? We carry with us at all times who we believe ourselves to be. This is why Satan loves having access to our identities, because he knows having that gives him an upper hand in getting us to continue believing his untruths.

Identity

I remember two vivid childhood memories that make me cry. But to fully understand, first you need to know that when I raised my daughters I was rigid about how much time they spent watching television. I was a psychology major at the time and was convinced watching television was mindless and counterproductive to developing creative, analytical thinkers. I wanted my daughters to grow up thinking for themselves and engaging in creative expression so TV was restricted to thirty minutes per day.

I, however, was raised with a television in my bedroom from a very young age (this could explain so much). I was glad my parents didn't have beliefs about television compromising my abilities. I loved my TV watching privileges and I loved my room.

The wallpaper in my bedroom had a black and white background that created a grid. The thin black lines crossed in such a way that it reminded me of graph paper. But the large yellow, green and orange flowers changed the intention of the design from a rigid, lined design to fun. The prolific, misshapen flowers were definitely the focus of the wallpaper.

My carpet was lime-green shag I had to manage with a carpet rake. The flowers on the wallpaper looked exaggerated because of the mirrored wall tile surrounding my louvered closet doors, multiplying the number of flowers in my room. The mirrored tiles refracted the patterned walls like a prism bending the colors of light. The light fixtures in my room hung from the corners by wired chains because it was the seventies and it enhanced the desired tone of the room. My matching furniture was white with gold trim and I thought that it was a great complement to my vibrant room. I slept and mindlessly watched television in my white canopy bed that was occasionally adorned with multi-colored beads.

I felt like a princess in a castle when I was in my bedroom. I could easily escape life and enter into my imaginary fantasyland where everything was happy, peaceful and very colorful. I loved dreaming about painting pictures that represented the hues in my dreams.

However, one specific commercial, brought into my castle through the TV, would repeatedly wreck my happy place. I knew when I heard the music for the commercial about sponsoring a starving child my tears would soon accompany the music. I couldn't control my emotions when I saw the pictures of skinny, dark-skinned children crying because the voice-over was declaring their hunger. Yes, I was the child who wanted to send my leftover food, shoes, toys and money to the children in the television advertisement. My parents graciously allowed me to sponsor several children throughout the life of the commercials.

But the act of sponsorship didn't stop the pain that I felt for the hungry children. I would flop on my bed, cover my head with a velvet pillow and cry. I cared about these children and I was very dramatic. I was bothered by the fact that I had a comfortable bedroom, pretty clothes and all of the food I wanted and the children in the commercials were dirty and eating only rice. I remember always saying to myself, "There must be something I can do to help." I admit it was an extreme reaction to a commercial.

My second emotional response was several years later. Every time I heard news reports about the Vietnam War I fell apart. My ability to calmly listen to the news was hijacked by my tears. I remember kneeling beside my bed and crying for the war to end and the children and innocent people to be protected. My heart broke for the children in both scenarios who didn't have the help they needed. The ache in my heart was intense and would last for days. I didn't formally know Jesus at that time, but I knew about Him and would cry and ask Him to let me help hurting people someday.

Destiny is always within us

Many years have passed and I still respond with tears for hurting children and broken adults. Jesus often reminds me that those early experiences were more than emotion; they were signs of who I am and what He designed me to do.

The passion I feel for abused people has led me into fulltime inner-healing ministry. I come alive when I pray for hurting people and watch Jesus change their hearts and often their lives. It makes me very happy helping people realize the truth about who they are and how living in the truth defeats the Devil's plan for their lives.

When we encourage people who don't know who they are to listen to the voice of God, it helps them remember the passions in their hearts. The things that break our hearts are often road signs that can help navigate us toward our destinies. We simply need to learn to trust ourselves.

We often ignore our truest thoughts and our passions because we don't trust them. The voices of the world are loud and persuasive and often lead us away from our destinies. God's truth allows us to believe in ourselves and reach the dreams He puts in our hearts when He made us. Taking time to be still and ask God to remind you of the desires of your heart and the destiny of your life is always worth your attention.

It should be remembered that 'sin' in its literal sense means to fall short of the target, to miss the mark. Lies involved in the hiding of true identity are often connected to sin. It is all-too-common for people to allow some sin of theirs to define them.

It makes me sad when I hear people define themselves by what they have done, or by the sin that is controlling them, saying things such as, "I am a druggie," "I am an adulterer," or "I am a liar." And on a regular basis I hear people in my office describe themselves as abuse survivors. Their behaviors, their strategies for dealing with their pains, or the traumas of their personal stories, have merged with their identities. They have believed the lie that their shortfalls define them and not who God has told them they are.

People also often define themselves by their emotional behaviors, telling people, "I am shy," "I am an extrovert," "I am emotional," "I am not emotional," instead of understanding who God designed them to be.

It is important for us to remember when we began lying to ourselves in order to end the cycle of destruction a lie is creating. We need God to transform us. Asking God to reveal the origins of lies is helpful because if we attempt to identify the beginning of an issue without God's help our logic will often interfere. Sins, emotions or traumas have the power to lie to us, deceiving us about who we are. But if we will take time to meditate and listen to the Holy Spirit the lies we are empowering and assuming as our identity will be revealed.

Social media and identity

We have a new challenge to address when trying to help insecure people. Many people disregard the power of social media's ability to lie to them. Yet many people solicit public affirmation and allow electronic comments to influence how they feel about themselves. The voice of the world is very seductive and its voice has broadened and become instantly available. So we must now include the fact that social media makes it possible for broken people to refine their false personas by creating profiles of who they think they are or who they want us to think they are.

Hollywood is another avenue that offers people the opportunity to create unrealistic standards for rating themselves. Insecure women often devalue their physical bodies if they don't look like the actresses in movies or the models in magazines. This deception has become so common that many women artificially enhance their bodies and facial structure to copy the appearance of celebrities they want to look like or to deny their actual ages. This dramatic behavior is always rooted in lies. The Devil loves to convince us there is something wrong with us physically, emotionally and mentally. He wants us to believe our outward appearance is more important than the condition of our hearts and he wants us to think we are inferior to airbrushed Hollywood stars.

I know many physically beautiful people who have hardened hearts. I know plenty of physically flawless women who are no deeper than their eye shadow. Many women sit in my office and confess they feel worthless, useless and unattractive if they are not dressed up, adorned with jewelry and freshly applied make-up. They cry when they tell me how ugly they feel because they believe their body weight is more important than their morality.

I also know a lot of traditionally 'unattractive' people who have tender, loving hearts and the character of Jesus when it comes to facing the challenges of life. They know who they are and where they are going in life. I enjoy the confidence that emotionally healthy people radiate. God is after our hearts, not our physiques.

I believed many lies about myself as a young girl because I didn't fit in the same category as my mom. I compared myself to her all the time. I loved to play kick ball, shoot basketball, get dirty and act dangerously. My mother never did. She always looked pretty and was dressed up. I hated wearing dresses unless they were tie-dyed. Mom was classic and comfortable in the formal world. I would rather paint a picture, write a poem, or design various ways to utilize denim as clothing than ever attend a formal event. In fact, because my beautiful mother seemed to be created for elegant events and I was not, for years formal events brought out the worst parts of me because I believed lies about who I was. It is easy for comparison to become the lie that deceives us even if the comparison is within our own natural, healthy, and loving family.

His ways are not our ways

In the Bible Samuel was in charge of finding a new king for Israel. It makes sense that his criteria included stature, strength and intellect. After all who wants an ugly, dull leader? A man's ability to direct an army, instruct officials, influence others, and rule with authority is often related to his appearance. We usually view as powerless leaders who are short, skinny or young. It is a cultural norm to equate greatness with good looks and stature. This ideology hasn't changed for centuries. We still base numerous decisions on first time appearances. Judgment, especially that based on physicality, appears to be timeless. However, God told Samuel not to consider appearance or height in his decision-making. Given the prevalence of media-driven images which are our main source of information about officials today, it is probably wise to use God's standards for electing leaders and look more deeply.

The Lord directed Samuel to anoint the least likely candidate as the new king. David was a young, reddish shepherd boy. Can you imagine your reaction to a young, immature, electronic geek with little to no life experience being promoted over an older wiser man or woman who had worked for the company for years? A young man who receiving the coveted promotion over the more experienced candidate simply because he loved God and had good character?

Most people do not care about the condition of an employee's heart if they have an impressive résumé and the appropriate appearance for the job. But Samuel took God's advice and chose the least probable candidate. Samuel poured oil over David while his older, taller, more mature brothers watched. The Bible says that from that day on the Spirit of the Lord came upon David in power. How often do we misjudge people based on how they look? How often do we lie to ourselves because of our appearance?

People who dress in traditional, conservative attire often fool us. We often think because a person looks professional that he or she is wise, kind and lives a very productive life. We also misjudge people who dress in non-traditional clothes or clothes we personally disdain. Many people view tattooed, pierced, neon-colored hair and black clothing as a sign of rebellion.

If we are honest about profiling we can admit to ourselves that we all do it. I, personally, am guilty of automatically thinking women who are always dolled-up ('high-maintenance girls,' I call them) are uptight or insecure. I never understand why women feel more valuable in heels and lipstick than athletic clothing. Before concluding I am a horrible person, though, ask God if you have any secret judgments. What automatic assumptions are you making based on nothing more than how someone looks?

A place of acceptance

Church should be a place where everyone is welcome regardless of their appearance. I love to look around our church on Sunday mornings, seeing the variety of people who feel at home. We have some people who enjoy dressing in traditional clothes, many who dress according to the hipster trend, artists who look like leftover hippies, Amish families who chose to honor their roots with their clothing, and our share of good old rednecks. I love that our church has many expressions of family.

Although outward appearances are diverse in our fellowship, we are committed to growing in our abilities to unconditionally love each other and encouraging people to find their true selves. We strive, with intentionality, to not exclude people based on how they look or where they are in their spiritual-journeys. Our church, as a whole, is learning who we are as a spiritual family and we are learning who we are as individuals.

It is important for spiritual communities to understand how important it is to be skilled in the ability to help people connect with their true selves. This cannot be accomplished if churches believe everyone is already living from their true identity simply because he or she is a Christian. If churches believe salvation resolves all of our broken issues, we will not be positioned to help Christians who are hurting.

I encourage spiritual communities to embrace inner-healing training that teaches them how to help people transform. Such help can only be achieved when churches understand sanctification is a process and that the Holy Spirit is the one who transforms us into the likeness of Jesus - if we give Him permission to do so.

I want to encourage those struggling with knowing who they are by saying the Lord knows who you are and what He designed you to do. In the book of Jeremiah encouragement from the Lord says, "Because I formed you in the womb I knew you, before you were born I set you apart; I appointed you as a prophet to the nations" (Jeremiah 1:5).

If you are unsure about who you are or what you were designed to do, take time to ask Jesus who He says you are. We have spiritual identities that can only be realized in the presence of the one who created it.

Questions to Consider

- Do you know who you are?
- Do you have people in your life who encourage you?
- Are you helping others discover who they are?

CHAPTER THIRTEEN
Living a Connected Life

Have you ever listened to people defend their reason for living isolated lives? "I am around people all day at work, when I come home I don't want to be around people," or "I don't have any energy to listen to other people's problems," and, my favorite, "I don't like people." These are common mantras of those choosing to disconnect from society and live 'off the grid' lifestyles.

A remote location might appeal to many people who feel the effects of a busy schedule and a large family. But Christians who reject relationships are missing the vision Jesus has for the church because a life surrendered to Jesus is a life connected to other people. Even if you had a wonderful childhood, know who you are, are spiritually mature, and are devoted to God, it is not possible to experience the fullness of the Christian life and live in isolation.

The temptation to isolate

Christians have always struggled with the temptation to isolate themselves from the world in an attempt to be spiritual. Sections of the early church withdrew from society to devote all their time to worship, prayer and religious practices. We might consciously think such a lifestyle is excessive, yet people still seem to struggle with the temptation to live a separatist lifestyle. We currently define it as 'living off the grid.'

I interact on a regular basis with young adults who are disillusioned with traditional church. They have allowed their negative church experiences to restrict their interactions with other Christians or their attendance at any denominational gathering. Many Millennials wear hipster clothing, live in post-modern decorated houses, talk with philosophical boldness, but they are lonely. They want to belong, yet they resist spiritual communities because they react against traditional religion.

Whether our premise for retreat is to seek God and become holy, avoid painful experiences, take part in a popular non-conformist lifestyle, or fear our story will overwhelm people, living life alone is unhealthy.

The climate of our present society rewards isolated behavior and holds independence in high regard. The western mindset is fixated on looking out for ourselves and developing skills to become the alpha dog; controlling other people but never entering into intimate, vulnerable, relationships.

It is fashionable for Christians to believe they don't need anyone and that the most spiritual practice is living in a prayer closet. The scripture does not say to live in a prayer closet. The scripture says we should avoid praying out loud to get attention. Matthew 6:5-6 says, "When you pray, you are not to be like the hypocrites; for they love to stand and pray in the synagogues and on the street corners so that they may be seen by men. Truly I say to you, they have their reward in full. But you, when you pray, go into your inner room, close your door and pray to your Father who is in secret, and your Father who sees what is done in secret will reward you." This scripture is often used as an excuse to hide ourselves away and pray.

So there is a tension present here within the Kingdom of God because the Kingdom is, at the same time, both personal, private and internal and relational, public and shared. What the scripture is truly saying is that our praying should be in a private, humble manner that pleases God. It suggests that when we pray our focus should be on the Lord, not on seeking approval from other people for our well-crafted prayers. Though the prayer may be in a public, community setting or even a shared activity, the personal relationship honored by, and the focus of, the prayer is the private relationship between you and God, not you and other people. Matthew is not suggesting we isolate ourselves from other Christians or that praying in a closet is better than praying in church.

Transformational communities

Many people have experienced negative interactions with immature Christians. I have had many of them myself. But I know life with God is greater than life without Him, and excuses will distance us from the truth.

If we are encouraging people to connect with a spiritual community, we need to make sure our spiritual communities are sensitive to why people resist a life of faith and what, exactly, is happening in the community that helps them substantiate the legitimacy of their resistance. Communities should be places where disappointed, disconnected people feel safe, loved and encouraged. Church should be a place where disillusioned people can regain trust or build trust.

I have entered the doors of many churches and felt as if I was being scanned for acceptance into a private club. You know, those moments when you are the only one in the room in jeans when all others are wearing formal attire, or when you attend a church wedding and a very gracious stranger informs you that you are not dressed correctly. How ironic that these offensive interactions occur when Christians gather to learn how to be like Jesus.

A few years ago I sat down at an evening wedding wearing a black dress, black tights and my favorite pair of cowboy boots. Only a few moments passed until a woman approached me (in my opinion dressed like someone 50 years her elder) and informed me that it was inappropriate to wear black to a wedding. As the woman walked away, I turned to lady beside me - also wearing a black dress - and attempted to lighten the atmosphere by saying I wasn't aware the fashion police were patrolling the event or I would have added feathers or a hat to my outfit. This is a funny scenario to envision, but sadly, this same attitude greets many newcomers who visit churches.

I admit, it can be challenging to learn how to love broken, hurting people, welcome them into our spiritual communities, and demonstrate the kindness of Jesus if they are rude and defensive. It is still the right thing to do. We should love people unconditionally and not define them by their dysfunction or appearance.

When people enter our spiritual communities who are locked in sin, or simply abrasive, there is a tendency to believe that should change before we embrace them. We often place them in categories based on their lifestyles and react accordingly. We might tolerate a person who steals from the company he works for, but never embrace a person who gets drunk. We might be willing to overlook an extra-marital affair if the person doesn't dishonor his parents. Occasionally, we overlook all sinful, rude behaviors if the person is financially generous.

There is no end to this judgmental mindset. Jesus doesn't want anyone trapped in sin, whether visible sin or hidden, but He loves every person unconditionally and has provided a way for them to be free from sin when they are ready. When we help a person fall in love with Jesus, his or her heart is open to change.

We cannot manipulate another person's willingness to transform. We cannot manipulate people to act properly. We can demonstrate a better way.

One of the most challenging dynamics of the shared life is learning to serve others when we live in a culture that devalues servant-hood. We must remember that life with Jesus is counter-culture. Society tells us to look out for ourselves, Jesus says to serve others and that it is better to give to others than receive things for ourselves (Galatians 5: 13-14, Acts 20:35).

I have found this to be a truth in my own life, because it makes me much happier to do things for other people rather than have people serve me. Although I enjoy having friends who are free to speak into my life, I am happiest when I help a hurting person connect with Jesus or introduce them to someone who will become a good friend to them.

It is challenging to learn how to give ourselves to other people and not neglect ourselves. Religion tells us we should disregard our needs and only give attention to others. Wisdom tells us to take care of ourselves so we have the capacity we need to help others.

There is a tension in living life with broken people that I want to be honest about. When we embrace extremely broken people into our lives and our communities, we become vulnerable to the very real possibilities of disappointment and hurt.

This has become very familiar to me over the past twenty years. Several people I embraced and invested in chose to tell lies about me, discredit me and distort our times of prayer. Although I am a forgiving person, regret often remains even after forgiveness is extended. Over the years I have had to grow in wisdom in my approach to dysfunctional people and in my ability to care for those who may not value their healing as much as I.

Our care for other people cannot be allowed to compromise our own safety or our own health. We must know how to guard our hearts and minds in order to succeed in the tension of loving ourselves and loving other people.

Joy comes from Jesus

The Apostle Paul tells us in the book of Romans that the Kingdom of God is within us and that righteousness, peace and joy come from the Holy Spirit that resides within the hearts of those who belong to Jesus (Romans 14:17). This is an internal reality affecting our emotions and influencing our behaviors. In fact, sometimes we can identify a person's level of spiritual maturity by the peace and joy that rests on him or her.

Society encourages us to be like the beautiful, rich, celebrities who value fame and fortune. Jesus encourages us to develop lifestyles of peace and joy. It is important to know that joy and peace can only come from Jesus because it releases us from striving to 'do the right things' to make ourselves feel good. Although life experiences can make us happy, the joy of the Lord is lasting and a gift from Him.

Watching misdirected Christians is confusing for those who are observing and contemplating life with Jesus. Many Christians look and act the same as non-Christian people. They are fixated on money, possessions and outward appearances and will engage in immoral behaviors to meet their goals or try to make themselves happy. Some Christians are more exclusive, critical, and unrighteous than those who have no spiritual declaration at all.

Some spiritual people are more dismal than those having no religious attachment. Misery can stem from many sources, but this is partly due to the fact that many Christians have not given Jesus access to the secret places in their hearts. And many miserable people don't have any truly deep friends, positive relationships, or have authentic, genuine connection within their spiritual family.

My husband recently had a pastor come into his chiropractic office pretending to want an adjustment. When this man was seated in the adjusting room with my husband he became angry. As he began yelling his disapproval of Ray owning a vineyard and making wine his red face affirmed his disdain for my husband. He proceeded to yell (in my husband's clinic) that my husband was a disgrace to the town and he could not be a Christian and be connected to wine.

He huffed, puffed and stormed out of the clinic. This man not only left his strong opinion behind, he left proof he was more focused on his personal opinion than relationships. He was stronger in judgment than love and more filled with anger than the joy of the Lord.

Spirituality

The word 'spirituality' appears to cause a great divide for people who try to define it. Society refers to a spiritual person as a person who is kind, gentle and loving toward people, animals and the planet. In a broad sense, spirituality is defined by one who is connected to something bigger than oneself who is searching for the meaning of life.

This dialogue about 'spiritual' is not new. The conversation is ancient. Believing human development has an inherent magical power within our minds that evolves into a 'consciousness of divinity,' and that this inherent, internal strength is evidenced by our humanitarian behaviors, is quite ancient. However, it is also incorrect by definition because it separates spirituality, daily life and a higher power. The Apostle Paul calls this philosophy foolish (1 Corinthians 3:18-20).

In some realms, spirituality is defined by how often one attends church and the number of good deeds correlated to their denominational theology they do outside of the church building. Many include appearance in their definition of a spiritual person, defining it by what a person wears or doesn't wear. And there are also those who say that a person isn't Godly if everything the person does is not related to ministry.

To me, 'spirituality' is simply defined by a person's acknowledgement of God and his or her genuine love for Jesus and desire to be like Him. This is seen in how he or she lives their life.

I believe when we are devoted to Jesus everything we do is spiritual. I do not believe there is a separation between spiritual life and daily life for those who belong to Jesus. I consider it sacred when I am playing with grandchildren, having meaningful conversations with friends about our lives, taking a walk, reading a book, talking to a stranger about Jesus or praying for an addict. I also believe spirituality is progressive in nature and that some people are more mature in their spiritual lives than others.

It is appropriate that people can have seasons of confusion about life with God and that they learn, grow, and change. But though I can have strong opinions on various matters, I refuse to engage in philosophical conversations about Jesus. Although I am comfortable with disagreement and can navigate confrontations I don't think there is value in spending large amounts of time arguing points of opposition. Philosophical rhetoric is non-productive, but the truth about God can change the hardest of hearts and loftiest of intellects.

Perhaps this is what Paul meant when he said our salvation has to be worked out (Philippians 2:12-13). It has to be realized. It is naïve to think that when we say 'yes' to Jesus all of our questions are resolved. I personally think the deeper we grow in God, the more questions we have. Many things about God are a mystery. No one has the answers and no amount of time devoted to vain philosophy will change this reality. We must learn how to rest in the mystery of God.

When I define a 'spiritual' person or those who make up a 'spiritual' community I am referring to Christian believers who acknowledge that spiritual development comes from the inner working of the Holy Spirit, not the philosophical evolution of man (Ephesians 3:16, Romans 12:2). A spiritual person knows external behaviors, appearances or using the correct Bible language is not a sign of a Godly life. This is important because people who are unfamiliar with God need to know that a person can display moral behaviors and be called spiritual yet not be Godly.

I can always tell when I am around a Godly person because they don't have to say anything to release God's peace and beauty to those around them. They bring stability and balance into unsettling situations and release love with few words.

The Apostle Paul wrote in Galatians 5:25 about spiritual people being able to live and walk in the Spirit. I have always interpreted this to mean that the Holy Spirit equips us to live in a balance that isn't derailed by life experiences. We receive inner strength from the Holy Spirit that is transferable; it translates into everyday life.

Spiritually mature people understand that life with God isn't free from pain and that God doesn't orchestrate bad things to teach us life lessons. Christians have the ability to handle stress and painful circumstances because we know God is walking through it with us. They rest in the promise that God will use all of our pain to accomplish what we need to become mature people of God (Romans 8:28).

I have also been around Christian people who do nice things for others, recite and cross reference scripture better than I can ever imagine myself doing, and yet they are mean, unstable and carry confusion and division into peaceful situations. They often have few, if any, friends.

We need to tell people the truth about spirituality so they will not reject an entire community because of immature Christians. The Kingdom of God consists of many varieties of people at various stages of spiritual development. Some people within a community don't know anything about Jesus, God or the Holy Spirit, but they are searching for a place to belong. Some people in the church are new to the Christian faith and need help learning how to act like Jesus. Some people are broken, hurting and want to be like Jesus, but are too afraid to give Him access to their heart so they continue carrying around their pain, sin and abrasive behaviors. However, there are also authentic spiritual directors within the church, mature Christians who represent Jesus well and are delighted to help people learn spiritual disciplines that lead to maturity.

The Holy Spirit connects lives

Spiritual communities are eclectic, with various doctrines and preferences in their approach to expressing the church, but the Kingdom of God can only be authentic if it is unified in its understanding that a shared life is an experience of the Spirit. I like Paul's language in defining this truth when he writes that community is the outworking of the gift of the Spirit. In fact, much of Paul's writing regarding the church is about living life from our internal connection with the Holy Spirit.

I think the best translation of authentic fellowship of the church is one emphasizing participation in the Spirit. Many things can be in common and many people bond through worthy causes, but the Kingdom of God is the only entity united by an inward spiritual reality that translates into a shared life centered on the Holy Trinity and held together by the bond of love.

This view contradicts many Christian communal attempts which define 'spiritual belonging' as 'church membership.' A mindset like that is fantastic if you want to run a financially successful private club, but does not constitute Paul's definition of the Christian church and a life marked by the gifts of the Spirit (1 Corinthians 12:13). I like this scripture verse because it validates that the Kingdom of God is not defined by gender, nationality or status but united through one baptism and one Spirit.

We should agree that the church of Jesus is not a human creation but a gift from God. That gift should be protected, nourished and noticed by others for her peace. And we must not confuse 'peace' for 'weakness' - because the Kingdom of God is intended to impact the world.

Supernatural power

A spiritual community should be a place where we can learn about God's power. It is the context in which we can learn the Kingdom of God is more than words (1 Corinthians 4:20). When we are connected to Christian people who embrace the supernatural nature of God, the gifts of the Spirit are demystified and become a normal part of life.

It amazes me how many followers of Jesus do not believe in God's miraculous power to heal people, deliver people from oppression or completely release divine grace to change the course of a person's life. These are often the same people who don't believe in the Devil and his ability to disrupt our lives.

Many Christians have decided that the power of Jesus and the miraculous no longer exist. They believe miracles were restricted to the early disciples of Jesus and that present day Christians no longer need supernatural gifts. A friend of mine once told me if we believe a lie, it might as well be the truth because we will live as if it is true. If we believe the gifts of the Spirit are not applicable to us, we will live as such. We will approach our spiritual lives thinking all spiritual power for our lives is in God's hands and that we have none.

Jesus told his early disciples that when they were around people to heal the sick, raise the dead, pray for leprous skin, and tell demonic spirits to get out or away from people. He told his disciples they should do this without hesitation because He didn't hesitate giving them the Holy Spirit that enabled them to pray with power (Matthew 10:8).

Christian believers today are also called disciples of Jesus and have access to the same Holy Spirit power. In fact, Jesus said that we should believe in miracles and that we can do even greater things than what has already been done because it honors God. In John 14:11-14 Jesus says, "Believe me when I say that I am in the Father and the Father is in me; or at least believe on the evidence of the miracles themselves. I tell you the truth, anyone who has faith in me will do what I have been doing, and he will do even greater things than these, because I am going to the Father. And I will do whatever you ask in my name, so that the Son may bring glory to the Father. You ask me for anything in my name, and I will do it."

This is important because many people who are searching for a meaningful spiritual life come into our church communities expecting a dead, passive God who has little interaction with planet Earth. They have a worldview of Jesus restricted to a picture hanging on walls in ornate buildings of a bearded man in a robe.

People need to know the good news about Jesus and how He is alive and active and wants to be their friend. Jesus is also a powerful God who can deliver us on a daily basis from our sins, heal our bodies, souls, and spirits and release us from the Devil's grip. People need to know when they invite Jesus into their heart and decide to become disciples, they too have access to God's supernatural power so that they can help others.

Living a connected life begins with a heart that loves God and cares about other people enough to invite them into your life. It requires a willingness to invest time, energy and sometimes money to help people learn how to trust others enough to begin truly connected relationships.

It is easier to live an isolated life, but it isn't the best way to live life. The problem with isolation is that it is unhealthy and leads to dysfunction. Connectedness requires intentionality and is often hard work. When you sow into people you will get tired and most likely there will be times when you will be discouraged, but the Bible says keep sowing and don't grow weary (Galatians 6:9).

Living a connected life can answer many questions about spirituality when the experience of life is translated and expressed through the power of the Holy Spirit. Life with God is a universal picture of love. This is the picture of Jesus people need to have, not the bearded man in an ornate frame. Our spiritual communities must be the frame that displays this picture to ourselves and others.

The connectedness of the Christian life begins in the hearts of those who belong to God when they create a family that is both individual and global.

Questions to Consider

- Are you isolated?
- Are you inclusive?
- Are you connected to a spiritual community?

CHAPTER FOURTEEN
Defeating Darkness

Religious deception is a clever tool that Satan uses on a regular basis. Consider the effectiveness of convincing a person that evil does not exist. The possibilities are endless. When people are deceived about Satan and his abilities they are blinded to his activity in their lives.

The Bible tells us evil spirits can afflict us physically, emotionally, and spiritually giving examples of demonic spirits oppressing people in specific areas and influencing precise behaviors. Deafness, dumbness, convulsion, blindness, infirmity, fever, insanity, suicide, self-destruction, torment, murder, divination and lying are all included in the web of deception.

Deception is often subtle and can be discounted or reasoned away. I have prayed with many people who downplay the grip the Devil has on them, yet they admit that they feel like they are in bondage. One reason people dismiss this particular kind of evil is because Hollywood has painted unrealistic pictures of people being possessed by demonic spirits that are surreal and scary. Or we have preconceived ideas of demonic activity and what that means. It is easier to entertain that Satan's influence affects those practicing witchcraft, but we don't associate lying, judgment or pornography with demonic spirits. Darkness isn't always overt, but it is always damaging.

Addiction presents itself often in my office. The faces change, but the story is the same. People who love God and their families are depressed and suicidal and can't break away from the compulsions owning them. These people often have secret lives of sexual addictions. They spend extreme amounts of time and energy hiding their idolatrous lives and fighting against the invisible forces keeping them bound.

Deception can become so intense that it is eventually owned and defended. Although people may want prayer for freedom, when darkness in their lives is confronted they respond with elaborate defenses justifying their behaviors. This is why I always begin by asking people how serious they are about freedom. I ask what it feels like to consider making a choice to end the cycle of destruction in their life. They usually get angry and tell me their choices are not their own. They often feel entitled to their addictions and blame other people for their sins.

I don't excuse sin, but I understand how demonic oppression leaves people feeling like they don't have options. This is an example of how evil spirits can create emotional, mental and spiritual deception in a person's life that controls them. Deception is progressive in nature and its tentacles reach into a person's mind, emotions and body. The tentacles extend into the past, strangle the present and stretch into the future. Deception has the potential to control and eventually ruin a person's life.

The lies of deception are crafty and invisible, but their fruit is obvious. And deceivers love to keep lies buried in the dark because secrets must partner with darkness to maintain their life. When light is shone on something, darkness recedes. Once a secret is spoken, especially to ourselves, it begins to die.

Satan is the father-of-lies, and many of his lies which entrap people are about God's identity or a person's identity. When a person is under the influence of demonic spirits they often believe Satan is more powerful than God and that there is no light at the end of darkness - but he isn't and there is. We need to help people understand that unconfessed sin and unforgiveness are open doors to demonic spirits. They are doors God will help them close if they ask Him.

Open doors

I wish I could say that everyone who comes into my office for prayer genuinely wants to be set free, but it would not be true. Some people come for prayer to make them feel better without any intention of changing their behaviors. Some people come for prayer to appease loved ones who are concerned about them. Many people choose to continue defending their addictions, blaming other people, and accepting their self-cast role in their life as a victim. This allows them to continue letting deceptions destroy their lives.

However, there are also those who are serious about freedom and willing to do their part to defeat the wiles of the Devil. I enjoy watching God transform lives when people ask for help and are able, and willing, to believe they have the power of self-direction in their lives. Confession is the first step to freedom and it closes an open door to secrecy.

It is wonderful to watch people realize the truth about God and Satan, good and evil and how their choices can either connect them with God's truth or the Devil's deception. Choice is a powerful tool in our life that can help us overcome the toxicity that comes from destructive thinking. Toxic thoughts drive our behaviors and influence our health.

I love teaching people the truth about who God says they are and the spiritual power that is available to them as a followers of Jesus (1 Thessalonians 1:15, 1 Corinthians 4:20). When people awaken to spiritual authority and grasp the power they have against evil in the name of Jesus, deception loses its grip on them and light begins shining into their lives (Mark 6:7,13, Matthew 10:1). When this happens it releases hope. And hope is a catalyst that encourages the difficult choice to do the work of transformation.

Spiritual communities are a great place to teach people the truth about deliverance. When communities help people uncover who they are in Christ and teach them how to defeat darkness, we create sustainable communities of Christians who can stand against the storms of life.

Jesus loves people. He cares about people and He wants to heal people. Jesus came to set the captives free. Healing and deliverance is very natural for Jesus. So it should also be a normal part of our daily lives and our communities of faith. I want people trapped in addictions, in secrets, in deceptions to know there are people in our spiritual communities who love them, care about them and know how to help them.

The disciple Matthew tells us Jesus approached disease, pain, seizures and demonic-oppression in the same manner. Jesus calmly healed people (Matthew 4:24, 12:22, 17:18, Mark 9:28, 29 Luke 6:17). I can imagine Jesus touching, hugging and compassionately looking at a hurting person and simply telling the demonic spirits to get away from him. And a few minutes later, without drama, telling another person's body to be healed. My imagination lets me think of Jesus chilling out by a body of water meditating on what He heard from the Lord, and caring for those around Him.

I perceive Jesus as a master at spiritual multi-tasking. I never envision people feeling shamed or judged by Jesus when He prayed for them. I picture people feeling loved by a man who cared enough about them to help them. I also believe Jesus made eye contact and called people by their names and wasn't distracted by things around Him.

I am sure that Jesus was a great example of the importance of being fully present when interacting with people. This should be our model when we pray for people who need deliverance from physical, emotional, and spiritual oppression. I want people to feel loved when I pray for them. I don't ever want them feeling judged by me, like an object or a project I don't truly, genuinely care about. I don't want people to feel like I am distracted and not focused when I pray for them. I want to represent Jesus in such a way that it draws people closer to Him.

Knowing God

Ruth's husband was an addict. Ruth's life and family were torn apart by the choices of her husband. Ruth chose to forgive her husband, release him from her judgment and her life. Ruth couldn't reconcile with her husband because he wasn't sorry. For reconciliation to take place a person must take responsibility for his behavior, admit he was wrong and experience genuine remorse for hurting another person. Forgive is more than words.

Ruth's husband was only sorry that his addiction was found out. He didn't own his destructive behavior or acknowledge how it hurt his family. Instead of taking responsibility for his behavior, he played the victim card and found ways to blame Ruth for his addiction. Ruth understood the dynamics of reconciliation and the fact that she could not take responsibility for her husband's choices.

Ruth knew Satan would love for her to blame herself, enter a state of depression, derail her life with God, become physically and emotionally sick, and believe lies about her husband's deception. Satan loves to find ways for us to indict ourselves for other people's choices. Misplaced blame is an effective demonic scheme that continues to hook many people.

Ruth amazed me as I watched her turn to God for comfort and other people for wisdom. She would meet on a regular basis with people in our community who loved her and cared about her broken heart and shattered family. She invited caring people into her pain to make sure she was listening to God's truth and not allowing pain to influence her decisions. She sought spiritual direction. Her spiritual counsel affirmed that lament, and releasing pain was an appropriate way to process her shock and agony.

I watched as Ruth shifted from pain, anger and sadness to peace and resolve. I watched as she made good decisions for the sake of her children and her future. Ruth still tells me she could not have gotten through the painful season in her life so easily without the care of a healthy spiritual community and wisdom about the importance of lamenting pain to trusted friends who affirmed her. I witnessed God's transforming work in the middle of a dark situation because Ruth knew who she was as a Christian and believed in the supernatural power of God to bring good from evil.

Delivering people from demonic oppression can be a natural part of our daily lives. Defeating darkness doesn't have to be weird, awkward, or dramatic if we know the truth about God and Satan. Sometimes Jesus defeated darkness in people's lives by laying hands on them and praying and sometimes He simply spoke to evil spirits and told them to go (Luke 4:40-41; 13:11-13, Matthew 8:31).

In fact, such deliverance should be part of our everyday lives if we are Christian believers. Sometimes we need to pause and lay hands on people and pray for them. Sometimes we need to deal with demonic spirits on behalf of a hurting person. But we don't have to be in a formal ministry setting to set people free from demonic oppression. We can set captives free while drinking coffee and having conversations about life because the power of prayer is not about our posture or words. It is about the authority we have in the name of Jesus.

I remember sitting in a restaurant with a woman I didn't know while she told me how she was stuck in the pain of her childhood trauma. She had been in therapy for many years and processed the abuse, but was still tormented by nightmares, panic attacks, and lies about her identity. I asked if I could pray for her and she agreed.

I was getting reading to pray for her when she got serious, closed her eyes and bowed her head. I think this was her trained way of preparing herself to receive prayer. I smiled and asked her to look at me. I prayed a quick, calm prayer telling the demonic spirit that was bothering her to leave in the name of Jesus. The woman looked at me with a strange expression I could not interpret. Then she asked me to explain what I did and how I did it. She said she needed to understand what was going on because the bad thing that always bothers her left when I was praying.

Although we were in a restaurant praying for deliverance, it was not awkward. My prayer was conversational. It was relational, taking place over lunch and a friendly chat with a person I only met moments before.

We help people who are afraid of darkness by showing them we have faith in God's power to deliver them. We wage spiritual warfare rooted in recognizing the lying voice of our soul's enemy. And we live out of our confidence in Christ when we resist that enemy and watch him flee (James 4:7). We do well when we commit to a life of honoring beauty - not darkness – and declaring that nothing will consume us but God.

We can demonstrate God's love when deliverance is a normal part of our daily lives. To create spiritual communities comfortable with setting people free from demonic oppression it must become a normal part of our church life. We must intentionally become communities of faith which release the tormented from demonic oppression in a manner that is powerful and supernatural yet ordinary and everyday.

"He called his twelve disciples to him and gave them authority to drive out evil spirits and to heal every disease and sickness" (Matthew 10:1)

Questions to Consider

- Who has greater access to your heart, mind and story: Satan or Jesus?
- Do you have confidence in your spiritual authority promised you by God?

CHAPTER FIFTEEN
The Power of Words

Words have the power to change lives. In fact, words have a life of their own. Words can actually lead us to life or death and they can encourage or discourage the direction in which we move. Words enable us to express our experiences and share our stories with other people.

We need to recognize the power of our words and how they influence our lives and the lives of others. Solomon said that death and life are in the power of the tongue, yet we often discount the significance of what we say (Proverbs 18:21). The power of words can be positive or negative.

It isn't wise, but it is common, to speak before we think. Words spoken without consideration frequently release negative effects over the person receiving them. Have you ever reconsidered the good things about yourself because of what someone said to you? Has discouragement taken root in your heart when an outspoken person felt the need to tell you that your thoughts and dreams were wrong?

Although we are not always aware of the impact of words they are often prophetic declarations over our lives. It is easy to recall negative conversations and the dark cloud that remains afterwards. But the fragrance of positive words releases hope that can stir our forgotten dreams. There is something magical about someone telling us they see hidden treasure in us when we are not aware of it. Every heart welcomes affirmation because prophetic words encourage us long before their fruit is seen.

I spent many years getting my formal education with no consideration of writing as something I had interest in doing. Yet as

I sit here writing these words I remember a grade school English teacher telling me some day I would write books that would help people. I appreciated my teacher complimenting me, but during adolescent years not once did I consider the reality of becoming a writer. I dreamed of being an artist and living a creative, non-conformist lifestyle. Many years later I smile as I reflect on the power of a teacher who spoke into my future. Though unaware of the abilities or desires of my own heart to do so, Mrs. Moscow at Elm School in Martins Ferry, Ohio saw something in me and declared it over my life.

Declarations are made in our hearts long before we activate them with words. I am part of a community that believes in the power of words and the role they play in giving voice to our longings. Our spiritual community encourages giving voice to the declarations already inside out hearts.

'Declaration-dinners' are the avenue we have created for giving language to the dreams God has placed within us. Each January small groups gather in various homes where we share a meal. Part of the night is dedicated to declaring, to each other and God, the desires of our hearts for the upcoming year. My husband and I agree it is one of the most fruitful get-togethers of the year. It is a time to reflect on our pasts and activate our futures as we agree with God in prayer.

This concept began around our pastor's kitchen table with 12 friends who were dining and sharing their hearts for the upcoming year. One man declared he would own the house he was looking at across the road, even though it was not for sale, because he wanted to live on Roachville Road. Another person declared the upcoming year would be the year he would meet and marry his wife. A musician declared writing profound songs. Someone declared the release of the business of his dreams. Declarations continued and glasses were raised as toasts of agreement drifted toward Heaven as our incense to God and affirmation to each other.

Things declared

I love how testimonies follow declarations. Within the year the man who declared he would own the house across the road purchased it, the declared songs were written and recorded and the bachelor became a husband.

Declaration-dinners have grown and developed into a vital part of our spiritual family. That initial declaration-dinner continues bearing fruit in our community as the number of them in the area continues increasing. There are many stories of God honoring the unity of these gatherings and releasing movement in the lives of those who open their hearts to God and those with whom they share life.

The gatherings are unique to the host and each group mirrors the personalities of the attendees. Some of the dinners meet around candlelit tables adorned with china, long stemmed wine glasses, and flowers creating an atmosphere to be aware of God's extravagance. Others share and declare with pizza and paper plates releasing a casual atmosphere showing God's presence in the everyday. Some people meet in restaurants while others prefer a potluck meal, creating an eclectic tone where sentimental foods from each household represent the group's diversity. The style of the dinner is not important. The power rests in the unity of people sharing a meal and their hearts with each other and inviting God to join them.

Declaration-dinners are a wonderful example of our symbiotic relationship with God. He places desires within our hearts; we agree with them and say 'Yes' to them. When we say 'Yes' and 'Amen' to what Jesus has in mind for us there is a spiritual shift that releases activity into our daily lives. When we are living an intimate life with

Jesus He will grant the desires of our hearts that are in agreement with Him (Psalm 37:4). This can also be phrased as God's desires becoming our desires. A spiritual symbiosis occurs in our lives when we become friends with Jesus and trust Him to define our lives and write our stories.

Declaration-dinners are one way we can honor God with the things He places in our hearts. It is also a practical way we can agree with and trust God with our lives. When we trust God to write our stories we can rest assured He knows the best path for each chapter of our lives even when our lives don't match our expectations.

A personal story of transition and transformation

Kimbra was in transition when she made her declarations for 2015. She was searching for a place to live in the midst of changing jobs and moving toward her desire to work in full-time inner-healing prayer ministry. I became friends with Kimbra when she completed some of her required counseling hours for her degree with me in prayer ministry. I also invited her to live with us while she searched for an apartment. Kimbra and I had many conversations about God writing our stories through times of peace and pain. We had no idea at the time of our conversations what the future held.

It amazes me that Kimbra made her declarations before I invited her to live with us because she declared that she would embrace the family that God connected her with for the upcoming year. Kimbra understands the significance of a spiritual family structure within the Kingdom of God and that God places people in families to make connections that surpass our understanding.

Kimbra also declared she would become 'experienced with Jesus' in 2015. She admitted she didn't know how to define the phrase 'experienced with Jesus,' but she knew it indicated a deeper level of intimacy with Him and she wanted that. This was a bold declaration because trusting the sovereignty of God doesn't come with a peaceful guarantee.

An unexpected chapter

It was a wet, drizzly Monday morning when Kimbra was scheduled to meet me at my office for a ministry session with an out-of-town couple. Kimbra was never late for such sessions. I remember thinking it would be nice if it stopped raining before evening when we would be moving Kimbra's belongings into my house.

Transition has a way of overwhelming us and thoughts have the ability to distract. So when Kimbra was not on time as usual it made sense that she was running late. Her car was filled with the bags and boxes of her life. She was thinking about all of the transition in her life and the uncertainties of her future - not returning to her usual housemates or the familiar house they shared with friends. Instead, she was moving in with a family she barely knew. Her life was changing and her mind was racing to keep up.

It is only a ten-minute drive to my office from where Kimbra had stayed the night before. After thirty minutes I did not think she was running late; I knew something was wrong. I had a sense of heaviness and darkness surrounding her.

It was one of those moments that didn't make logical sense, knowing the condition of another person about whom I had no information. But in my spirit I felt something and in my mind I saw something. At the time I did not realize this was a spiritual experience, or that the Holy Spirit was giving me insight. However, at the very moment that I had the ominous sensation I received a text asking if I knew about Kimbra's wreck.

A photo of the accident accompanied the text. Kimbra's car had reacted to the rainy road conditions by hydroplaning, going airborne and slamming into a tree, crushing the vehicle. Her car had been reduced to a flat envelope of metal and, realistically, I did not see space for any human. This picture left almost no room for the interpretation of a person surviving.

My tears represented my conflicted emotions as I scrambled for some way to have hope Kimbra was alive, gracefully dismiss the people sitting across from me awaiting prayer from Kimbra and me, and get to the hospital. My thoughts were interrupted with their suggestion of driving to the hospital with me to check on Kimbra's condition. They knew Kimbra from previous ministry sessions and were also greatly concerned about her status. I agreed with their compassionate plan and we quickly left my office.

Arriving at the hospital, approximately twenty people from our church were gathered in the waiting room anticipating a medical update. The intense concern on everyone's face for Kimbra's life was appropriate for anyone who had seen that photo of her car.

We learned that the accident had not only crushed Kimbra's car but also the left side of her body. Sometimes we have a preconceived expectation of what it means for God to be part of a situation. We discount His intervention if it doesn't match our expectation. Yet I actually felt the kindness of God at that moment. The fact that Kimbra had not been instantly killed was a visible sign of the hand of God.

Because she was technically living with us, and there were no immediate relatives in Kimbra's life to contact, I was granted permission to enter the ER to see Kimbra. I was the first non-medical person to see her. I confess that hospitals, injuries, physical traumas are not my strong suit. I am not the best representative to enter a hospital trauma room. Before I pushed back the ER curtain to enter the room where Kimbra was I quickly said, "Jesus help me, I'm not good at this!" then slid open the curtain. I stepped into a space of divine peace as I felt God's assurance that Kimbra was going to be completely healed. I knew deep in my spirit that Kimbra would recover. But what I saw tried to steal my trust.

Kimbra was hooked to electrodes, monitors and numerous other devices unfamiliar to me to assist the trauma team in evaluating her condition. The nurses and attending physician informed me she was unconscious due to brain trauma and not very responsive. I leaned down and whispered a prayer in her ear.

Her eyes opened and she blinked her eyes. The oxygen mask prevented a smile, but I wonder if it would have appeared if she were not so restricted. The nurses looked at me in surprise saying, "What did you say to her? That is the first sign of response we have seen." I smiled and said I was praying for her.

I believe the human spirit is always receptive regardless of the condition of the body or brain. My prayer was simple and intentional. I spoke to Kimbra's spirit and blessed it to be stronger than the broken condition of her body, the numbness of her brain, and the pain in her heart. The human spirit that has been activated by the power of Christ through salvation can bypass the physical restrictions of our souls because it is in communion with the Holy Spirit.

Romans 8:10 assures us that, if we belong to Jesus, the Spirit of Christ makes our spirits righteous. I encouraged Kimbra's spirit to receive the healing that was on God's heart for her. I whispered to her what the Lord had whispered to me right before entering her room that she was going to be OK. The physician telling me she was going to be transported to a major hospital in Louisville interrupted my prayers. The doctor's words did not affect my faith in God's ability to heal Kimbra.

The comfort of scripture

Two scriptures collided in my mind as the urgency in the Emergency Room intensified. I was thinking and picturing Jesus walking through cities and villages long ago, healing people with whom He came in contact and also imagining the man in the Bible who had so much faith in Jesus that he asked Jesus to heal his sick servant who was many miles away (Matthew 9:35; 8:5-10). It was strange and exciting to feel both aspects of Jesus at the same time. I had faith that Jesus was walking through the ER releasing healing and I had faith that he would accompany Kimbra to Louisville and continue healing her broken body.

Unconscious hours turned into days in the Louisville Hospital as Kimbra slowly regained consciousness. There were weeks Kimbra did not know her recovery story, but those who loved and cared for her did. Everyone stepped into a needed role without prompting and met the needs of a hurting young woman who Jesus put on their hearts.

I loved that people who aren't usually connected to each other were united around this healing. The Holy Spirit is always at work in ways that we do not know connecting, restoring, revealing Jesus in times and places where we least expect Him.

The fact that God is omnipresent was evident in the way the Holy Spirit was personal and present to Kimbra, healing her body while He led others to the hospital. Many people still talk about how they felt compelled to drive to University of Louisville Hospital and pray for Kimbra at specific times. Several women in our church felt driven to spend the night with Kimbra at the hospital to give her a voice in her unconscious state. Kimbra did not spend one night alone in the hospital.

I think it is fair to say Kimbra experienced supernatural provision through human acts. She received the love of Jesus through caring people. Kimbra acknowledges that she grew closer to God through the pain of a horrific trauma. It is unproductive debating the author of Kimbra's pain, but it is evident God used her pain for growth.

There are two camps within the Christian faith about why bad things happen to good people. Many Christians believe God causes traumatic things in our lives to teach us lessons and help us grow and become like Jesus. Job is often quoted in defense of this stance because God granted Satan permission to test Job's spiritual devotion. Satan claimed Job was only righteous because he was protected and blessed by God and if Job experienced suffering he would not remain faithful. God allowed Job to suffer. The story of Job is often presented as an absolute answer for any tension resulting from tragedy within a Christian's life.

Others believe God is good and does not devise pain in the lives of those who love Jesus to help them mature. This doctrine often references passages such as Psalm 100:5 or Psalm 136:1 where the Bible says God is good all of the time. They conclude if God is good all of the time He does not possess evil, pain, or trauma to release to those who follow Him. This doctrine concludes painful life experiences are the result of natural causes, human choices and the fact that Satan is alive and active on planet earth.

I believe this debate will continue and there will always be people who credit God with the activities of Satan. People will always struggle with good and evil and how both are present in the world and in the lives of Christian believers. I personally think our focus should be not on the fact that this tension exists or why it does, but rather on the fact that God promises to be with us through painful life experiences and use it for good. We must learn to see the beauty of God in every event. This will allow Jesus, not some concept or debate about fate, to be our center (Romans 8:28).

It is a wonderful to know the promises of Jesus will be with us even when we don't understand why bad things happen in our lives. It is even more amazing learning to see God in the midst of our pain. I knew Jesus was present in Kimbra's trauma and I saw the big and small movements He made in her recovery. I personally don't believe the Lord caused Kimbra's car accident in order to answer her declaration about wanting to be more 'experienced in Jesus.' But I knew He would use all of her pain to make her so.

It is a profound gift to see the beauty of God in our stories and it is life changing to recognize the kindness of the Lord during pain and suffering. I don't think God was trying to teach Kimbra a lesson about Jesus by directing her car to impact a tree at an uncontrollable speed. But I did witness His faithful presence during her recovery and His intervention in writing the future of her story. Today, I listen to Kimbra share new chapters of her story and how she saw Jesus at different times and places on her path to recovery.

We aren't always aware of how our story will unfold. Kimbra likes plans and she likes to be in control. Kimbra thought she knew the next chapter of her life when she was to move into our house for a few weeks. She made declarations and plans. A nearly-fatal automobile accident interrupted her control and her plans, but her story continues to reveal the goodness of God and her testimony continues to strengthen her faith.

Life is supernatural

In our life with God, we cannot separate the everyday from the spiritual realms. The natural world is a mirror reflecting the spirit realm and vice versa. Spiritual activity is always happening and it is always related to the events and people in our lives. Our experiences in daily life often reflect what God is doing in our spirit and in our hearts. Just as Kimbra's car and body were broken in the natural world, things were also shaken in the spiritual realm presenting opportunity for God to reveal himself to Kimbra in new ways.

Kimbra declared she would embrace the family with whom God connected her for the new season in her life. And she declared she would see Jesus in new ways through her spiritual family. Both of those declarations were true, but it should be understood - Kimbra's declaration of family extends far beyond my home. Her story of healing has involved and touched an entire community.

Healing is often a process

As I write this, it has been twelve months since Kimbra's accident. Her body has completely recovered, her heart knows new levels of peace, and her mind understands the power of a supernatural God and His mercy to answer prayers. Kimbra is part of a family, a spiritual family made up of people from an entire community, which cares about her. Kimbra knows Jesus is writing her story and she is learning to see the beauty and love of God in the midst of pain and suffering. She has witnessed the supernatural work of God in a personal way through her own healing and experiences with Jesus, and also through the way the Spirit touched so many throughout our community to help this young woman get whatever she needed on her journey.

Questions to Consider

- Are you ready to make a declaration for your life?
- Do you recognize the beauty of God in the midst of pain and suffering?

CHAPTER SIXTEEN
The Cost of Community

We want people transformed and relationships built at the same speed as a fast food order. Hurry up! Get it together! Stop it and do the right thing! We have short attention spans and low emotional capacity for needy, broken people. Yet communities are composed of needy, broken people. When we are honest with ourselves we admit we don't always posses the capacity required to interact with people who are draining.

Ray and I have had many people live with us over the years with many different stories. Some housemates were very easy to live with and others challenged every bit of grace I had. We have had abuse survivors live with us who were trapped in the past and couldn't relate to daily life, creating endless days of drama in our home because they were fixated on demonic spirits, darkness and the details of their past.

The atmosphere in our home is usually peaceful and we don't traditionally communicate by yelling. However, some of the people who have lived with us have brought new levels of emotion into our home because they felt safe enough to release years of anger. I watched many people change the climate in our home from serenity to chaos in a matter of weeks.

I remember many nights I dreaded going home after work because I didn't know how one particular houseguest would release her repressed pain. On my drive home I would try to convince God that our hospitality had expired. I began to question our initial decision to invite the woman into our home. I would replay the original conversation Ray and I had about offering love and shelter. I began questioning my wisdom, thinking perhaps I had heard from the wrong source when we invited such a broken person to live with us. Surely, if God orchestrated this stay it would be easier. Perhaps kindness and generosity are overrated became a mantra I tried defending. I was confident Jesus was not in favor of the peace in my home being challenged.

Many years have passed since that experience and I now understand a shared life comes with a price. Scuffmarks on painted walls, stained carpet or torn furniture are outward signs of the costs of hospitality. Fatigue, stress, frustration, disappointment and diminishing capacity are often internal signs of servanthood. The reality is that living life with other people costs time, energy, money, and space. It wrecks a tightly planned lifestyle and is a challenge for perfectionists who want their homes and their hearts to remain undisturbed.

Developing lasting relationships requires time and is built by investing in people's lives. It is un-realistic thinking relationships or communities are built by casual interaction. Lasting friendships develop slowly and have lifecycles that are both positive and negative. When we authentically relate to each other we learn how to celebrate and grieve together because we understand that growing a healthy community is hard work and it can't be sustained if we enter it with naïveté.

The shared life

The early Christian community as described in the Bible lived shared lives and expressed their devotion to God and each other around the dinner table. The language of breaking bread has changed over the years, but the power of fellowship remains the same (Acts 2:42-47). Enjoying a meal with people is a sacred experience that is often disregarded as insignificant. Surrounding a dinner table is symbolic of many things on many levels and shouldn't be belittled as only meeting a physical need.

A wise friend of mine encourages people to intentionally use specific task from their daily lives, such as making the bed, doing dishes, drinking hot tea as opportunities to craft prayers that connect our communication with God to everyday tasks. This allows the material objects of normal life to become spiritual symbols of our lives with God. I like this practice because it affirms that daily life is sacred. I like this practice because it is simple and I can welcome it into my regular routine.

I believe the most practical way to develop a healthy community and get to know people is by sharing a meal in your home. The best way to deepen relationships with casual friends is also around your table. There is a spiritual connection that occurs when we invite people into our homes and create an intimate, open space for each person's story to be heard.

Everyone has a story and it breaks barriers when we open up the emotional places in our heart with each other through the narrative of our lives. There is also an emotional connection that occurs when we engage in a person's journey. The scripture says when the early church met for meals and conversation joy and sincerity were released (Acts 2:47). I can relate to this because I love entertaining and hosting dinners in my home. I like the energy it gives my house when people trust Ray and me enough to talk about themselves. And it makes others happy when we care enough to listen.

The presence of God

There is a lot of talk within the Christian community about how to invite the presence of God into a gathering or bringing Heaven to Earth. I think one of the best ways to teach people how to connect with God is to teach them how to connect with other people. And I believe the easiest way to connect with people is sharing a meal together.

Inviting people to dinner is the same as inviting Jesus into your home. Teaching people how to host is a spiritual practice worthy of our attention.

I think many people miss the principle of being a good host and focus on their cooking abilities. I know there are different skill levels in cooking and that some meals are more pleasant than others, but to focus on our culinary ability misses the main point of creating an environment conducive to meaningful conversations. I am not a trained chef and I do not compete for culinary attention. However, I know the value of honoring those I invite to dinner. I know what makes me feel honored when I am a guest in someone's home. I also know when I have been invited, but not truly welcomed.

Although it is good to know a person's story, learning the details of a person's life also opens the door to challenges because many stories reveal pain, trauma, dysfunction, addictions, sin and desperation. Confessions shared over dinner are often invitations for help.

Some people are aware of their needs, but most people are in denial. A healthy spiritual community should be equipped to help people find freedom and deliverance from what holds them captive without people feeling judged or afraid of being rejected if they don't want help. It is easy to help people who are self-aware and want help. It is more difficult listening to people's traumatic history or watching them justify self-destruction and ungodly behaviors that have become their norms.

The cost of sacrifice

It is often easier for us to love people who make wise choices for their life and label those who don't. This is conditional love and not the love Christ extends to us or wants us to extend to each other. It is the heart of Jesus that we learn to love people who are broken, awkward and unaware of what they need. Peter tells us Jesus is patient with how long it takes a person to realize what they need and the pace at which they turn to Jesus for help (2 Peter 3:9).

It's wise to ask ourselves if we are patient when people are slow to seek help or do the right thing. It is difficult for me to be patient and watch Christians and non-Christians take too long to ask for help because I know Jesus is eager to help them. I confess, it seems like I often want people to be healed and delivered more than they do. And I get frustrated when it takes too long to see change in people's lives.

I have had many people ask me for help only to realize they were not ready or willing to do the work required. However, those who are not yet ready to do the hard work to resolve issues in their lives are always ready to be loved and accepted.

This fact is helpful to keep in our minds because it is harder to be patient with the lost or broken or deceived when you are concentrating on their unchanging behaviors. Having that focus challenges the ability to be long-suffering. But when we concentrate not on the behavior but on unconditionally loving and accepting a person, as Jesus does for us all, our own patience is much more easily found; patience necessary to help the broken in whatever stage of readiness they are in with truly asking God for His healing. My personal strategy for strengthening the skill of patience is by embracing people in my life who are not ready for God's help.

When people who are trapped in addictions ask me for help, I begin by suggesting we deal with the addiction. It is difficult for anyone to examine their inner-reality while they are numbing themselves with various sedatives. I often suggest that addicted people detoxify from their substance abuse before we begin inner-healing prayer work.

It amazes me how many times people say that they truly want to be healthy and free from addiction, but they are not willing to let go of the destructive vices that makes them 'feel good.' Or how often people trade a destructive addiction for a healthy addiction, but use it in the same manner for avoidance. This is because addressing addiction means being honest with ourselves. Let's face it: denial is easier.

Many people trapped in addictions are insecure about who they are and not intimately connected to Jesus. They have information about Jesus, but they have not experienced Jesus. I have particularly noted that many young men trapped in addictions have daddy issues influencing their abilities to relate to God as a father because their dad paid them little to no attention. They know their dads, while also not truly knowing their dads. This leads to knowing about themselves, but they also don't know who they are, especially in relation to their father. This influences a man's capacity to embrace being a son of God. They know God is the Father, and Jesus is His son. So they know who Jesus is, but at the same time have no experiential grid for what such a relationship can actually be.

The best thing to offer a person in this position is an invitation into your family and for older men to treat them with the love of a father. Healing has many expressions and the love of family is always an opportunity to release the love of Jesus. This is a great opportunity for healing, but it is still true that embracing needy people requires time and energy; but anything of value is costly.

Healing communities should also note that when people spend years in addictions it often creates a selfish, narcissistic approach to life that keeps the person focused on self in a very unhealthy way. A selfish person can easily transfer this attitude to the spiritual life in a way that presents pride and superiority while resisting family or community.

We don't want to admit it, but we need each other. It is impossible to know who you are apart from God and those who love you. It is impossible to break the power of addiction on your own. Even though people present stoic, independent attitudes, they still need to be connected to caring people who love them - people who are not intimidated by their stories or behaviors in order to break the residual affects of addiction.

If you are a helping person who doesn't have an extreme personality or extreme behaviors when you are in pain, you could be in danger of judging those who do. It is tempting to transfer our life experiences and how we handle stress onto the person we are trying to help. We often have thoughts toward others rooted in comparing their behavior to our own.

We need to understand that everyone is at different stages in their journey and everyone's story contains drastically different chapters influencing their ability to seek help and implement change. One of the biggest challenges within a spiritual community is learning to love people who are not ready to do the right thing.

It is important not to push Jesus on people who are not ready to invite Jesus into their addiction, sin, dysfunction or pain. I believe the prerequisites for inner-healing to happen are safety, love and acceptance. It has been my experience that when people feel loved, and not judged, their sense of safety will encourage them to deal with their pain and sin.

Until they are ready for help, people who are not ready to own their negative behaviors must be taught appropriate ways to relate to others. Many addicts feel entitled to project their inner turmoil onto other people and, in turn, their loved ones end up paying a high price for their choices. We must help each other learn to be present to those around us and not allow unresolved issues to excuse emotional or physical detachment. Disconnecting is not an appropriate option for a person searching for freedom. It is wise to ask for help from those around us who have the abilities to help us and not seek approval from those who will approve our dysfunctions or offer immature counsel.

Tensions

There is a tension between loving a person unconditionally and not agreeing with his or her sin. I want people in my life to know I love and value them, but that I will not compromise Biblical standards to agree with their choices. I share this so our awareness can lead us to action as we agree to have the difficult conversations with those who come to us for prayer.

Perhaps you are also living life with people who are choosing sin over change. They seek prayer, but it is not for the obvious need in their lives. They might go so far as to create an appearance of spiritual progress to those in the community, but in their homes they do not treat their families with love and respect or practice the discipline of being present to them. I have seen this specific pattern repeat itself numerous times though the faces and families change.

It is naïve to believe those in the midst of transformation always tell us the truth about their progress. We must love and care enough about people to allow them time to change. We must trust the timing of the Lord while we speak the truth they need. Jesus is a gentleman and will not violate a person's choice. We must grant Jesus access to our inner worlds before He will come. And He will come. But there is also a tension in allowing people time and space to change while at the same time encouraging them to heal.

It is not our job to change people - it is our job to love them and teach them how to connect with the Lord so He can transform them. Extending kindness includes showing people the power of Jesus to change them. But transformation is not instantaneous. Transformation is a progression.

The Bible says sanctification is the process of becoming more like Jesus. Poor theology tells us salvation instantaneously makes us completely like Jesus. Oh, how I wish that to be true. Salvation does instantly make it possible for us to become like Jesus. But our quest to become more like Jesus is a lifelong event. Understanding the process of transformation should help us to be patient with those who are slow to change. It should also give us grace for the places in our own lives that haven't yet been redeemed.

A big part of our personal story is refined when we take the time to slow down and listen to God. When we are busy and preoccupied with our lives, it becomes normal to only hear God in the earthquakes or fires in our lives and miss the whispers of the Lord. God often speaks to us in a still small voice, and if we are caught up in the noise of our lives, we can easily miss him (1 Kings 19:12). It is a challenge to teach people to turn off all of the voices in their lives that are competing with the voice of God. Meditation is a wonderful antidote for a hectic life and contemplation can develop awareness of the gentle messages of God. Are you willing to sacrifice your time for a person who needs help in discerning the voice of God?

Inner-healing danger

It is common in charismatic communities for people to repeatedly seek prophetic ministry instead of developing a personal contemplative lifestyle. This can lead to keeping an individual stuck at one stage of their spiritual maturity and should be discouraged. People get stuck because they become more dependent on an inner-healing session and the person leading the session than Jesus.

The danger is not one-sided, either. The person praying must be vigilant, also. We should desire prophetic words so we can encourage, comfort and exhort others, but we also must grow in our abilities to discern them so we do not misuse them. I have had many 'prophetic words' given to me that were merely a person creating an opportunity to voice their opinion and mask it with the phrase, "The Lord said you should..." This can be damaging to people who are personally insecure, unsure about Jesus, or unfamiliar with prophecy.

Prophetic ministry is intended to encourage people, not direct their lives. The life direction comes from the individual's interactive, personal relationship with Jesus – the work the Spirit does with the person inside themselves when they are relating with God, not relating with the person praying for them. Yes, there is a tension here: there is a balance between showing broken, searching people God through a community of unconditional love and their need to be alone with God and feel His love and power at those times.

There is a great need for spiritual communities to teach people how to experience God for themselves. A person's spiritual life becomes sustainable when it is personal and not dependent on other people hearing from God for them. Studying scripture is a foundational principle conducive to our personal knowledge of God, but speaking one-to-one with Him is the avenue to spiritual maturity and knowing our true identity. Helping people identify the voice of God is one of the major keys to developing a lasting prayer life because our inner-truth is the avenue to intimacy with the Father.

I want to emphasize that this is a challenge when we embrace confused people who don't know God personally. Some people are needy, tending to cling to us in unhealthy ways because they don't know how to turn to Jesus. They don't have a grid for allowing Him to fill the voids in their life. So prayer for others, prophetic ministry or inner-healing work given by a spiritually mature community are all part of welcoming the broken and searching. It is a worthy endeavor for faith communities to offer hope, direction, healing and deliverance. But the goal is the training and personal education of people to pursue God on their own on a regular basis in practical ways. This is a tension we must understand, be comfortable with, and hold on to when we pursue God because that pursuit is both communal and personal.

Overcoming division

We can call people to higher lives when we value them above our religious traditions. This is important because when we are united through the love of Jesus there are no denominational barriers.

Denominational boxes usually restrict God and determine how we relate to each other. Traditional, conservative boxes are often filled with scriptural knowledge about God, but can veer away from knowing God personally and de-emphasize the importance of living shared, emotionally open lives. Charismatic Christians can often fill their boxes with experiences, defining life with God through their individual, personal signs and wonders and not how well they care for each other. The contents of both boxes - the head knowledge of God and the heart experience of God - contain truth. Both boxes should be embraced simultaneously because the fullness of an infinite God cannot be limited.

It is true that the outline of our lives should be rooted in the principles of the scriptures, but we should not limit God to our denominational orthodoxies. It is also true God manifests Himself miraculously, sometimes uncomfortable for suspicious Christians, but these outward signs are not intended to be the sole evidence of God's presence. We are designed to experience God on a supernatural, personal level and learn to listen to His voice. We are also intended to study the Bible and allow it to be our guide in discerning all we hear. Knowledge of God and intimacy with God is a marriage that will last as long as we don't divorce them.

When we become aware of the constraints our minds puts on our spiritual lives it is an invitation to experience the divinity of God. When we open our God-boxes to the Holy Spirit, they actually disappear as we realize God cannot be contained. He is too vast to be restricted by our thoughts or our doctrines.

Our communities should consider how to best help people un-clutter their lives and minds, learning to listen to Jesus rather than defending religious boxes. This often requires letting go of things we use to distract us. There is a measure of life that comes only when we talk to God, and God alone, and deal with the idols in our hearts. Some people don't seem to realize God is aware of all the things we try hiding from Him. Many people spend years and great amounts of energy hiding things from a God who already knows.

I am a fan of friendship and this book is about the transforming power of community. But the ultimate importance for a community of faith is helping people experience the shelter of God. The community must be directive toward an inseparable connection with the Holy Spirit, not with the community itself. The focus of a spiritual community needs to be making individuals truly know they can have an intimate relationship with God, their Father. Because hurting people need to know God really can be their refuge and that they can trust Him with the things hindering them or that they've hidden away (Psalm 91:21, 46:1).

When God is our center He becomes our shelter. But it is a challenge to run to Jesus if you have never had people to turn to for help. We often fall for the lie that other people have it all together, don't struggle, never need help from their community and don't need God's protection. In reality, we all have seasons requiring help from others and we always need the Lord.

Since the Kingdom of God is righteousness, peace and joy and the Kingdom of God is within us, the answer to pain and suffering is never far away. The Holy Spirit within us allows us to recover from pain and return to joy if we will choose to do so. When you choose joy you will also experience yourself growing stronger. When we choose joy we are choosing power because the delight of the Lord is our strength (Nehemiah 8:10). Returning to joy is a practical way we can experience divine protection because joy and strength are companions.

Words of intervention

I was recently reading a Bible story that is a great reminder of the power of choice. Abigail's husband, Nabal, is scornful and dismissive of David's messengers when David and his men had just recently assisted Nabal's shepherds. Upon hearing contemptuous words as repayment for his kindness, David vows revenge on Nabal and all the men of his household. David marches to kill Nabal, but on learning this Abigail immediately sets out with food, gifts and apologies to David for her husband's foolishness and smallness of character. Due to Abigail's intervention, David reconsiders his plan for revenge (1 Samuel 25).

Abigail's actions remind David of who he truly is, what his identity in the Lord is. In fact, David thanks God and praises her actions and words because they "...kept His servant from doing wrong" (1 Samuel 25:39). Abigail called forth David's true identity in the Lord which David was hiding from himself through making poor choices motivated out of his pain.

This story contains a number of lessons of which it is wise to be aware. First, we should note that the Lord uses women in ministry in very powerful, impactful ways. We must not create spiritual communities restricting women from ministry. When spiritual communities confine women to taking care of children and cooking, we are missing the fullness that God intends for his church.

We should also see that when Abigail received word David intended to kill her husband she took action immediately, which God honored. When Abigail heard the condition of David's heart and his plan to implement his hate and anger through violence, she intentionally made plans to intervene. Abigail went to David. Abigail did not wait for David to ask for her help, she did not call the family together and plan an intervention, nor did she set aside a long period of time to pray and ask God what to do. She took action.

When she was with David, she first approached him in humility, asking his permission to speak into his life. Abigail spoke truth about God and His ways saying, in effect, if you extend mercy to others God will grant mercy to you. She continued to speak Godly principles about judgment and vengeance belonging to God and how David should release vengeance and judgment to the Lord.

The narrative tells us David received her words and that his response was praise to God. I think it is fair to say Abigail's words were blessed by God and that David not only heard them, but he experienced the power of them. Through interaction with others, David heard the Lord speaking to him when his own heart was deaf due to his anger at being treated so poorly. The power of intentional words changed the condition of David's heart and his decision. David recognized the love he felt in Abigail's words as coming from God. Our words have the same power over people.

There is an encouraging message we can apply to those in our lives who are trapped and need the same type of supernatural intervention. We often hesitate to speak truth to those who we know are struggling because we are waiting for God to tell us to talk to them. I know I am guilty of this very issue. I frequently convince myself that if people want my help they will ask for it. I think the story of David and Abigail tells us that there are times when we should intentionally go and speak about God to those who need help.

Abigail reminded David of his true identity through humility and the power of her words; through taking action and speaking into his life in a manner of respect and care for him. She did all this while also sharing food with David and his men - a grateful generosity her husband, blinded by his own prejudices, refused to extend to David. In fact, Abigail's husband, Nabal, even went so far as to judge David and his men quite poorly when David had done nothing wrong and was actually contributing to Nabal's well-being! Abigail knew such smallness, such exclusion and judgment was not going to help her family's situation. It was not going to sway David into letting go of his pain, anger, and resentment, put aside his false, worldly self and remember his real identity through the truth of God's love and peace and unity.

But instead of excluding David, as her husband had, Abigail did speak to David. And she didn't merely give her opinion, she spoke truths about God and the way life with God operates. I am encouraged by the results of Abigail's intentionality. Her words changed David's mind, which in turn changed his plan. David was so grateful with Abigail's intervention it released worship!

Being like Abigail is what it means to live a shared life in the Lord. This short Bible narrative is an excellent illustration of what I am proposing as a model for our spiritual communities. We must help those who God brings into our lives, being aware of the risks of doing so, but still choosing to receive, aid, and love them. They are unlikely to be marching on our households with swords, but even if they were we should not be intimidated by their pain, anger, choices or where they are in their journeys. We must still remind them God knows who they are by choosing to welcome, help, and honor them.

My belief is that we all are created in the image of God, with an identity breathed into us by the Lord. A multitude of things can blind us, or help us blind ourselves, to that sense of self: The dynamics, fear or lack of blessing from our natural family; life redirected by traumas and pains and lies; our soothing behaviors being adopted as our identity; having no concept of what honoring is or how to give or receive it; rebuffing the experiences of others who have gone before on similar roads; connecting to screens and not real people; deceptions from the father-of-lies; confusion about

God and unauthentic, unwelcoming, or judgmental churches; not knowing we can choose whose story to believe about our self - the world's, imperfect people's or God's; or not accepting the supernatural power of the Spirit to speak our true identities to us and defeat the darkness around us.

Those in a spiritual community seeking to love one another unconditionally and speak the truths of God we've learned from our own experiences can help each other remember God is our Father. And that He wants to remind us of our true selves. He wants to release to us the peace and joy that comes from knowing who we really are in His eyes.

I pray that our spiritual communities will not allow judgment to cloud our love for one another. I pray that as we create authentic communities we will welcome the diverse needs of all people and not allow anything to become bigger than Jesus and the power of the Holy Spirit to transform lives. I pray we may recognize the beauty of contributing to others and grow in love for the family of God.

I began this book by saying it was not a book about my niece, Sarah, and the tragedy which befell her and her family. That remains true. It is not a book about tragedy – not Sarah's or the assorted tragedies which befall diverse peoples, from small towns or large, at different times throughout their lives, from childhood to adulthood.

This is a book about how we recover from tragedies; from individual difficulties which left an ache in an otherwise happy life to the aftermath of horrific events affecting entire towns and making national news.

This is a book about the many paths we can all take to deal with those tragedies which can be paths leading us further and further away from where we truly want to go.

This is a book about how we can help one another find better paths and what should be waiting for us when we truly arrive where we need to be.

This is a book about what I have seen resolve tragedies: The identity of God the Father and our personal willingness to know His, and our own, true nature; the character of Jesus and our private choice to emulate it in how we see ourselves and show it to others; and the power of the Holy Spirit and our individual readiness to receive it and share it.

God knows who we truly are, loves us for it, and can show us how to see ourselves and each other the way He see us. He views us as His blessed children who walk in the light, can believe we are who He says we are, and are ready to demonstrate to one another just what that looks like. Regardless of what façade our natural family or society or we have come to believe is our self, our Father knows our true identity. He wants us to see it and will bless our search to know it, too. Our communities of faith must be welcoming, genuine, non-judgmental places for those seeking God and their true self.

Younger or older sibling, we all share one Father. Boisterous, reserved, joyful, discerning, impulsive, considered... He blesses us all and blesses us with each other and our diversity. Our Father invites us to His supper with the rest of our spiritual family. Our spiritual communities must be places where all of us, with our various natures and stories, know we are loved unconditionally for who we are so we can come together and share His table.

Questions to Consider

- Does desire for a shared life outweigh your concerns of its cost?
- Do you trust God's promises that He is your strength?
- Do you share your table?

A Note from the Author

As an inner-healer I am committed to the ministry of the gospel and the process of transformation and its application to daily life. I believe we can not experience the fullness of God, or develop a mature spiritual life, apart from relationship with God and other Christian people. I believe the answer for a sustainable life of faith is found by engaging in healthy, spiritual community. I hope this book, Sharing a Table: Knowing the Love of God in Community, has encouraged you to share your life with others. May God bless your journey.

Contact Information

If you would like to contact Dr. Candyce Roberts for personal ministry, register for the Emerge School of Transformation or have Candyce speak at your gathering or event you can contact her at:
info@CandyceRoberts.com
or visit her website:
CandyceRoberts.com

56162444R00121

Made in the USA
Lexington, KY
14 October 2016

MW00560058

CODEX
ORKS

BY ANDY CHAMBERS

UUUER STUFF: Gavin Thorpe   **MINIATURES DESIGNERS:** Brian Nelson, Mark Bedford, Norman Swales & Alan Perry

COUER ART: David Gallagher   **INTERNAL ART:** Alex Boyd, John Blanche, John Wigley, Wayne England & Neil Hodgson

THANKS TO: Pete Haines, Adrian Wood, Roine Atte, Pat Marstall, Gary James, Mark Adamthwaite, Ray Snyder and to everyone who wrote in or emailed us about Orks

PRODUCED BY GAMES WORKSHOP

Citadel & the Citadel logo, 'Eavy Metal, Games Workshop & the Games Workshop logo and Warhammer are trademarks of Games Workshop Ltd registered in the UK and elsewhere in the world.

Bad Moon, Bigboss, Blood Axe, Boss Snikrot, Boss Zagstruck, Codex Dreadnought, Evil Sunz, Freebooterz, Ghazghkull Mag Uruk Thraka, Gretchin, Mad Dok Grotsnik, Nazdreg Ug Urdgrub, Nobz, Ork, Redskull Kommando, Vulcha Boyz and Wazzdakka Gutmek are all trademarks of Games Workshop Ltd.

All artwork in all Games Workshop products and the images contained therein have been produced either in-house or as work for hire. The copyright in the artwork and the images it depicts is the exclusive property of Games Workshop Ltd.

© Copyright Games Workshop Ltd, 1999. All rights reserved. British Cataloguing-in-Publication Data. A catalogue record for this book is available from the British Library.

Second Printing

UK GAMES WORKSHOP LTD. WILLOW RD, LENTON, NOTTINGHAM, NG7 2WS	**US** GAMES WORKSHOP INC. 6721 BAYMEADOW DRIVE, GLEN BURNIE, MARYLAND, 21060 6401	**AUSTRALIA** GAMES WORKSHOP, 23 LIVERPOOL ST, INGLEBURN, NSW 2565	**CANADA** GAMES WORKSHOP, 2679 BRISTOL CIRCLE, UNITS 2&3, OAKVILLE, ONTARIO L6H 6Z8	**JAPAN** GAMES WORKSHOP, WILLOW RD, LENTON, NOTTINGHAM, NG7 2WS

PRODUCT CODE: 60 03 01 03 002   Games Workshop World Wide Web site: http://www.games-workshop.com   ISBN: 1 869893 38 7

Greetings Warboss, welcome to *Codex: Orks*, a book dedicated to collecting, painting and gaming with an Ork warband in the Warhammer 40,000 battle game. The Ork way is brutal and savage, using sledge-hammer tactics coupled with the ferocity of a bag of wolverines. If you're looking for the Warhammer 40,000 equivalent of a barbarian horde you're in the right place!

ORKS

Orks are the most widespread and warlike race of aliens in the bloodstained galaxy of the 41st millennium. From the depths of the core to the distant ghost stars beyond the galactic rim burgeoning Ork empires rise and fall. In terms of sheer numbers and planets Orks occupy more of the galaxy than any other single race and were they unified they would soon crush all opposition. However the Orks' passion for violence is so unquenchable that they spend most of their time warring amongst themselves and any Ork leader worth his followers' respect would never dream of voluntarily following another. But once in a generation an Ork leader will emerge who is powerful enough to defeat his rivals and dominate their tribes. His success will draw others and soon a great Ork Waaagh! is underway, a movement of millions; part migration, part holy jihad as the Orks seek

new worlds to conquer and races to enslave. The violence of Ork warriors unleashed is truly terrifying and the ferocity of the Ork Waaagh! evokes fear even amidst the holy spires of Terra.

WHY COLLECT AN ORK ARMY?

First off because Orks can fight anyone, even other Orks! No matter who your opponent is you can fight them with no qualms about whether you've got a realistic match-up. In the Warhammer 40,000 background Orks are the classic antagonists, a constant threat to all other races and are in a permanent state of war.

Orks are also an ideal army for the player who wants to field everything at once. Individual Orks are tough, capable warriors and mercifully cheap in points, so an Ork force can field a solid body of troops and still have plenty of room left to include warbikes, big guns, Dreadnoughts and other nasties. In battle the Ork army is a real horde, a solid mass of troops and vehicles which will make even the most hardened Space Marines player balk.

The Orks themselves are excellent hand-to-hand fighters. Even the most basically equipped Ork fights better in close combat than many races' assault specialists, and a whole mob of Orks can overrun most enemy units with ease. Better still, the Orks' confidence in their own fighting abilities means that mobs have to be decimated before they even think about retreating and Orks which do fall back are likely to join up with another mob and renew the attack. This makes the Orks' brutal style of combat easy to emulate on the tabletop, and even if they lose you can win a moral victory if you have the right sense of bravado and mutter things like "You haven't heard the last of us, meddling Space Marine!".

Ork barbarity is also highly entertaining in itself. If you want a straight laced army that takes itself seriously try the Eldar or Sisters of Battle! A good Ork player can have a laugh at the expense of his Gretchin slaves getting blown to bits when they're sent into a minefield, or when one of the Mekboyz' insane weapons blows up or a supercharged vehicle smashes into a wall.

The crude, barbaric style of an Ork army lends itself well to painters more interested in fielding a big force than an immaculately painted one. By using basic painting techniques an Ork force can be easily assembled, with its sheer mass of warriors compensating for their individual simplicity. Nearly everything the Orks use is hand built and heavily personalised, be it weapons, armour, vehicles or bioniks. This offers modellers a vast range of possibilities for converting and scratch building, making Ork armies the most varied, individualistic creations in the Warhammer 40,000 game.

Sir, despite repeated efforts at alerting sector command to the alien threat emanating from the Alacanth, Redwold and Tyr systems no action has been undertaken. Naval scouting forces have noted a sharp increase in the build-up of Ork ships within these systems and the recent loss of the Falchion class cruiser Tempest in the Tyr system has rendered further reconnaissance impossible. It is imperative that further information is gathered by whatever means possible to ensure the continued security of the Kolchis system. >>>>>>>>>>>>>>>

Date: 2763994.M41

Sir, my thanks for the recent intelligence on Ork activity in the sub-sector. This, combined with my own sources, makes it clear that an Ork Waaagh is imminent. The central figure appears to be Warlord Gorbad of the Redskulls tribe. Gorbad has conquered all neighbouring tribes on Redwold, Tyr and Alacanth over the last four years and is now building heavy armaments and invasion ships. Rumours abound of two (or more) space hulks being sighted in the Redwold system and the Emperor's Tarot produces ever more dire portents of strife. I would suggest, nay, request that a pre-emptive strike be made on Redwold to cripple the Ork's shipping and eliminate their leader before this dangerous situation gets further out of hand. I would also note that the Angels of Absolution have recently fought on Belami and would make an eminently suitable strike force. >>>>>>>>>>

Date: 2800994.M41

Sir, I find it inconceivable that slaying the Ork's leader would not result in the dissipation of the Waaagh. You assure me that another Warlord would simply take his place, but surely a period of internecine warfare would occur as his rivals fought to take control? I only pray that the Angels of Absolution will undertake to raid on our behalf. >>>>>>>>>>>>>>>>>

Date: 2851994.M41

The outer early warning beacons have detected an alien fleet moving into the Kolchis system. Patrol ships have been dispatched to investigate and planetary defence forces have been placed on full alert. >>>

Date: 2967994.M41

The Ork fleet of Waaagh Gorbad has breached our orbital defences and even now Ork attack ships and assault boats are landing forces on the planet. Fast-moving spearheads have isolated the capital from the outer mines. Early estimates place the attacking ground forces at the equivalent of sixteen regiments, with one hulk, four cruisers and twenty plus attack ships supporting from orbit. >>

Date: 2093995.M41

All outer defences overrun. Orks are engaged in street fighting throughout the capital. Supplies running low and fighting forces shattered. Collapse of all resistance estimated at six days maximum.

Commend our souls to the Emperor. >>>

<<<<<< NO FURTHER TRANSMISSIONS >>>>>>

Transmitted: Kolchis
Received: Ryza
Telepathic Duct: Astropath-Terminus Sondavi
Author: Commander Heironys
Date: 4255994.M41

Transmission intercepted at Inquisition station 574363/b/Mk3.

Addenda: Full transcript suppressed for reasons of Sector security by order of Inquisitor Marles. Full transcript available via archive Xeno. Arc/uis/897.delta Security clearance Vermillion. Cross-ref: Angels of Absolution. Belami Incursion. Waaagh Gorbad. Warlord Gorbad. Redwold. Alacanth. Tyr. Ryza.

Appended note by Inquisitor Marles: The sacrifice of Kolchis has given Ryza an additional seven month build-up, somewhat less than the period required by Solar Hostarax but greater than would have been gained by prematurely instigating the Waaagh by taking action. Exhaustion of the Kolchis mines was estimated within twelve standard years.

And at this time
the brazen god of war
cast up a great lord
to lead the savages forth

The Book of War

This section of *Codex: Orks* contains information on the different troops and vehicles an Ork Warboss (ie YOU!) can use. The list allows you to fight battles using the scenarios included in the Warhammer 40,000 rulebook, but also provides the basic information you'll need to field an Ork army in scenarios you've devised yourself, or that form part of a campaign.

The army list is split into five sections. All squads, vehicles and characters in the army list are placed into one of these sections, depending upon their role on the battlefield: *Headquarters (HQ), Elites, Troops, Fast Attack* and *Heavy Support*. Every model included in the army list also has a points value, which varies depending on how effective it is on the battlefield.

Before you can choose an army for a battle you will need to agree with your opponent upon what scenario to play and the points each of you have to spend on your army. Having done this you can proceed to pick an army as described below.

USING A FORCE ORGANISATION CHART

The army list is used with the force organisation charts from a scenario. Each chart is split into five categories that correspond to the sections in the army list, and each category may have one or more boxes. Each light-toned box indicates that you *may* make one choice from that section of the army list, while a dark-toned box means that you *must* make a choice from that section.

Note that unless a model or vehicle forms part of a squad or a squadron it counts as a single choice from those available to your army.

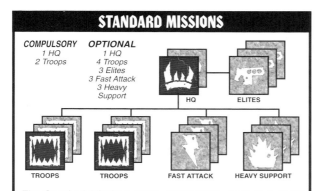

STANDARD MISSIONS

COMPULSORY	OPTIONAL
1 HQ	1 HQ
2 Troops	4 Troops
	3 Elites
	3 Fast Attack
	3 Heavy Support

*The Standard Missions force organisation chart is a good example of how to choose an army. To begin with you will need at least one HQ unit and two Troop units (dark shaded boxes indicate units that **must** be taken for the mission). This leaves the following for you to choose from to make up your army's total points value: up to 1 HQ unit, 0-3 additional Elite units, 0-4 additional Troop units, 0-3 additional Fast Attack units or 0-3 additional Heavy Support units.*

USING THE ARMY LISTS

To make a choice, look in the relevant section of the army list and decide what unit you wish to have in your army, how many models there will be in it, and which upgrades you want (if any). Remember you cannot field models that are equipped with weapons and wargear not shown on the model. Once this is done subtract the points value of the unit from your total points, and then go back and make another choice. Continue doing this until you have used up all your points. Then you can get on with the serious business of unleashing your deadly Ork Waaagh!

ARMY LIST ENTRIES

Each army list entry consists of the following:

Unit Name: The type of unit and any limitations on the maximum number of choices you can make for that unit type (0-1, for example, indicates that only one unit may be included in the army).

Profile: These are the characteristics of that unit type, including its points cost. Where the unit contains different warriors, there may be more than one profile.

Number/Squad: The number of models allowed in the unit, or the number of models you may take for one choice from the force organisation chart. Often this is a variable amount, in which case it shows the minimum and maximum unit size.

Weapons: These are the unit's standard weapons.

Options: Lists the different weapon and equipment options for the unit and any additional points for taking these options. It may also include the option to upgrade one mob member to a character. If a mob is allowed to have models with upgraded weaponry (such as big shootas or rokkit launchas), then these must be given to ordinary squad members, not the character.

Special Rules: This is where you'll find any special rules that apply to the unit.

ORK SPECIAL RULES

The following special rules apply to all Ork units except where noted.

MIXED ARMOUR

Due to the wide variety of wargear and the Ork Mobbing Up rule it is entirely possible for some units to include models with different armour saves. Because of this the normal casualty removal and armour save rules are altered slightly.

The opposing player rolls to hit and wound for whichever unit he is firing with as normal. However, when the Ork player makes armour saves before removing casualties from a unit that has mixed armour saves he uses the best armour saves as long as the Orks wearing that type of armour are in the majority (ie, they outnumber Orks with worse saves in the unit). This represents the heavily armoured Orks making more obvious targets and the lighter armoured Orks using them as cover! Any casualties removed after saving throws have been taken must come from amongst the most heavily armoured Orks first (ie, the ones with the best saving throws take the hits).

If heavier armoured Orks are in the minority use the worse armour saves and take the casualties from the lightly armoured Orks instead.

For example: A Warboss and his bodyguard of five Nobz suffer 6 wounds from enemy fire. The Warboss and three of his bodyguard are wearing mega armour so the Ork player rolls his saving throws using the 2+ mega armour save (as the models with mega armour outnumber the other models in the mob). Unluckily he fails two saves and 2 wounds are suffered. Because the Nobz have 2 wounds each, one mega armoured Nob is removed as a casualty. If the enemy fire had an Armour Penetration of 2 or better, three mega armoured Nobz would be removed as casualties (ouch!).

ORK MOB RULE!

An Ork mob has to check morale and test for pinning from barrages and snipers in the same way as any other unit. However, if the mob fails a test it will immediately 'check size' by rolling 2D6. If the score is equal to or less than the number of Orks (not including Gretchin) left in the mob then the Orks carry on, confident in the belief there are enough of them left to win. Their courage is bolstered by their comrades, spurring them on to battle. This means that an Ork mob of twelve models or more will always fight on, regardless of any casualties it might have received.

Mobbing Up

Orks falling back can attempt to regroup as normal if there are enough of them left, but this rarely happens as Orks will only withdraw once most of them are dead. However, an Ork unit of any size can attempt to join another mob or in other words 'mob up'.

When Orks fall back they can move towards any Ork mob that lies behind their own position. If any withdrawing Orks get within 6" of the new mob once moves are complete then the withdrawing mob can attempt to join up with the new one. Make a 2D6 roll against the Leadership value of the mob which is falling back. If successful the two mobs combine together (mob up) and the previously withdrawing mob can immediately move up to 6" so they are in proper formation.

Only Ork foot troops will mob up in this way – Slavers and Meks in charge of Grot mobs or Big Gunz, Stormboyz and warbikes may not mob up.

Victory Points after Mobbing Up

A mob of Orks which mobs up counts as destroyed for victory points purposes. An Ork mob which gains additional Orks from another mob joining up with them is not worth any more victory points than it was before, it will still use its starting strength and points value for working out victory points.

THE POWER OF THE WAAAGH!

When a big mob of Orks charges they form a solid mass, blazing away with their shootas and screaming Waaagh! at the top of their lungs. The sheer momentum of their charge is stunning and opponents are in danger of getting bowled over by a scrum of Orks all trying to get into combat first.

To represent the Power of the Waaagh!, when an Ork mob charges into close combat check its size by rolling 2D6. If the score is equal to or under the number of Orks left in the mob they charge in with a rousing "Waaaaaaaaagh!". All the Orks in the mob double their Initiative characteristic for the rest of the assault phase. In future assault phases the Orks revert to their normal Initiative values. If the 2D6 roll is greater than the number of Orks left in the mob the Orks charge in as normal and attack with their basic Initiative value.

Orks who make a sweeping advance into the enemy also use the Power of the Waaagh! The test for this is made at the beginning of the assault phase so any casualties from enemy fire will reduce the chances of them managing to maintain their momentum.

He was an avalanche from an unexpected quarter. He was a thunderbolt from a clear sky.

Commissar Yarrick on Ghazghkull Thraka.

GRETCHIN MOBS

Gretchin are notoriously cowardly by Ork standards so in battle they are led (or rather driven forward) by an Ork Slaver. In the case of these units Morale checks are made against the Ork's Leadership value – but there is no Mob Rule for Gretchin. Grotz don't count when it comes to counting heads!

Gretchin are affected by Morale checks for losing an assault just like normal troops. However, Gretchin who fail a Morale check caused by enemy shooting or tank shock or which fail to regroup after falling back from close combat, 'go to ground' and hide with almost preternatural skill; in the blink of an eye they disappear under rocks, behind foliage, and whatever else they can hide in. The Gretchin mob is removed and the Slaver is left in place to indicate their position (as he starts the thankless task of rounding them up again). If no Slaver is present (ie, he has been slain or was not included in the mob for some reason) the Gretchin mob may not regroup and counts as being destroyed.

Gretchin can attempt to regroup each turn as long as the Slaver is still alive, even if the Gretchin mob has been reduced below 50% of its original strength or the enemy is within 6". If the Gretchin have gone into hiding, when they regroup they are replaced on the tabletop in coherency with the Slaver but not more than 6" from him. Whilst they are hiding Gretchin cannot be harmed.

Ork Slaverz trying to regroup Gretchin can be attacked as normal by shooting and in close combat. The Slaver may not move, shoot or initiate an assault (although he can still fight back if attacked in close combat). If the Slaver is killed the Gretchin mob counts as being destroyed.

ORK ARMOURY

In most cases characters are upgraded from ordinary Boyz. Where this is the case the character keeps the basic weapons and wargear of the mob he's part of – for example, a Stormboyz Nob has a slugga, choppa and jump pack. This doesn't prevent you from picking extra weapons for him from the Armoury although the restrictions on the number of weapons that can be carried always apply.

Ork characters may have up to two single-handed weapons, or one single-handed weapon and one two-handed weapon. You may also pick up to 40 points of extra wargear for each character from the Wargear lists (80 points for an Ork Warboss and 60 points for a Big Mek or Painboss). The full Wargear rules are on pages 34-37. You can not take duplicate items for the same model with the exception of Grots or squigs and all wargear and weapons must be represented on the model.

SINGLE HANDED WEAPONS

Choppa	2 pts
Power claw	25 pts
Slugga	1 pt
'Urty syringe (Mad Doks only)	5 pts

TWO-HANDED WEAPONS

Big shoota	12 pts
Burna (Mekboyz only)	10 pts
Grabba stik (Slaverz only)	5 pts
Kombi weapon: shoota/rokkit launcha	5 pts
Kombi weapon: shoota/skorcha	8 pts
Kustom force field (Mekboyz only)	20 pts
Kustom mega-blasta (Mekboyz only)	15 pts
Rokkit launcha	8 pts
Shoota	2 pts
'Uge choppa	10 pts

WARGEAR

Ammo runt	4 pts
Attack squig	6 pts
Big horns/iron gob (Warboss & Nobz only)	6 pts
Bionik arm	10 pts
Bionik bonce	10 pts
Bosspole (Warboss & Nobz only)	3 pts
Cybork body	10 pts
Dok's tools (Mad Doks only)	1 pt
'Eavy armour	8 pts
Frag stikkbombz	1 pt
Grot oiler (Mekboyz only)	6 pts
Grot orderly (Mad Doks only)	6 pts
Krak stikkbombz	2 pts
Kustom job: More Dakka	4 pts
Blasta	3 pts
Shootier	2 pts
Mega armour (Warboss & Nobz only)	30 pts
Mega boosta (mega armour only)	10 pts
Mekboy's tools (Mekboyz only)	2 pts
Squighound (Slaverz only)	5 pts
Stikkbomb chucka (mega armour only)	1 pt
Super stikkbombz (Mekboyz only)	5 pts
Tankbusta bombz	3 pts
Waaagh! banner (max. one per army)	20 pts

ORK VEHICLE UPGRADES

Any Ork vehicles (apart from warbikes) may be fitted with the following additional equipment. Any upgrades chosen must be shown on the vehicle model. Dreadnoughts may only choose upgrades marked with an (*). No duplicate upgrades may be taken for the same vehicle.

Armour plates*	5/10 pts
Big grabber	5 pts
Boarding plank	5 pts
Grot riggers	2 pts
Bolt-on big shoota (wartrukks and battlewagons only)	10 pts
Red paint job	3 pts
Reinforced ram	5 pts
Searchlight*	1 pt
Spikes 'n blades (not wartrukks)	5 pts
Stikkbomb chucka*	3 pts
Turbo boosta	5 pts
Wrecker ball	5 pts

Mega Armoured Warboss and Bodyguard

If an Ork Warboss is equipped with mega armour any members of his bodyguard Nobz that are also equipped with mega armour will be able choose up to a total of 80 points of wargear each (including the mega armour).

Grots and Squigs

Some Ork wargear takes the form of Gretchin slaves or squigs (short for 'squiggly beasts' – animals that Orks eat or train for simple tasks). Grot slaves and squigs must be represented by a separate model and become part of whichever mob the character they are with belongs to. They must also stay within the 2" coherency distance of the unit.

Note that the special rules for Grot morale only apply to mobs of the little green blighters, not to any Grots that are chosen as wargear. An Ork character may choose up to a maximum of three Grot slaves and/or squigs. If the character becomes a casualty, his attendant Squigs and Grots are also removed.

HEADQUARTERS

As the monstrous and all powerful leader of the warband the Warboss gets first pick of any wargear and the best fighters to make up his bodyguard with. Some Warbosses also include Mekboyz and Mad Doks in their bodyguard — often with their own small entourages of Grot slaves and squigs. Others just get in their wartrukks with a select band of hard nuts and lead their Boyz by the simple expedient of careering into the middle of the enemy force first!

0-1 WARBOSS										
	Points	WS	BS	S	T	W	I	A	Ld	Sv
Warboss	60	5	2	5	4	3	4	4	9	6+

Your army must include a Warboss.

Options: A Warboss may be given any equipment allowed from the Ork Armoury.

Bodyguard: The Warboss may be accompanied by a bodyguard (see entry below). If he has a bodyguard then the Warboss and his bodyguard are treated as a single unit during battle. Note that the bodyguard does not count as a separate HQ choice (it does not use up a HQ 'slot').

Wartrukk: If the Warboss and his bodyguard number ten models or less (including squigs, Grots, etc) they may be mounted in a wartrukk at a cost of +30 pts. See below for details.

SPECIAL RULE

Independent Character: Unless accompanied by his bodyguard (see below) the Warboss is an independent character and follows all the rules for independent characters as given in the Warhammer 40,000 rulebook.

WARBOSS'S BODYGUARD

NOBZ

	Points/model	WS	BS	S	T	W	I	A	Ld	Sv
Nob	20	4	2	4	4	2	3	3	7	6+

Number: The Warboss may be accompanied by between five and ten Nobz.
Options: The Nobz may be given any equipment allowed from the Ork Armoury.

MEKBOYZ

	Points/model	WS	BS	S	T	W	I	A	Ld	Sv
Mekboy	10	4	2	3	4	1	2	2	7	6+

Number: If the Warboss is accompanied by a bodyguard he may also be accompanied by up to two Mekboyz.
Options: The Mekboyz may be given any equipment allowed from the Ork Armoury.

MAD DOKS

	Points/model	WS	BS	S	T	W	I	A	Ld	Sv
Mad Dok	10	4	2	3	4	1	2	2	7	6+

Number: If the Warboss is accompanied by a bodyguard he may also be accompanied by up to two Mad Doks.
Options: The Mad Doks may be given any equipment allowed from the Ork Armoury.

The wartrukk is a lightly armoured, fast transport vehicle used by Orks for getting the Boyz into battle quickly. It allows them to thrust deep into enemy lines and capture forward positions.

TRANSPORT: WARTRUKK					
	Points	Front Armour	Side Armour	Rear Armour	BS
Wartrukk	30	10	10	10	2

Type: Fast, open topped.   **Crew:** Orks.
Weapons: The wartrukk is armed with either a big shoota at +8 pts or a rokkit launcha at +5 pts.

0-1 BIG MEK

	Points	WS	BS	S	T	W	I	A	Ld	Sv
Big Mek	25	4	2	4	4	2	3	3	7	6+

Options: A Big Mek may be given any equipment allowed from the Ork Armoury for Mekboyz, and also any equipment that can normally only be chosen by the Warboss and Nobz.

Bodyguard: The Big Mek may be accompanied by a bodyguard as detailed below. If the Big Mek has a bodyguard then he and the bodyguard are treated as a single unit during the battle. Note that the bodyguard does not count as a separate HQ choice (it does not use up one of the HQ 'slots').

Wartrukk: The Big Mek and his bodyguard may be mounted in a wartrukk at an additional cost of +30 pts. See the wartrukk entry on page 8 for details.

SPECIAL RULE

Independent Character: Unless accompanied by his bodyguard the Big Mek is an independent character and follows all of the rules for independent characters as given in the Warhammer 40,000 rulebook.

BIG MEK'S BODYGUARD

MEKBOYZ

	Points/model	WS	BS	S	T	W	I	A	Ld	Sv
Mekboy	10	4	2	3	4	1	2	2	7	6+

Number: The Big Mek may be accompanied by between three and five Mekboyz.

Options: The Mekboyz may be given any equipment allowed from the Ork Armoury. Mekboyz are highly individualistic and have a violent aversion to 'standardised' weapons. For this reason no Mekboyz in the bodyguard may be equipped with the same combination of weapons.

Occasionally a Mekboy will exhibit the kind of ambition usually only seen amongst Nobz. Although he can never aspire to lead a whole warband the Mekboy will gather other Mekboyz as followers and gain in power and stature. It is common for a Big Mek to leave his warband or be outlawed by its Warboss for getting too big for his boots. Outlaw Big Meks and their followers will hire out their services to warbands, searching for a war big enough to satisfy their obsession for building the biggest, shootiest war machines around.

0-1 PAINBOSS

	Points	WS	BS	S	T	W	I	A	Ld	Sv
Painboss	25	4	2	4	4	2	3	3	7	6+

Options: A Painboss may be given any equipment allowed for Mad Doks from the Ork Armoury.

Bodyguard: The Painboss may be accompanied by a bodyguard as detailed below. If he has a bodyguard then he and the bodyguard are treated as a single unit during battle. Note that the bodyguard does not count as a separate HQ choice (it does not use up a HQ 'slot').

Wartrukk: The Painboss and his bodyguard may be mounted in a wartrukk at an additional cost of +30 pts. See the wartrukk entry on page 8 for details.

SPECIAL RULE

Independent Character: Unless accompanied by his bodyguard the Painboss is an independent character and follows all of the rules for independent characters as given in the Warhammer 40,000 rulebook.

Veteran Painboyz become increasingly obsessed with perfecting their own methods of 'serjery' and eventually drift away from their Warboss. Left to their own devices, they will indulge in ever more extreme eksperiments. Any Ork brave/stupid enough to venture into a Painboss's lab has to be careful otherwise it may wake up to find itself with a new set of mechanical lungs that allow it to breathe underwater even though it probably only went in to get a bad tooth removed!

PAINBOSS'S BODYGUARD

CYBORKS

	Points/model	WS	BS	S	T	W	I	A	Ld	Sv
Cybork	13	4	2	4	5	1	2	2	7	5+

Number: The Painboss may be accompanied by between four and nine Cyborks.

Weapons: Sluggas and choppas.

Special Rule: The Cyborks have an invulnerable saving throw.

ELITES

Stormboyz are fierce Ork warriors who are willing to gamble with their lives (and their sanity) by strapping on crude Ork rokkit packs to blast them towards the enemy.

STORMBOYZ										
	Points/model	WS	BS	S	T	W	I	A	Ld	Sv
Boyz	15	4	2	3	4	1	2	2	7	6+
Nob	+11	4	2	4	4	2	3	3	7	6+

Mob: The mob consists of between five and twenty Ork Stormboyz.

Weapons: Sluggas and choppas.

Options: The entire mob may be equipped with frag stikkbombz at +1 pt per model and krak stikkbombz at +2 pts per model.

Character: For an additional cost of +11 pts one of the Stormboyz may be upgraded to a Nob. The Nob may be given any equipment allowed from the Ork Armoury, except mega armour.

SPECIAL RULE

Jump Packs: The mob is equipped with jump packs. See the Warhammer 40,000 rulebook for details.

Kommandos are the most slippery, cunning and untrustworthy Orks in any warband. On the other hand they are the best at slithering closer to an enemy battleline or sneaking around a flank without raising the alarm.

KOMMANDOS										
	Points/model	WS	BS	S	T	W	I	A	Ld	Sv
Boyz	10	4	2	3	4	1	2	2	7	–
Nob	+11	4	2	4	4	2	3	3	7	–

Mob: The mob consists of between five and ten Kommandos.

Weapons: The models in the mob may be armed with either a shoota or slugga & choppa (you may have a mixture of weapons within the mob).

Options: Up to one model in the mob can be armed with either a big shoota at +8 pts, rokkit launcha at +5 pts or burna at +6 pts. The mob may have frag stikkbombz at +1 pt per model, krak stikkbombz at +2 pts per model and/or tankbusta bombz at +3 pts per model.

Character: For an additional cost of +11 pts one of the Kommandos may be upgraded to a Nob. The Nob is allowed to have any equipment allowed from the Ork Armoury, except for mega armour.

SPECIAL RULES

Infiltrators: Kommandos are Infiltrators and follow any special scenario rules for Infiltrators.

Slippery: Kommandos sneak through cover quickly and easily, so they roll an extra D6 when they move through difficult ground.

'Ard Boyz wear heavy armour pieced together from steel plates and equipment scavenged from defeated foes. Their thick armour combined with the natural toughness of Orks means that 'Ard Boyz are able to wade through the fiercest fire fights with barely a scratch.

'ARD BOYZ										
	Points/model	WS	BS	S	T	W	I	A	Ld	Sv
Boyz	12	4	2	3	4	1	2	2	7	4+
Nob	+16	4	2	4	4	2	3	3	7	4+

Mob: The mob consists of between five and twenty 'Ard Boyz

Weapons: The models in the mob may be armed with either a shoota or slugga & choppa (you may have a mixture of weapons within the mob).

Options: Up to three models in the mob can be armed with either a big shoota at +8 pts, a rokkit launcha at +5 pts or a burna at +6 pts. The entire mob may be equipped with frag stikkbombz at +1 pts per model, and/or krak stikkbombz at +2 pts per model.

Character: For an additional cost of +16 pts one of the Boyz may be upgraded to a Nob. The Nob may be given any additional equipment allowed from the Ork Armoury.

SKARBOYZ										
	Points/model	WS	BS	S	T	W	I	A	Ld	Sv
Boyz	11	4	2	4	4	1	2	2	7	6+
Nob	+9	4	2	4	4	2	3	3	7	6+

Skarboyz are veteran warriors who bear the scars of dozens of battles. These Orks have grown exceptionally big and strong and have brawny, gnarled arms bulging with slabs of muscle from fighting in numerous conflicts.

Mob: The mob consists of between five and twenty Skarboyz.

Weapons: The models in the mob may be armed with either a shoota or slugga & choppa (you may have a mixture of weapons within the mob).

Options: Up to three models in the mob can be armed with either a big shoota at +8 pts, a rokkit launcha at +5 pts or a burna at +8 pts. The entire mob may be equipped with frag stikkbombz at +1 pt per model, krak stikkbombz at +2 pts per model.

Character: For an additional cost of +9 pts one of the Boyz may be upgraded to a Nob. The Nob may be given any additional equipment allowed from the Ork Armoury.

0-1 FLASH GITZ										
	Points/model	WS	BS	S	T	W	I	A	Ld	Sv
Boyz	9	4	2	3	4	1	2	2	7	6+
Nob	+11	4	2	4	4	2	3	3	7	6+

Some Orks are so obsessed with guns that they will scrape together all the wealth they can to get the best kustom shoota they can afford. Other Orks call these over-equipped nuttas 'Flash Gitz'.

Mob: The mob consists of between five and twenty Flash Gitz.

Weapons: Shoota.

Options: The entire mob may be given the same kustom job for their shootas chosen from the Wargear section: *Shootier:* +2 pts per model, *Blasta:* +3 pts per model or *More Dakka:* +4 pts per model. Up to four models can have either a big shoota at +8 pts, a rokkit launcha at +5 pts or a burna at +6 pts.

Character: For an additional cost of +11 pts one of the Gitz may be upgraded to a Nob. The Nob may be given any equipment allowed from the Ork Armoury.

TROOPS

SLUGGA BOYZ										
	Points/model	WS	BS	S	T	W	I	A	Ld	Sv
Boyz	9	4	2	3	4	1	2	2	7	6+
Nob	+11	4	2	4	4	2	3	3	7	6+

Slugga Boyz are the heart and soul of most Ork warbands. They are normally formed into huge mobs and are armed for close combat with hefty, razor-edged choppas and the big-bore Ork pistols known as sluggas.

Mob: The mob consists of between ten and thirty Boyz.

Weapons: Slugga and choppa.

Options: Up to three models can have either a big shoota at +8 pts, a rokkit launcha at +5 pts or a burna at +6 pts.

Character: For an additional cost of +11 pts one of the Boyz may be upgraded to a Nob. The Nob may be given any equipment allowed by the Ork Armoury.

SHOOTA BOYZ										
	Points/model	WS	BS	S	T	W	I	A	Ld	Sv
Boyz	8	4	2	3	4	1	2	2	7	6+
Nob	+12	4	2	4	4	2	3	3	7	6+

The deafening clamour of a mob of Shoota Boyz opening fire is legendary. Each Ork will try to outdo his neighbour by letting fly with the most ammo and the loudest gun. Hitting the target is less of an objective than terrorising the enemy!

Mob: The mob consists of between ten and thirty Shoota Boyz.

Weapons: Shoota.

Options: Up to three models can have either a big shoota at +8 pts, rokkit launcha at +5 pts or burna at +6 pts.

Character: For an extra +12 pts one Boy may be upgraded to a Nob and given any equipment allowed from the Ork Armoury.

Stikk Bommas are special among Ork society for one reason — they know that when you pull the pin out of a stikkbomb, you throw the bomb and not the pin!

Ork burnas are powerful cutting torches used in battle to melt enemy armour. When he is within distance the Burna Boy can crank open the nozzle and unleash a torrent of flame to incinerate foes, even those skulking in woods or behind walls.

Tankbusta mobs are formed from Orks who have survived tank attacks and learned how to beat them. Small mobs of Tankbustas work among the larger mobs of Boyz to hunt down enemy tanks or bunkers.

0-2 STIKK BOMMAS									
	Points/model	WS	BS	S	T	W	I	A	Ld	Sv
Boyz	10	4	2	3	4	1	2	2	7	6+
Nob	+11	4	2	4	4	2	3	3	7	6+

Mob: The mob consists of between ten and thirty Stikk Bommas.

Weapons: Slugga, close combat weapon, frag and krak stikkbombz.

Options: Up to three models in the mob can be armed with either a big shoota at +8 pts, a rokkit launcha at +5 pts or a burna at +6 pts. The mob may be equipped with tankbusta bombz at an additional cost of +2 pts per model.

Character: For an additional cost of +11 pts one of the Boyz may be upgraded to a Nob. The Nob may be given any equipment allowed from the Ork Armoury.

0-2 BURNA BOYZ									
	Points/model	WS	BS	S	T	W	I	A	Ld	Sv
Boyz	9	4	2	3	4	1	2	2	7	6+
Mekboyz	+9	4	2	3	4	1	2	2	7	6+

Mob: The mob consists of between five and ten Burna Boyz.

Weapons: Slugga and choppa.

Options: Up to four models in the mob can be armed with a burna at +6 pts. The entire mob may be equipped with frag stikkbombz at an additional cost of +1 pt per model and krak stikkbombz at an additional cost of +2 pts per model.

Character: For an additional +9 pts the Burna Boyz mob may be led by a Mekboy. The Mekboy may be given any equipment allowed from the Ork Armoury.

0-2 TANKBUSTAS									
	Points/model	WS	BS	S	T	W	I	A	Ld	Sv
Boyz	11	4	2	3	4	1	2	2	7	6+
Nob	+11	4	2	4	4	2	3	3	7	6+

Mob: The mob consists of five and ten Tankbusta Boyz.

Weapons: Slugga, close combat weapon, frag stikkbombz and tankbusta bombz.

Options: Up to three models in the mob can be armed with a rokkit launcha at +7 pts each.

Character: For an additional cost of +11 pts one of the Boyz may be upgraded to a Nob. The Nob may be given any equipment allowed from the Ork Armoury.

SPECIAL RULE

Tank Hunters: The mob always passes Tank Shock tests and adds +1 to all Armour Penetration rolls.

The building shook as the Leman Russ approached, dust and fragments of masonry rained down on Krug and his mob from what was left of the roof. They waited back from the shattered walls and out of sight with unusual patience for Orks. It wasn't until they heard the first thwack!-booom! of the tank's battlecannon that they brought their rokkit launchas up to the windows. The tank was right outside, cutting down the last of a mob of Gretchin with its heavy bolters and presenting its flank to the apparently empty building the Tankbustas occupied. Their three rokkits roared down at it on smoky yellow tails. One corkscrewed away at the last instant and plowed into the ground, one was a dud which ricocheted off with a clang, but the other tore a great chunk out of the vehicle's side armour and sent a track whipping away like a wounded python. Krug and his boyz were up and running before it had even slewed to a halt, Grognatz and Arik clamped their bombz to its side and ducked away before a fiery blossom lifted its turret clean off and the engine blew with a teeth-rattling concussion.

GRETCHIN MOBZ

	Points/model	WS	BS	S	T	W	I	A	Ld	Sv
Gretchin	3	2	2	2	2	1	2	1	5	–
Slaver	9	4	2	3	4	1	2	2	7	6+

Mob: The mob consists of one Slaver and between ten and thirty Gretchin.

Weapons: The Gretchin are armed with grot blastas.

Character: The Slaver may be given any equipment allowed from the Ork Armoury.

SPECIAL RULES

Living Shield: Orks are adept at using Grots to draw enemy fire. Any Ork mobs which are shot at 'through' a Grot mob can claim a 5+ cover saving throw. Each save made by the Orks means one of the Grots must be removed as a casualty.

Better Footing: Orks are also adept at using Grots to clear a path through difficult ground, sometimes by the simple expedient of stepping on them! If a Grot mob is in difficult ground any Ork mobs moving through the same difficult ground may re-roll the dice for how far they move. Mega armoured Orks may not use this benefit (the Grots would just go 'splutch').

Mine Clearance: Grots are sometimes charged across minefields to make the mines safe(!) before the Orks have to cross. If a Grot mob moves into a minefield take off 3D6 Grots as casualties and then remove the minefield marker. If there aren't enough Grots in the mob to satisfy the casualty quota the minefield remains in play and the Grot mob is wiped out.

In every society there are those who are on the bottom of the heap. In Ork society this position is most definitely held by the Gretchin, or Grotz as they are also known. They are often enslaved against their will and forced to serve their brutal Ork masters. Quite literally downtrodden (and kicked and beaten), the Grotz are always at the wrong end of things — including the food chain!

FAST ATTACK

TRUKK BOYZ

	Points/model	WS	BS	S	T	W	I	A	Ld	Sv
Boyz	9	4	2	3	4	1	2	2	7	6+
Nob	+11	4	2	4	4	2	3	3	7	6+

Mob: The Trukk Boyz mob consists of between five and ten Ork Boyz.

Weapons: The Boyz have either a shoota or a slugga & choppa. The mob may contain a mix of differently armed Boyz.

Options: Up to one of the Boyz can have a big shoota at +8 pts, a rokkit launcha at +5 pts or a burna at +6 pts.

Character: One of the Boyz may be upgraded to a Nob at an additional cost of +11 pts. The Nob may have any equipment allowed from the Ork Armoury.

Wartrukk: The mob must be mounted in a wartrukk at an additional cost of +30 pts. See the wartrukk entry on page 8 for details.

SPECIAL RULES

Bailin' out: Trukk Boyz have plenty of experience in jumping on and off trukks (and landing on their heads), so they will only suffer a wound on a D6 roll of 6 instead of a 4+ if their trukk is destroyed.

Trukk Boyz, or trukkers as they are also called, have invested loads of time and energy in getting a wartrukk as their own personal transport. They are much envied by the foot-slogging Boyz for their ability to get into the fight quickly.

WARBUGGIES/WARTRAKS

	Points	Front Armour	Side Armour	Rear Armour	BS
Warbuggy/trak	30	10	10	10	2

Squadron: The squadron consists of between one and three Warbuggies/Wartraks.

Type: Fast, open topped.

Weapons: Each vehicle may be armed with one of the following: twin-linked big shoota at +16 pts, twin-linked rokkit launcha at +10 pts, a kustom mega blasta at +20 pts or a skorcha at +8 pts.

Most warbands are accompanied by a ramshackle band of vehicles that hurtle around the battlefield blasting at anything they can. The most crazed krews are known as Speed Freeks as they have completely succumbed to the Ork predilection for going far too fast.

Ork Warbikes are one of the strange miracles of Ork technology, possessing an immensely powerful armament for their size. Ork Bikers love nothing more than to roar around the battlefield, unleashing hails of shots in all directions. Often they will ride straight into the middle of their enemy, their fingers firmly on the trigger, riding over the bodies of those who fall to their murderous advance.

WARBIKE SQUADRON

	Points/model	WS	BS	S	T	W	I	A	Ld	Sv
Boyz	30	4	2	3	4(5)	1	2	2	7	6+/5+
Nob	+22	4	2	4	4(5)	2	3	3	7	6+/5+

Squadron: The squadron consists of between three and ten Ork warbikes.

Weapons: Twin-linked big shootas.

Options: Some warbikes are stripped of their big shootas and their riders fight as pure assault troops instead. In this case the warbikes cost 20 pts and the riders are armed with sluggas and additional close combat weapons (chains, tyre irons etc).

Character: At an additional cost of +22 pts one of the bikers may be upgraded to a Nob. He may be given any equipment allowed from the Ork Armoury with the exception of mega armour.

SPECIAL RULES

Short Ranged: The bouncing, rattling progress of warbikes is not conducive to hitting accurately at long range. Therefore the warbikes' big shootas are limited to a maximum range of 18".

Hard to Hit: As warbikes career across the battlefield they kick up vast quantities of dust and oily exhaust fumes. This gives them a 5+ saving throw as if they were in cover. Furthermore if an enemy shoots through a unit of warbikes to hit another Ork unit behind it the Ork unit behind counts as in cover too. The warbikes' pollution cover has no effects in close combat.

Psycho Bikers: Ork Bikers are the worst kind of speed-crazed loons there are. They are unlikely to even notice casualties over the roar of engines so they are completely immune to the effects of morale and pinning.

Psycho Blastas: In an assault Bikers use their big shootas to blast the enemy at point blank range, breaking through their lines in a storm of shrapnel. This means that warbikes that charge into close combat strike first and make a special close combat attack that works like a shooting attack on the enemy in the first round instead of fighting normally (ie, roll three D6, hitting on a 5+ but with a re-roll to hit, any hits are resolved with a Strength and AP of 5). Once the warbikes have resolved their shots their opponents may fight back.

HEAVY SUPPORT

Big gunz are batteries of crude Orkish artillery manned by a swarm of Grot slaves. They are used to pound enemy lines into submission and knock out tanks from a distance while the ferocious mobs of Boyz close in to butcher the enemy infantry in hand-to-hand combat.

0-2 BIG GUNZ BATTERY

	Points/model	WS	BS	S	T	W	I	A	Ld	Sv
Big Gun Krew	30	2	2	2	2	1	2	1	5	–
Slaver/Mek	+9	4	2	3	4	1	2	2	7	6+

Mob: The battery consists of between one and three big gunz and two Gretchin krew per big gun.

Weapons: All of the weapons in a battery must be of the same type, either lobbas, Zzap guns or kannon. Rules for these weapons can be found in the Wargear section.

Options: You may include up to three additional Grot krew per gun at a cost of +3 points per model.

Character: It is common for a Slaver and/or a Mek to command the krew of a battery of big gunz. You may include up to one Slaver and up to one Mek at an additional cost of +9 points each. The Slaver or Mek may have any equipment allowed from the Ork Armoury.

SPECIAL RULE

Hits on the Battery: When a battery of big gunz is fired at, randomise any hits between the krew and the gunz themselves by rolling a D6:

1-4: Hits the Krew; **5-6:** Hits a big gun.

Hits against the Gretchin krew are resolved as normal, Gunz count as vehicles with an armour value of 10, any penetrating or glancing hits destroy them. For Morale checks, use the number of Krew, not Krew and Gunz.

LOOTAS										
	Points/model	WS	BS	S	T	W	I	A	Ld	Sv
Loota	10	4	2	3	4	1	2	2	7	5+
Nob	+11	4	2	4	4	2	3	3	7	5+

Mob: The mob consists of between five and ten Lootas.

Weapons: Shootas plus see options below.

Options: Lootas are allowed to use the options of one of the following squad types as detailed in the army lists in the Warhammer 40,000 rulebook:

Space Marine: Tactical squad, Devastator squad, Scout squad (note that Orks with sniper rifles hit on a 4+ not a 2+).

Imperial Guard: Infantry squad, Fire support squad, Anti-tank squad.

For example: You might choose to use the weapon options for an Imperial Guard Infantry squad for your Lootas. This would give them up to one plasma gun (+5 pts), melta gun (+8 pts) or flamer (+3 pts) and one heavy weapon which could be either a heavy bolter (+5 pts), missile launcher (+10 pts), lascannon (+15 pts), autocannon (+10 pts) or mortar (+10 pts). Alternatively, a squad's options from any one army list entry may be used as long as both players agree.

Character: For an additional cost of +11 pts one of the Boyz may be upgraded to a Nob. The Nob may be given any equipment allowed from the Ork Armoury.

SPECIAL RULE

Looted Weapons: If you roll a 1 to hit with a looted weapon, a hit is scored on the unit shooting with the weapon, instead of the target. The opponent gets to roll To Wound etc. Blast marker weapons score a single hit but do not place the template. The Ork player gets to allocate any wounds, and they don't have to be allocated to the model who fired the weapon that rolled the '1' (the 'Ooops... Sorry Mate!' rule).

Ork Lootas scavenge the battlefield after the fight is over and strip weapons, armour and equipment from their enemy's dead. Most of the gear is sold on to Meks or other Orks but the Lootas keep the few prize working weapons for themselves and set about figuring out how to use them.

ORK DREADNOUGHT					Armour				
	Points	WS	BS	S	Front	Side	Rear	I	A
Ork Dreadnought	70 + wpns	4	2	5(10)	12	12	10	2	2(3)

Krew: The Ork Dreadnought has a crew of one Ork.

Weapons: It is armed with two Dreadnought close combat weapons (power claws usually), and two chosen from among the following: rokkit launcha at +5 pts each, big shootas at +8 pts each, kustom mega blastas at +15 pts each, skorchas at +5 pts each. You may have two of one weapon type if you wish or two different weapons.

Options: The Ork Dreadnought may replace one or both close combat weapons with extra weapons for the additional cost shown above. Each extra weapon chosen must be the same as one of the two main weapons and makes one of the main weapons twin-linked. If one close combat weapon is replaced the Ork Dreadnought is reduced to its basic 2 Attacks, if two are replaced the Ork Dreadnought is reduced to its basic Strength of 5.

Ork Dreadnoughts possess the three main elements of Ork warfare — they're big, shooty and stompy! They are often created by the combined skills of Meks and Doks because the pilot is 'wired-in' to the control systems so that the huge armoured vehicle moves as if it were his own body. Other Dreads are not so sophisticated and are controlled by a wild array of levers, buttons and gears.

KILLER KAN					Armour				
	Points	WS	BS	S	Front	Side	Rear	I	A
Killer Kan	45	4	2	5(10)	11	11	10	2	2

Krew: The Kan has a crew of one Ork.

Mob: Your mob may consist of between one to three Kans.

Weapons: The Kan is armed with a Dreadnought close combat weapon and a big shoota.

Options: A Killer Kan may replace its big shoota with a rokkit launcha or a skorcha for free.

Killer Kans are smaller and less sophisticated Ork Dreadnoughts. Although lightly armoured, they retain the deadly power claws of their larger cousins making them dangerous foes at close quarters.

Mekboyz build all sorts of variants on the basic Battlewagon design but they all bristle with guns and have plenty of space for carrying a mob of Boyz into battle. Any captured vehicle that finds its way into a Mekboy's hands will be cannibalised into a Battlewagon once its weapons start to break down and run out of ammunition.

Orks use all kinds of captured vehicles either looted from the battlefield or built in Ork-controlled Imperial factories. In time successive rebuilds and modifications will turn most looted vehicles into creations that are the equivalent of a Battlewagon.

Corporal Brecht's monocular brought the scene below into sharp focus. A crude earth ramp had been thrown up to the armoured flank of the Ork's attack ship and an opening cut through the buckled plates and leaking pipes. A stream of Gretchin slaves were hauling boxes of ammunition and cans of fuel down the slope. As he watched a heavy tracked vehicle nosed its way out of the ship's cavernous interior and a thrill of fear coursed through him as he recognised the familiar hull of a Basilisk under a barbaric array of spikes and armour plates. He crawled back to the rest of the patrol who were warily watching back down the defile in case any more Kommandos were in the area. "Get on the link," he shouted to Arhaus, "And tell the Captain we've got big problems, it looks like the greenskins salvaged tanks from Kolchis and they're on their way."

O-I BATTLEWAGON

	Points	Front Armour	Side Armour	Rear Armour	BS
Battlewagon	120	13	12	10	2

Type: Tank, open topped.

Weapons: The Battlewagon is armed with three twin-linked big shootas. You may upgrade any of the twin-linked big shootas to a twin-linked rokkit launcha or a skorcha for free.

One of the twin-linked big shootas may be replaced with a big gun – either a lobba, Zzap gun or kannon at +15 pts.

Options: In addition the Battlewagon may mount up to five bolt-on big shootas at +10 pts each. These must be fired by the Ork mob onboard (see page 37).

Transport: The Battlewagon may carry up to twenty Orks.

O-I LOOTED VEHICLE   PTS: VARIABLE

You may include a one looted vehicle worth 51+ points or one to three vehicles worth 50 points or less. Even though you can include more than one vehicle they count as a single Heavy Support choice.

Type: A looted vehicle may be chosen from one of the following army list entries in the Warhammer 40,000 rulebook:

Space Marines: Rhino, Razorback, Predator Annihilator, Predator Destructor, Land Raider.

Imperial Guard: Chimera, Hellhound, Griffon, Leman Russ battle tank, Leman Russ, Demolisher, Basilisk.

Although the cost for a looted vehicle remains the same as it was in its 'parent' army list its Ballistic Skill is reduced to 2 because it's crewed by Orks! Also note that the model for a looted vehicle must be converted and/or painted appropriately to show it is being used by Orks; simply borrowing a Leman Russ from an Imperial Guard army is not allowed!

Weapons: Variable, see below.

Options: The looted vehicle may be given any weapons options permitted from its army list. For example, a Leman Russ battletank may be given a heavy flamer or heavy bolter sponsons at a cost of +10 pts each. A looted vehicle may only use Ork vehicle upgrades.

SPECIAL RULES

Looted Vehicles: Make a Breakdown test for each looted vehicle at the start of each turn. Roll a D6, on a 1 roll again on the table below:

D6   RESULT

1   May not move this turn, roll again on this table next turn.

2-3   May not move this turn

4-6   Don't press that – Waaagh! The vehicle lurches forward 2D6" straight ahead. Make Dangerous Terrain, Tank Shock tests etc as if the vehicle were moving normally. The vehicle counts as moving the distance rolled on the dice and may not make any further moves this turn.

Oomans are pink and soft, not tough and green like da Boyz. They'z all the same size too – no big 'uns or little 'uns, so they'z always arguing about who's in charge, 'cos there's no way of telling 'cept fer badges an' ooniforms and fings. Anuvver fing – when they do sumfing, they try to make it look like somfink else to confuse everybody. When one of them wants to lord it over the uvvers, 'e says "I'm very speshul so'z you gotta worship me", or "I know summink wot you lot don't know, so yer better lissen good". Da funny fing is, arf of 'em believe it and da over arf don't, so 'e 'as to hit 'em all anyway or run fer it. Wot a lot of mukkin' about if yer asks me. An' while they'z all arguin' wiv each other over who's da boss, da Orks can sneak up an' clobber da lot.

STARTING A WAAAGH!

Collecting an effective Warhammer 40,000 army is a big challenge when you are first starting out. Picking the right mobs to make your warband a force to be reckoned with can be tough! To help out we've provided this handy guide to help get you started on building your first Ork army.

WHERE TO BEGIN?

The first objective of any Warhammer 40,000 gamer is to collect a force that can be fielded in battle. The Ork army list gives details of all the different mobs you can get in a warband – their size, armament and so forth. Although there are several several ways to build an army, by far the most commonly used is the aptly named Standard Missions force organisation chart. Use this and you won't go far wrong.

As you can see from the Standard Missions chart shown on this page, one HQ and two mobs of Troops are compulsory (dark-toned choices *have* to be included in your army). These form the basis of your whole army and so make a splendid starting point for collecting and painting. Once you have built up this core force you'll be able to fight a standard scenario, albeit a fairly small one.

The photo below shows a fairly typical starting force of Orks. For our HQ choice we have included a Warboss as the all-conquering leader and for the two Troops choices we've selected a mob of Slugga Boyz and a mob of Shoota Boyz. Each of these mobs can be from ten to thirty models strong, but we've gone for mobs of sixteen models each as a good compromise between these extremes. If

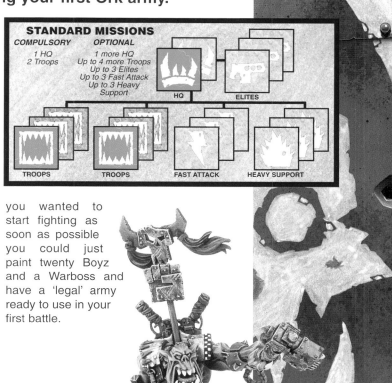

you wanted to start fighting as soon as possible you could just paint twenty Boyz and a Warboss and have a 'legal' army ready to use in your first battle.

Extraordinarily huge and powerful, the Warboss is the toughest warrior in the whole Ork army.

An Ork force made up of a Warboss (HQ), a Shoota Boyz mob (Troops) and a Slugga Boyz mob (Troops).

WHAT'S IN THE ARMY?

Da Boyz form the heart of an Ork army, constituting the ferocious mass of warriors it needs to win a battle. All Ork Boyz excel in close combat and the more Boyz that get stuck in the better! Using big mobs of Orks is important because it stops their assaults being broken up by enemy fire. Specialist Orks such as Tankbustas and Burna Boyz should be used for tackling important objectives or especially tough enemies.

Da Wheelz give an Ork army mobility and firepower but are vulnerable to enemy shooting. They are best used in support of the main advance, pinning down an enemy and distracting them while Da Boyz close in to attack.

Da 'Ard Stuff has thick armour, powerful weaponry and inflicts tremendous carnage in assaults. If Da 'Ard Stuff attacks alongside Da Boyz the enemy can be forced to divide their firing, giving both elements a good chance of survival.

Da Big Gunz give supporting fire so that the most dangerous enemy units can be blasted to bits at long range. Big Gunz are vulnerable to enemy shooting and assaults so they need to be placed where they will be protected by other mobs.

EXPANDING YOUR ARMY

Adrian Wood's Waaagh! Grishnak.

Andy: armed with your Warboss and two Troops units you have a core force for your army. However, you'll soon want to expand it by adding new units, though deciding exactly what to add can be a tough choice. The approach I find best is to add in one unit from each category which you don't already have – a Fast Attack unit, a Heavy Support unit and an Elite unit. At this stage it will be useful to try out these different parts of the army and see which suits your tactics best. Later you may decide to add more choices from one or other of these categories based on your experience in games, or you may want to add more Troops instead, but having a bit of each to begin with will be a useful way to start learning how your army works.

To give you some helpful pointers we've included two armies collected by experienced Greenskins, Adrian 'Grand Warlord' Wood and myself. As you can see, both armies include a powerful core force of Boyz, but there the similarities end. Adrian has a lot of Wheelz in his army (Fast Attack choices, that is) because experience has taught him to move quickly to pin down the enemy. I, on the other hand, have gone for more Big Gunz and 'Ard Stuff (Heavy Support) to try and land a 'knock out punch' which will send the enemy reeling if it connects! The mark of an Ork army is the endless variety of miniatures, so both armies contain loads of great conversions.

Andy Chambers' Blitz Boyz

ORK TACTICS

On this page are some different battle plans for an Ork army. These are just the basic ideas, and leave plenty of room for you to tailor these tactics to your own forces and different opponents.

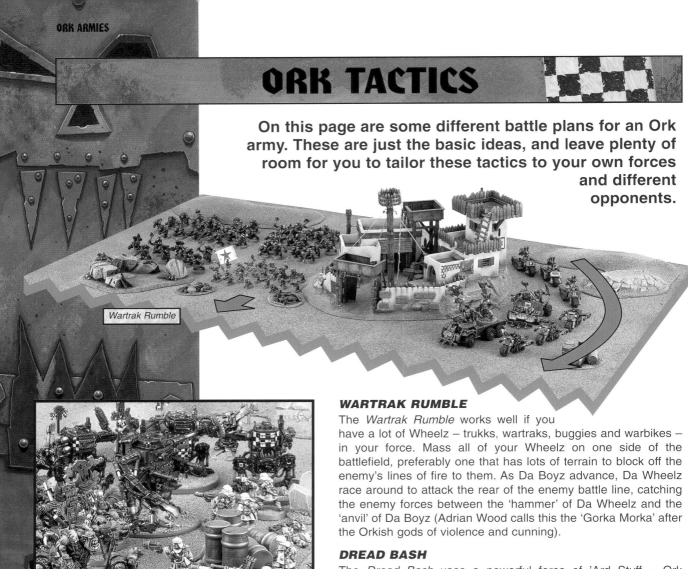

Wartrak Rumble

Dread Bash

WARTRAK RUMBLE

The *Wartrak Rumble* works well if you have a lot of Wheelz – trukks, wartraks, buggies and warbikes – in your force. Mass all of your Wheelz on one side of the battlefield, preferably one that has lots of terrain to block off the enemy's lines of fire to them. As Da Boyz advance, Da Wheelz race around to attack the rear of the enemy battle line, catching the enemy forces between the 'hammer' of Da Wheelz and the 'anvil' of Da Boyz (Adrian Wood calls this the 'Gorka Morka' after the Orkish gods of violence and cunning).

DREAD BASH

The *Dread Bash* uses a powerful force of 'Ard Stuff – Ork Dreadnoughts and Killer Kans – to give an armoured spearhead to Da Boyz' attack. Deploy your 'Ard Stuff along a short part of your battle line, backed up by your toughest mobs of Boyz. As with the *Wartrak Rumble*, try to use any available terrain to cut down on the amount of incoming enemy fire as your force advances, but don't hide or dawdle, close in quick! Use your 'Ard Stuff to tear a hole in the enemy forces so that Da Boyz can pour in and start destroying their battle line.

SWAMP 'EM

When you *Swamp 'Em* you need a force made up mostly of Da Boyz and loads of Gretchin slaves. Deploy Da Boyz across a broad front and place the Gretchin out in front as cannon fodder, but have one or two units of Boyz behind the line so that other Orks which fall back can mob up with them. The enemy should have too many targets to be able to stop them all with shooting, so you will start to overrun his battle line in several places. The mobs furthest back will then arrive, reinforced by Orks which have mobbed up with them, and finish off any pockets of resistance.

Swamp 'Em

PAINTING ORKS

So your head's full of cunnin' plans on how to crush your foes, but what about painting all those greenskin warriors? In this section we'll impart some of the tricks of the trade when it comes to painting Orks.

ORK SKIN

Goblin Green drybrushed over Dark Angels Green, followed by a mix of Goblin Green and Bleached Bone drybrushed on as a highlight.

Painting Ork skin is the most important thing in creating an impressive Ork army.

There are as many ways of painting Ork skin as there are Ork gamers and each one has their own style. Some like to paint their Orks simply, so they can paint lots at the same time. Others prefer to carefully highlight and shade their models for maximum effect. Whichever way you paint your Orks, bear in mind that you will be painting dozens of them, so choose a style that allows you to paint lots of models easily. A single coat of Goblin Green on a mass of Ork Boyz looks fine.

Goblin Green, this time painted over Dark Angels Green and then highlighted with a mix of Goblin Green and Bleached Bone.

There are a few simple tricks you can use to add more detail to your models. For example, a wash

Goblin Green washed with Green ink then drybrushed with a mix of Goblin Green and Bleached Bone as a highlight.

of Green ink will add instant shading to your Boyz. Another trick is to drybrush on a lighter green to highlight the detail. We've included some examples of painting Ork flesh on this page, but you can use all sorts of combinations of Green ink wash and different colours for highlighting. Feel free to experiment.

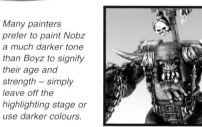

Gretchin and Nobz can be painted differently to Ork Boyz. This Grot has been painted with a mix of Goblin Green and Bleached Bone to make it paler and weaker-looking than Da Boyz.

Many painters prefer to paint Nobz a much darker tone than Boyz to signify their age and strength – simply leave off the highlighting stage or use darker colours.

PAINTING METAL

Use Boltgun Metal to paint your guns and choppas. It looks that good after a single coat and can be highlighted with Chainmail. A wash of Rust Brown ink will make your guns look weather-worn. In comparison, Tin Bitz is a much darker and browner metal colour. Used as a base colour and highlighted with Boltgun Metal, you get even dirtier looking guns.

TEETH

You can paint teeth and horns with Bleached Bone – a couple of coats will look good even over black. If you want your model's teeth to look more discoloured, use a wash of Rust Brown ink. You can also use Bubonic Brown or Codex Grey as a base colour for teeth. We painted the horns on this Nob with Scorched Brown first, then the ridges were painted on with Bubonic Brown and then Bleached Bone.

DRYBRUSHING

One way to paint Orks is to drybrush them, which is a way of highlighting models, particularly if they have textured surfaces. Start with your base colour and either lighten it with Skull White or choose a lighter version of it (eg, Bleached Bone is a lighter version of Bubonic Brown). Wipe away most of the paint on a tissue and lightly brush over the raised areas of the miniature. The colour in the brush will come off onto the detail, highlighting it. The more you drybrush over the model, the lighter the model will look, so you can easily vary the look of all your models within a mob. You can paint armour, fur, vehicles and Ork skin this way if you like.

The skin of these Orks (painted by Adrian Wood) has been drybrushed – the muscles particularly suit this style of painting. The skin was first painted a base colour of Dark Angels Green and was then drybrushed with a mix of Dark Angels Green and Goblin Green. Adrian then drybrushed the whole model with Goblin Green followed by a mix of Goblin Green and Rotting Flesh. Finally the model had the lightest drybrushing of Rotting Flesh. Excessive, but it looks good!

◄ *This is the end result of Adrian drybrushing over Dark Angels Green as discussed above.*

To make the shading look nice and crisp Adrian painted on final highlights with a mix of Goblin Green and Rotting Flesh.

THE ORK CLANZ

Ork warbands often belong to a specific Ork clan which has its own colour schemes, glyphs and markings. On the next few pages you can see examples of these that you can use to paint your army…

GOFFS

Goff clan Orks think they are the toughest, most no-nonsense warriors around and wear a uniform that is sombre black with some white and red detailing. Black and white checks are especially popular.

This war buggy is equipped with a ram.

Nob with power claw and bosspole.

Shoota Boy

Stormboy

Slugga Boy

Ork with converted big shoota.

The Warboss and his retinue mounted in a huge converted wartrukk.

SNAKEBITES

Snakebite Orks are distrustful of technology and prefer good old-fashioned stuff. Their warriors wear leather and furs for the most part, with some red and white markings.

Nob with big horns and bosspole.

These three Snakebites were made from bits from Warhammer 40,000 and Warhammer Orcs.

Shoota Boy

BAD MOONS

Bad Moons warbands are wealthy and well-equipped. Their ostentatious yellow clan colour is used as markings in a 'dog-tooth' pattern or as a background colour for black flames.

Nob with bosspole.

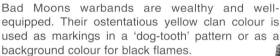

This wartrukk is fitted with a ram and a wrecker ball.

Slugga Boy

Stikk Bommas

Ork with converted rokkit launcha.

Nob with kustom shoota and bosspole.

DEATHSKULLS

Deathskull warbands are expert looters and scavengers and use blue as their clan colour, which most Orks think of as a lucky colour. Deathskulls often daub their bodies with blue warpaint to bring extra good fortune to their scavenging exploits.

Slugga Boys

BLOOD AXES

Blood Axe warbands are seen as being tainted by un-orky ideas picked up from human warriors on the battlefield and for this reason they are mistrusted by other Orks. Blood Axes often use camouflage colours, although they appear rather lurid to human eyes.

Shoota Boyz

EVIL SUNZ

Evil Sunz are obsessed with speed and love to ride in fast buggies. Their vehicles and warriors are all predominantly red (red ones go faster after all!), with some yellow detailing. Yellow flames are a common motif, and easy to paint too!

To satisfy their need for speed, this Evil Sunz Mob have given their trukk a red paint job.

FREEBOOTERS

Freebooter warbands are either made up of mobs of lots of different clans or mobs that don't belong to a clan at all. They don't care just as long as they are where the fighting is!

FREEBOOTERS

A Freebooter warband is an ideal opportunity to make up your own warband's colour scheme, so if you don't see any clan colours you like – go Freebooter! Many Freebooter warbands are an amalgam of Ork mobs from several different warbands. This means you could use a mix of Orks wearing different clan colours to give them a really rag-tag, undisciplined appearance.

Alternatively, you can create your own entirely original colour scheme – for example you might decide that Orks would look groovy in white (Snow Orks!) or grey. It's worth thinking about having a 'trademark' feature for your colour scheme (this is true of any warband, but especially Freebooters). For example the Bloodied Fist warband might have Orks which all have their fists painted red, whereas the Death Jawz have white jaws and so on.

This Nob has no specific clan glyphs or colours, the only decorations are a few checks and a lightning flash.

Adrian's Ork Nob wears white warpaint that distinguishes his Trukk mob, 'Da Dragsterz'.

THEMED ARMIES

A themed army is one built around a single, distinctive idea. This might be a part of the background which appeals to you, or a style of play which you really like. For example, you might decide to collect a Goff warband around the idea that Goffs would never namby around with Wheelz, so the only vehicles you use are Ork Dreadnoughts: <u>lots</u> of Ork Dreadnoughts! Themed armies need a lot of planning, so they aren't very suitable if you're just starting out, but for an experienced gamer they are a great way of getting a unique and very personal force.

Clan Glyphs

- Goff
- Bad Moons
- Deathskulls
- Snakebites
- Blood Axes
- Evil Sunz

ORK GLYPHS

Orks use glyphs to symbolise the important bits of their kultur, like violence, bloodshed and... more violence!

Nobz: Nobility, authority, high rank

Snikk: Cut, kill, execute, assassinate

Bad: Evil, bad, wicked, brave, strong, tough

Grim: Ruthless, prowess, face, dangerous

Zag: Lightning, movement, fast strike

Grub: Cunning, find, dig, hide

Skraga: Skarboy, veteran

Dakka: Attack, noisy weapon, shoot, fight

Gor: Blood, red, slaughter, wound

Boss: Leader, officer, head Ork, Warlord

Regular Glyphs

Waaagh: Warband, tribe of, Watch Out!

Gull: Death, bones, skull, rocks, white

Wazza: Speed, Kult of Speed

Orks mix and combine glyphs together to create new ones, for example the Blood Axes glyph has been combined with a skull. If a glyph represents something important like a Waaagh!, Orks make it really big. Glyphs are often made out of metal and can be painted too.

PAINTING DA WHEELZ

Ork armies often include a lot of Wheelz, because they're cheap and drive around much faster than the slower moving mass of Da Boyz. I always used to find painting vehicles daunting until I learned some good techniques...

Choose the colour you want to paint your vehicle and paint the whole model all over. If you decide to paint your vehicle Boltgun Metal, just drybrush the colour onto the black undercoated vehicle, it looks great immediately. After that, paint the wheels and the crew as normal and the vehicle is finished. You can add transfers at this point as well if you want to. Sorted!

Ork warbike

SPRAY CANS

A very quick way to paint vehicles is to use spray cans. Simply choose the colour you want and either spray it over a black undercoat or directly onto the model (black is best though). You can also lightly dust the vehicle, using spray cans, over the base colour to make it look dirty or rusty. Afterwards drybrush on a lighter shade of your chosen base colour to bring the detail back out.

This wartrukk is fitted with a big grabber and painted in Boltgun Metal. You can use clan colours such as red and black if you like, to fit in with your army.

Big shoota

Rokkit launcha

Skorcha

Ork Dreadnought and Killer Kans

GUBBINZ

Ork vehicles are covered in bits and pieces commonly called 'gubbinz'. These bits can represent vehicle upgrades such as boarding planks and reinforced rams. However, more often than not gubbinz are either useful or decorative stuff that the crew have picked up, such as tools, trophies and fuel cans. Adding gubbinz is an easy way of modifying vehicles so that they don't all look the same.

GLYPH PLATES

Ork miniatures and vehicles often feature clan symbols such as the Evil Sun and the Bad Moon. In the case of the Evil Sun symbol on the warbike, shown above, the symbol has been painted the clan colour Blood Red, with the tusks and eyes painted just like a real face. You can paint these symbols (and indeed any Ork glyphs) in bright colours, or just leave them painted metal if you prefer.

TRANSFERS

Transfers have been applied to this wartrak and drybrushed with Boltgun Metal to make them look as if the paint has been chipped away.

Transfers look great on both Ork miniatures and vehicles and there are loads of different designs to choose from. To apply waterslide transfers, carefully cut out the transfer and leave it in a saucer of water for 30 seconds. Using a pair of tweezers and a brush, slide the transfer off its backing paper and onto your model. Then use the corner of a tissue to dab away any excess water from the model and leave for a few minutes to let it dry completely. You can also combine transfers together to make new designs, re-paint them different colours or highlight them.

DUST

Orks don't clean their vehicles, it's too much like hard work! Therefore buggies end up covered in dust and grime which is easy to paint onto your models. Just drybrush brown paint onto the vehicles or wheels and tracks.

Checks have been painted onto this wartrak's sides, forks, and big shootas, as well as the gunner's wrist band. The areas to be painted with checks were undercoated Skull White first and then the grid was painted on in Chaos Black. Note the extensive battle damage to the armour plate on the front of the vehicle as well as to the mudguard.

In order to get transfers to stand out against metal body work, it's a good idea to paint a black background on first. When applied on top, white transfers stand out from the vehicle as shown with the flame effects on the front forks of this wartrak.

MEK'S WORKSHOP

One of the great things about Ork conversions is that you can make them as crude and as rough as you like!

The 'porthole' was made from a bit of a light fitting.

This wartrukk is festooned with armour plates made from metal and plastic Ork vehicle parts, as well as others created from plasti-card.

Andy used tank turrets to make the bodies for his Ork Dreadnoughts.

This wartrukk has had traks added, a remodelled hull and an impressive skorcha conversion.

CONVERTING VEHICLES

Vehicles are perfect for converting; it's relatively easy to make one buggy look very different from another. One way is to swop the front plate of a buggy for part of a trukk, or replace it with a metal front plates from another vehicle. There are loads of different bits and pieces for Ork vehicles that you can use to make a unique looking vehicle. If you are a bit more adventurous, you can really start swopping bits around, as you can see in the examples above. Extra wheels look good, as do additional weapons, battered armour plates, etc. We suggest that you also carve some battle damage into the plastic with a modelling knife or a pin vice drill.

You can even have a go at making your own Ork buildings. This one was made from a furniture drawer!

ORK STRONGHOLDS

Orks often construct makeshift strongholds for themselves and these pieces of scenery are an excellent addition to your battlefield. As you can see above, there are already a fort and a stronghold available as card buildings. If you want, you can also add parts from the Battlefield Accessory set such as barrels and tank traps.

PAINTING TIPS

This page details lots of different tips that you will find useful for painting Orks. Look out for more in *White Dwarf* magazine.

BATTLE DAMAGE

Battleworn paint over metal looks great on Ork miniatures and is very easy to do. We used this effect on this Ork's shoulder armour. After painting the armour red, random shapes were painted onto it in Chaos Black. Then Boltgun Metal was painted over the black areas leaving a slight line of black showing. To finish it off, a little Mithril Silver can be painted on to make the metal look really worn.

PAINTING CHECKS

Painting checks onto models and vehicles is simple once you know how. Start by painting the area you want the

check pattern on with Skull White (or any other light colour). Then paint parallel lines horizontally and vertically in Chaos Black to make a grid. Finally paint alternate squares to create a chequered effect.

WARPAINT

One of the best ways to unify your mobs of Orks is warpaint. Choose the colour for the mob and paint marks onto the skin. Ork glyphs look good, as well as simple lines and dags. If the mob belongs to a particular clan, such as an Evil Sunz mob, use warpaint in the appropriate clan colour, in this case red.

DAGS

Also called dog-tooth pattern, dags are a good Orky decoration for both troops and vehicles. First paint a zig-zag pattern and then fill in each alternate triangle.

ORK CONVERSIONS
Individual Orks are just as much fun to convert as their vehicles.

Plastic Orks are perfect for converting, there are so many different combinations that you can really let your imagination run riot. Swapping arms, weapons and heads is the easiest way to change a figure. For instance, adding plates to their front, back and shoulders is a good way of making 'Ard Boyz.

Adrian Wood's crazy Storm Boy conversion.

Note the extra bolts and glyph trimmed off and glued onto this 'Ard Boy.

Brian Nelson's superbly simple conversion features the human head from the Ork sprue.

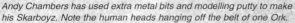

Andy Chambers has used extra metal bits and modelling putty to make his Skarboyz. Note the human heads hanging off the belt of one Ork.

Both these Deathskull Lootas are armed with Space Marine heavy weapons. These conversions are very simple: just cut off the shootas and add the Imperial guns.

This dynamically posed Ork is one of Dave Gallagher's conversions. The legs have been cut to create a headlong charge.

Dave's Ork with big shoota was made by adding an extra barrel length to the shoota and repositioning the legs and feet to get a recoil effect.

BIG TOOF RIVER

The Battle of Big Toof river was created as a display for Games Day '97. Ork fanatics throughout Games Workshop contributed hundreds of figures to create this truly awe-inspiring spectacle.

▲ *A scratch built Ork Fighta Bomma swoops over the battlefield.*

The huge Ork fort dominates one corner of Big Toof river. You can see mob after mob of the Ork defenders pouring onto the battlefield.

Can you spot the Vindicare Assassin? ▶

One of the centre pieces of the whole display is this enormous Gargant built from card, tubing and lots (and lots!) of scavenged bits from kits and other models.

Countless buggies sweep over the hill and onto the Imperial positions.

▶The Stormboyz jump Big Toof river in order to assault the Imperial Guard defenders.

◀ Leading one of the columns of Orks through the outlying Ork buildings is this huge scratch-built Squiggoth.

 ◀ ▲

Captured Imperial vehicles kustomised by the Mekaniaks strike out for the Imperial Tank forces.

31

SHOWCASE

On this page are some of the best Ork models that we've ever seen. The Golden Demon painting competition at Games Day always features loads of great Orky conversions!

Nigel Carman *converted his own Ghazghkull Thraka.*

Andy Chambers' *Waaagh! banner Nob.*

Ork Dreadnought by **José Antonio Romero.**

Steve Buddle *won the best Warhammer 40,000 Vehicle category at Golden Demon '97 with this imaginative looted Imperial vehicle.*

Adrian Wood's *scratch-built battlewagon.*

ORKS

This next part of the Codex is given over to all the bits and pieces that don't form part of the army list or hobby guide. This includes rules for new weapons and wargear detailed in the Ork Armoury and a selection of infamous Ork Warbosses and warriors to use as special characters in your games. In addition to these we have compiled a series of treatises and studies about the Ork race which continues to plague the Imperium. Hopefully these should be of some interest to players who are running campaigns or want to create their own clans and warbands – as well as being a good laugh of course!

TRANSMITTED: Midal II
RECEIVED: Genneman Prime
DESTINATION: Mars
DATE: 6738374.M4I
TELEPATHIC DUCT:
Astropath-terminus Melial
REF: AdMech/01159168298/GW
AUTHOR: Magos Biologis Rastex
TITLE: Preface: Growth patterns of Orks in variant societies

It is widely accepted as fact that prolonged periods of conflict lead to an increase in the size and strength of Orkoid individuals. Our research team set out to investigate whether this phenomenon had additional, further reaching, effects on Ork societies. We have spent the last two decades studying Ork communities in various regions of the Segmentum Obscurus, taking physical samples and comparing their exological composition. The evidence we have gathered is highly conclusive.

Orkoid settlements which have undergone long term isolation, with relatively few Orks [up to 10,000] show a decline in size and stature from those more regularly encountered. Samples taken from Ork colonies in the Paramar and Goliant Sectors, where Orks are low in density, showed a decrease in body mass of 15–19%. They were less physically aggressive [although still capable of tearing a man limb from limb if necessary]. To compensate for this reduction of stature, greater reliance is placed on their crude technology, with ranged fighting taking greater precedence over the brutal affair of close mêlée. This sub-type of Ork is not widely found, both due to their lack of numbers and also the fact that such developments take place in the most solitary and backwater conditions.

Conversely, Orks in greater numbers are much more likely to be fiercer in combat; more aggressive and short tempered; impatient and less likely to employ ranged weaponry with any noticeable effect. It appears that the greater the number of Orks present [on a global and interplanetary scale] the more the Orks' savage basic instincts prevail. Such specimens are physically larger than their scattered counterparts, and the muscle:mass ratio of their exological make-up is greater [in other words there is literally strength in numbers for the Orks].

Attempts to penetrate the so-called Ork enclaves of Gathrog and Dregruk in the southern regions of the Segmentum have proved unsuccessful. The Orks have dominated these areas unchecked since before the founding of the Imperium and it is, quite reasonably, surmised that within an area of only a few light years there are tens of millions of the creatures. It is possible that in such conditions the Orks' physical proportions are even more pronounced, with whole planetary populations the size of the sub-type known to our warriors as 'Skarboyz'. When one considers the size of the 'Nobz' and 'Warbosses' of even relatively small Ork armies, one shudders to think of the monstrous creatures that must dominate these cultures. Should ever such a monster be filled with a desire for conquest, it is a matter of much debate whether any military means at our disposal could stop them.

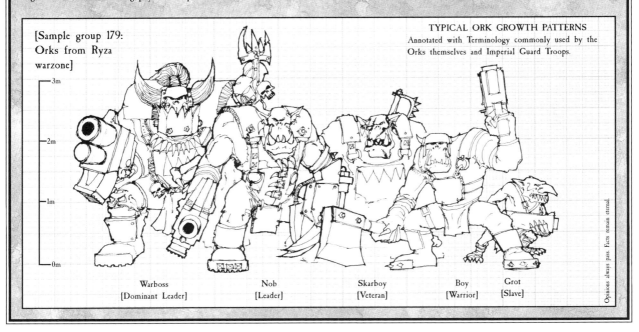

[Sample group 179: Orks from Ryza warzone]

TYPICAL ORK GROWTH PATTERNS
Annotated with Terminology commonly used by the Orks themselves and Imperial Guard Troops.

| Warboss [Dominant Leader] | Nob [Leader] | Skarboy [Veteran] | Boy [Warrior] | Grot [Slave] |

Opinions always pass. Facts remain eternal.

ORK WARGEAR

*T*he following rules describe how all of the specialised equipment used by Orks works during a battle. These rules tend to be more detailed than those in the Warhammer 40,000 rulebook, and supersede them if they are different. Anything not listed here functions exactly as described in the Warhammer 40,000 rulebook.

Ammo Runt

An ammo runt is a heavily overburdened Gretchin who carries a massive amount of extra ammo for his master. One Ork model in base-to-base contact with an ammo runt in the shooting phase is allowed to re-roll one To Hit dice. The ammo runt is removed once the re-roll has been used – it can be imagined that the runt has gone running back to camp to fetch more ammo for his master (but with typical Grot slovenliness will not return during the battle!).

An ammo runt may not be chosen as a casualty caused by enemy shooting (they stay well out of the way 'cos they're carrying lots of ammo!) but Blast markers and template weapons will affect them as normal. Ammo runts removed because they are 'used up' do not count for morale or victory points purposes.

	WS	BS	S	T	W	I	A	Ld	Sv
Ammo Runt	2	2	2	2	1	2	1	5	–

Attack Squig

Some varieties of squig are vicious predators with razor sharp fangs or a poisonous bite. Attack squigs are specially trained to accompany an Ork character and attack the enemy on command. They have the following characteristics:

	WS	BS	S	T	W	I	A	Ld	Sv
Attack Squig	3	0	3	3	1	4	2	3	6+

Choppa

Beloved of Ork Nobz in particular, choppas are usually immense axe-like weapons or brutal cleavers. Choppas frequently have a chainsaw edge to make them extra rippy when it comes to chopping through armour. In close combat choppas limit the armour saving throw an enemy model can have to a 4+ at best. So, for example, if a Space Marine in power armour or Terminator armour were hit and wounded by an Ork with a choppa they would have to roll a 4 or more to make their saving throw.

Big Horns/Iron Gob

Ork leaders commonly display their prowess by hunting down and killing dangerous beasts. The creatures they fight against the most are those with big horns or tusks which can then be displayed on the Nob's helmet for all the Boyz to see. If such a creature has a disappointing lack of horns or tusks the Ork leader will sport a huge metal jaw instead to show that he has got the biggest bite around! If a mob is led by a Warboss or Nob with either Big Horns or an Iron Gob they add +1 to their Leadership value. Note that the two may not be combined to get a +2 bonus.

Bionik Arm

Ork bioniks are typically crude but effective. Ork bionik arms are equipped with built-in weapons as standard – be they one-shot sluggas, retractable spikes, ferocious creatures in cages or something even more unsubtle. An Ork with a bionik arm causes one automatic Strength 4 hit in close combat with the equivalent of Initiative 6, but only if in base-to-base contact with the target. The plethora of spikes, blades and other hurty bits welded on to the arm mean it also counts as an additional close combat weapon. This may not be combined with mega armour.

Bionik Bonce

Orks with serious head injuries may well come back from the Mad Dok's with most of their cranium replaced by solid armour plates. An Ork with a bionik bonce adds +1 to its armour saving throw. This may not be combined with mega armour.

Bosspole

In addition to their Big Horns and Iron Gobs, successful Nobz have a trophy pole to carry interesting souvenirs from foes they have defeated in battle. The pole may be carried by the Nob (strapped to his back) or by a member of his mob (including a Grot but not a squig). An Ork mob trying to mob up with a mob carrying a bosspole may re-roll their Leadership test if they fail on the first try.

Burna

Burnas are cutting torches used by Mekboyz for carving up vehicle wrecks into useable chunks. However, a quick twist of the mixture valve and WHOOOSH! the burna spits out a blast of incinerating flames. A burna may be fired in the shooting phase with the stats shown below or used in close combat as a power weapon. It may not be used to shoot and fight in close combat within the same turn. In close combat, burnas roll 2D6 instead of 1D6 for armour penetration against vehicles.

Range	Str	AP	Notes
Template	4	5	Assault 1

Cybork Body

Critically injured Orks may survive to fight again after an extensive rebuild at the Mad Dok's. An Ork with a Cybork body can survive terrible injuries and so gains a 5+ invulnerable saving throw.

Dok's Tools

A Mad Dok with Dok's tools can have a go at 'fixin' one wounded Ork in the mob he is in each turn at the end of his enemy's shooting phase, even Orks reduced to zero wounds can be saved... perhaps! If several Orks have been wounded the Mad Dok can choose which to assist. Roll a D6 for his efforts and look up the result below.

D6	Result
1	**Aaargh!** The Ork suffers 1 wound. If reduced to zero wounds, remove the Ork as a casualty.
2-5	**Da patient is restin'....** The Dok achieves precisely nothing this time. If the Ork had been reduced to zero wounds remove it as a casualty.
6	**Job's a good 'un!** The Ork regains 1 wound, up to the maximum it started the game with.

'Eavy Armour

Ork 'eavy armour is made up of thick armour plates shaped to fit an Ork (sort of) and cover up its few vulnerable spots. This gives the Ork wearing it a 4+ armour save.

Grabba Stik

Grabba stiks are long catchpoles that Slaverz use to catch wayward Grots. In close combat a Slaver armed with a grabba stik can make its full number of attacks even if it is 2" away from an enemy model. The stik's effects may not be combined with any other special close combat weapons or attacks.

Grot Orderly

Mad Doks often have a small gaggle of Gretchin slaves that help fetch and carry, stitch wounds, etc. Each orderly in base-to-base contact with a Mad Dok gives him a +1 bonus on the dice roll for using Dok's tools, up to a max of +3. However the Grot's enthusiasm often exceeds its capabilities so a roll of 1 before bonuses always fails and inflicts a wound on the unfortunate patient.

	WS	BS	S	T	W	I	A	Ld	Sv
Grot orderly	2	2	2	2	1	2	1	5	–

Grot Oiler

Mekboyz use Grot slaves to carry their tools, hold stuff in place, bash in extra nails, etc. Each Grot oiler in base-to-base contact with a Mekboy gives them a +1 bonus to the dice roll for using their Mek's tools, up to a maximum of +3. Grot oilers sometimes get under the Mek's feet and pull the wrong wires out so a roll of 1 always fails.

	WS	BS	S	T	W	I	A	Ld	Sv
Grot Oiler	2	2	2	2	1	2	1	5	–

Kannon

Kannon are heavy guns mounted on wheeled carriages and crewed by Gretchin. They can fire either a big bore frag round for blasting infantry or a solid shell for punching through tanks. They are appallingly inaccurate but make very, very big holes when they hit!

Kannon may use frag or shell rounds: choose which you are firing with before rolling to hit. Frag rounds are resolved in the same way as ordnance but use the small Blast marker – place the marker (within range and line of sight) and roll the Scatter dice and a D6. The marker moves D6" in the direction indicated if an arrow is rolled. If a 'hit' is rolled the shot lands on target but if a 6 is rolled on the D6 a hit is scored and one of the Gretchin krew is killed in a nasty firing accident. Kannons firing shells roll to hit as normal and have a BS of 2.

Against vehicles shells count as an ordnance hit, so roll 2D6 for armour penetration and pick the highest results. Any penetrating hits roll for damage on the Ordnance Damage table, for glancing hits use the Glancing Hits table as normal. Kannon have the following characteristics:

	Range	Str	AP	Notes
Kannon (Frag)	36"	5	5	Heavy 1/Blast
Kannon (Shell)	36"	8	3	Heavy 1

Kombi-Weapons

A kombi-weapon is two weapons nailed/wired/welded together, and gives the Ork a choice of two weapons to fire with. An Ork that is armed with a kombi-weapon may choose to fire one of the weapons during the shooting phase. The shoota may be fired any number of times, but the other weapon is only allowed to be fired once per battle. Note that you may not choose to fire both of these weapons at the same time. A kombi-weapon may be upgraded with kustom jobs but the customising only applies to the shoota part of the weapon.

Kustom Mega-Blasta

A kustom mega-blasta is a marvel of Ork technology which works by firing a blast of energy at the target. However, if a mega-blasta rolls a 1 To Hit it scores a wound on the Ork carrying it (normal armour saves apply) or scores a glancing hit on the vehicle carrying it.

Range	Str	AP	Notes
24"	7	2	Heavy 1/Blast/gets hot!

Kustom Force Field

Mekboyz have an uncanny understanding of battlefield technology and will sometimes build or scavenge powerful force field projectors to protect the Boyz on the battlefield.

A kustom force field gives all models within 6" a 5+ cover saving throw, vehicles within 6" are treated as being hull down. The force field has no effect in close combat or against shooting within 6" of the operator.

Kustom Job: More Dakka

Mekboyz spend much of their time tinkering with weaponry to make it more powerful or faster to fire. More Dakka kustomisin' makes a shoota or slugga Assault 2 instead of rapid fire or pistol respectively (More Dakka sluggas may still be used in close combat however). A More Dakka kustom job may be combined with a Shootier kustom job to produce a S5, assault 2 shoota or slugga.

Kustom Job: Shootier

Just as popular as More Dakka kustom jobs, Shootier weapons use a larger calibre and heavier ammo to give them more punch. A Shootier kustom job makes a shoota or slugga S5 instead of S4.

Kustom Job: Blasta

A shoota or slugga with the Blasta kustom job has extra heavy duty armour piercing ammo or is radically altered so that it fires a lethal energy bolt capable of burning through armour. A Blasta kustom job gives a shoota or slugga AP3 at up to 12" range, increasing to AP2 if the target is within 6". But a shoota or slugga with the Blasta kustom job gets hot just like a plasma weapon, so on a roll of 1 To Hit the weapon scores a wound on its firer; normal armour saves apply. A Blasta kustom job may be combined with Shootier and/or More Dakka kustom jobs.

Lobba

These are artillery pieces crewed by Gretchin. They are called lobbas because they 'lob' their payload in a high arc onto the enemy. How they go about lobbing their munitions varies. Most look like big mortars or howitzers but rockets are popular too and there have even been reports of medieval-style catapults and trebuchets being used. Regardless of their type all lobbas work in the same way as standard barrage weapons – guess range and roll for scatter. However if a 'Hit' and a 6 are rolled together a hit is scored but one of the Lobba's Gretchin krew is killed in an unfortunate mishap (launched high into the air, crushed by the Lobba's recoil, etc).

Range	Str	AP	Notes
Guess 48"	5	5	Heavy 1/Blast

Mega Armour

Mega armour is a suit of massively thick and heavy armour plates over a powered exo-skeleton. Though slow mega armour has the advantages of giving a 2+ armour save and includes a shoota and power claw. However, an Ork in mega armour always moves as if in difficult terrain including during assaults, advances and fall back moves (but there's no extra penalty if it actually moving through difficult terrain). If you have a unit that includes several Orks with mega armour just make one roll to see how far the Orks get. Mega armour weaponry may not be changed for other types (because it's built in) but the shoota may be upgraded to a kombi-shoota and/or a kustom shoota. An Ork in mega armour may not use the following abilities, equipment or weapons: *jump packs, bikes, infiltration, bioniks, frag or krak stikkbombz or tankbusta bombz.*

Mega Boosta

Some mega armoured Orks get extra power boost units fitted to their suits to ensure that they don't miss out on any chances for a fight. If an Ork in mega armour has a mega boosta he is allowed to re-roll his dice for the distance he moves. If a unit of Orks in mega armour includes some with mega boostas and some without only the ones that have the boostas will gain the benefit of the re-roll, the others will only move the distance first rolled.

Mekboy's Tools

A Mekboy equipped with Mekboy's tools can attempt to repair a vehicle which has suffered an 'Immobilised' or 'Weapon destroyed' damage result, or to fix a big gun which has been destroyed. In order to attempt a repair the Mekboy has to reach the vehicle or gun in his movement phase and may not shoot or fight in close combat that turn. At the end of the turn roll a D6 and look up the result on the table below.

D6	Result
1	**Krunch!** Oops! If it wasn't broken before it is now! No further repair attempts can be made on the vehicle unless it becomes damaged again.
2-5	**Umm, dis bit goes dere...** The Mekboy makes no progress this turn. He can keep trying in his next turn or give up and go somewhere else.
6	**Job's a good 'un!** The weapon/big gun is fixed or the vehicle is made mobile again.

Skorcha

A skorcha is an Ork vehicle-mounted flamethrower which sprays a gout of burning fuel over the target area, reducing it to a burning shambles in seconds. Some kustom-kombi shootas are built to include a skorcha barrel and enough fuel for one shot. The skorcha has the following profile:

Range	Str	AP	Notes
Template	5	4	Assault 1

Squighound

Squigs are simple creatures genetically related to Orks that form an essential part of Ork ecology (or Orkology). Some are trained as guards and hunters, particularly by Slaverz. A Slaver with a squighound in base contact may re-roll Leadership tests and Morale checks for the Grot mob or Big Gun battery he is leading. The Squighound is represented by a separate model with the following characteristics:

	WS	BS	S	T	W	I	A	Ld	Sv
Squighound	3	0	3	3	1	2	1	2	–

Super Stikkbombz

Mekboyz can't resist improving something, even if it makes that something hideously dangerous in the process. Super stikkbombz are a case in point, each one is a bundle of krak bombz wired together to make one almighty bang.

Super stikkbombz work just like krak stikkbombz but have an armour penetration of 10+2D6. If a double is rolled on the 2D6 the attack is resolved as normal but the Mekboy using them is also caught in the explosion, he suffers a wound automatically but may attempt an armour save as normal.

Stikkbomb Chukka

A stikkbomb chukka allows a mega armoured Ork to use frag stikkbombz so that it can fight troops in cover simultaneously instead of striking last. A mega armoured Ork which chooses to use a stikkbomb chucka must attack with its basic Strength instead of using its power claw that turn.

Tankbusta bombz

These bombz are directional explosive charges the size of manhole covers. They are used by Orks against vehicles and fortifications which krak stikkbombz just aren't heavy enough to break. Tankbusta bombz are used just like krak grenades to attack vehicles and bunkers. However Tankbusta bombz double the D6 roll for penetrating armour, giving them an armour penetration of 6+(D6x2).

'Uge Choppa

'Uge choppas are unsubtle double-handed hitting implements easily capable of cleaving an opponent in two. An Ork with an 'uge choppa always strikes last in close combat but adds +2 to their Strength and their opponent's maximum save is reduced to 4+. An Ork using an 'uge choppa may not use any other close combat weapons at the same time.

'Urty Syringe

Mad Doks carry all kinds of crude, rusty, medical paraphernalia. Most of the saws, blades and hammers they carry make perfect close combat weapons, but a special favourite is a huge steel syringe filled with a toxic goo of the Dok's own devising. A Mad Dok armed with an 'urty syringe always wounds on a 4+ regardless of the victim's Toughness. 'Urty syringes have no effect on vehicles, Tyranids, Daemons, Eldar Wraithguard or the Eldar Avatar.

Waaagh! Banner

This banner is carried by a Warboss or his bodyguard to show how dangerous the warband is. It is decorated with glyphs declaring the warband's invincibility and mementoes of defeated foes. The banner has an almost religious significance to Orks and they will fight ferociously in its presence. Any mob that has one or more models within 12" of the banner may re-roll their *Power of the Waaagh!* test when they charge.

Zzap Gun

These guns are powerful, but unpredictable, energy cannon that are crewed by Gretchin. The gun automatically hits any single unit within range and line of sight. Simply pick a target and roll 2D6 to determine the strength of each hit (up to S10). If the gun rolls an 11 or 12 for its Strength it overheats, no hit is scored and one of the Gretchin is killed. If the weapon is mounted on a vehicle, there are no additional effects. Against vehicles the gun rolls its Strength on 2D6 as normal and then adds 2D6 to the Armour Penetration roll.

Range	Str	AP	Notes
24"	2D6	2	Heavy 1

ORK VEHICLE UPGRADES

Armour Plates
A vehicle with armour plates has extra protection against hits. Roll a D6 for each glancing or penetrating hit caused against it. On a 6 the hit is ignored because it's deflected by the armour. Armour plates will have no effect against ordnance hits 'cause they're just too big! There are two costs for armour plates. The cheaper one is for vehicles worth 50 points or less (including any other upgrades they have apart from the armour plates) the second is for vehicles that are worth 51 or more points.

Big Grabber/Wrecker Ball/
Reinforced Ram/Boarding Plank
Although these upgrades work in different ways their effects are the same. They allow an Ork vehicle to attack an enemy vehicle in close combat. The Ork vehicle must move into contact with the target vehicle during its movement phase but may not attack if it moved more than 12".

The Ork vehicle may shoot in the shooting phase as normal and then resolves an attack in the assault phase. The vehicle has one attack for each upgrade listed (ie, a vehicle with a boarding plank, big grabber and ram would have 3 attacks). Attacks hit on a 4+ regardless of the target's speed and are resolved with a Strength of 6. Walkers, skimmers, infantry and any other models that have a WS characteristic may not be attacked as these weapons are too cumbersome to be used against them.

Bolt-on Big Shoota
(Wartrukks and Battlewagons Only)
A bolt-on big shoota can only be mounted onto a Wartrukk or Battlewagon. It can be fired by one of the Boyz on board who is a passenger as long as the vehicle itself does not move more than 12" that turn.

Grot Riggers
An Ork vehicle with Grot riggers on board which becomes immobilised will be able to start moving again on a D6 roll of 4+. You can test to see if the vehicle becomes mobile at the start of each Ork turn.

Searchlight
Searchlights are only of any use in missions where the rules for night fighting are being used, such as the Night Fight mission. They allow one enemy unit spotted by the vehicle or Dreadnought to be fired at by any other Ork units that are in range and have a line of fire (the enemy unit has been illuminated by the vehicle's searchlight).

However, a vehicle or Dreadnought that uses a searchlight can be fired on by any enemy units in their next turn, as they can see the searchlight shining out into the darkness.

Spikes 'n' Blades (not wartrukks)
Enemy infantry which try to attack a vehicle that has spikes 'n blades in close combat and miss suffer a S3 hit. Wartrukks may not be fitted with spikes 'n' blades because da Boyz would get skewered by them when they jumped off!

Stikkbomb Chucka
A vehicle or Dreadnought equipped with stikkbomb chuckas can make a Tank Shock attack even though it isn't a tank. A vehicle may not move more than 12" and attempt to tank shock and a Dreadnought can only attempt a Tank Shock attack in its movement phase. In the assault phase it must move into close combat instead. If a proper tank is equipped with stikkbomb chuckas any tank shock it inflicts has an extra -1 modifier to the troops Morale check.

Turbo Boosta
A vehicle with turbo boostas can trigger them in any of its movement phases. The turbo boostas add D6" to its movement, but for shooting and disembarking troops the vehicle counts as moving at the speed it went before the turbo boosters were added. The extra D6" movement must be used to move in a straight line and if a 4+ is rolled the vehicle and any passengers onboard may not shoot or disembark that turn as they're too busy hanging on for grim death.

Red Paint Job
An Ork vehicle with a red paint job adds +1" to all of its move distances. So, for example, a fast Ork vehicle with a red paint job could move 13" and still fire one weapon and/or disembark troops or move 25" and not fire at all.

The big gunz boomed out with an earthshaking roar and their deadly cargo screamed overhead. Boss Grubnatz squinted over the shattered wall at the Space Marines deploying at the bottom of the hill. They were unfolding into neat ranks like a well-oiled machine, apparently oblivious to the explosions and shrapnel scything past. He hawked and spat a huge glob of green phlem over the wall. There were loads of them, almost as many of them as there were Orks in the ruins.

He ducked back down and looked over his own boyz. After months of fighting the survivors were getting bigger and tougher, their green hides thicker and more gnarled just like proper Orks. They were all excitedly slapping magazines into their shootas, cracking knuckles, sharpening fangs and blades and bragging about how many Marine-boyz they were going to kill. Grubnatz decided that he would have to keep an eye on young Skabsnik – the extra slabs of muscle he was growing and the truculent look in his eye showed he had started getting ideas about being Boss. He'd need to be taught a lesson pretty soon.

Time for that later, thought Grubnatz as he cursed them all roundly for being slackers and kicked them into a fighting line, no more than two or three to each gap in the wall. The last boyz were just in place as Space Marine bolter fire started blasting lumps out of the wall.

Grubnatz bounded to his feet and started blazing away, the boyz following suit. Up and down the ruins he could hear shouts and other mobs firing (though Grubnatz reckoned he'd got off the first shot). The noise alone was incredible, it pounded at his ears like a tribe of insane drummers. Great daggers of flame stabbed out from their shootas and hot shell casings spewed everywhere. The resulting storm of fire whipped across the armoured ranks and sparks flew as shots ricocheted off the Space Marines' armour, some of them fell but the line kept stubbornly advancing.

There was a flash and roar a split second before Grubnatz found himself hurled to the ground. A series of raucous explosions followed, rubble and dust flew from the walls with each concussion. Smoke and flames were snaking through the ruins as the boyz clambered to their feet. Several were wounded and some didn't get back up at all, even when they were kicked. Skabsnik was incautious enough to stand up right next to a gap in the wall and was blown to bits by bolter fire where he stood. Grubnatz felt vaguely disappointed that he wouldn't get to fight Skabsnik now that the stupid zogger had got himself perished. The Space Marines must be getting close now, time to back off to the courtyard. He led the dazed remnants of the mob in a crouching run back to the hollow shells of the buildings on the other side of the courtyard. Shots snarled and roared over their heads as they ran but nobody was hit.

There the big gunz were being readied for another shot. Slavers cracked their whips, eliciting thin shrieks of pain from the Grots struggling to push the guns into position and lug more ammo forward. Grubnatz took his boyz to join up with the remnants of Ruzgob's mob. Ruzgob and his boyz jeered them as they came up but it put more heart back in the boyz as they jeered back.

"Got chewed up an' spat out?" Ruzgob shouted.

"Dinna see you up there wormfood!" retorted Grubnatz.

"You was too busy runnin' like a runt", Ruzgob added emphasis by kicking his ammo runt a good three metres. It was an impressive kick but Grubnatz wasn't about to concede that. At that point armoured figures pushed through gaps in the outer wall and further exchanges of wit were cut short by the big gunz going off again with a crash that sounded like the end of the world.

The carnage was impressive, what was left of the wall was painted with bright red blood and armoured bodies were piled high around it. Ruzgob and Grubnatz led their boyz into the open and charged forward, howling and loosing off shots as they ran. The surviving Space Marines didn't run for it or even back away, though Grubnatz had fought Space Marines before so he didn't really expect them to, instead they levelled their bolters and started firing. Boyz were blown apart left, right and centre but they kept going, Grubnatz' boyz weren't going to be outdone by Ruzgob's skum. As they were about to barrel into the Space Marines a huge chunk of wall tumbled inward and the massive, armoured shape of a Dreadnought lurched through the gap with its cannon blazing at the charging mobs.

Without pause the Dreadnought plowed into Ruzgob's mob like a juggernaut and almost disappeared as Orks hurled themselves at it. The Space Marines charged to protect their Dreadnought and in an instant the whole courtyard had dissolved into a sprawling hand-to-hand combat. This was the time all Orks lived for – the roaring, blood-pumping, heart-racing mayhem of face-to-face fighting. Grubnatz brought his choppa down on the helm of the first Space Marine he reached but it glanced off the shoulder plate. The Space Marine raised a bolt pistol and blew a big chunk out of Grubnatz shoulder, which stung like crazy and made him really mad.

Grubnatz struck back with a roar, hitting at the joints in the Space Marine's armour; elbows, knees, neck – that was where they were vulnerable. In a few quick chops the Space Marine was face down in the mud and Grubnatz was blasting his slugga into the back of another one his boyz were having trouble with. Ricochets flew wildly but one shot hit something vital and the Space Marine crumpled. Grubnatz' arm was starting to stiffen up now from the wound but his blood sang with the joy of violence too much to take notice. He blazed away with his slugga, revelling in the solid kick of it each time it fired. When it was empty he threw it at the Dreadnought, which was busy ripping bits off the last of Ruzgob's boyz. He roared with laughter and swung his choppa to split the skull of a Space Marine who was trying to get to his feet – this was the life!

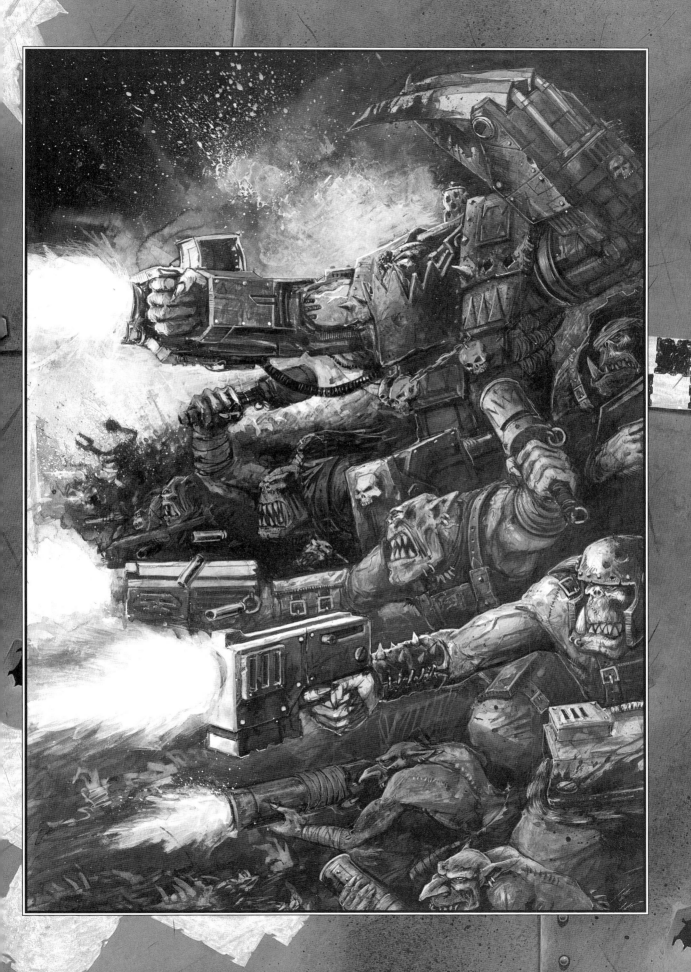

WARLORD GHAZGHKULL MAG URUK THRAKA

WARLORD GHAZGHKULL										
	Points	WS	BS	S	T	W	I	A	Ld	Sv
Ghazghkull	226	6	2	5	4(5)	3	4	4	9(10)	2+

An Ork army of at least 2,000 points may be led by Ghazghkull. If you include him then he counts as a HQ choice for the army. He must be used as described below, and may not have any additional equipment from the Ork Armoury.

Wargear: Iron gob, bosspole, mega armour, mega boosta, stikkbomb chucka, *Adamantium skull*, kustom shoota (S5 Assault 2).

SPECIAL RULES

Adamantium Skull: In some forgotten firefight long ago Ghazghkull took a bolter round in the head and was almost killed. He was saved by the 'skills' of Orky serjery and his own Ork hardiness.

The adamantium skull plate he now has adds +1 to his Toughness (as shown on his profile above). When Ghazghkull charges into combat he gets an extra free head butt attack against one model in base contact with him. The head butt is resolved as an attack made with an Initiative of 4, roll to hit as normal for a close combat blow and if a hit is scored roll to wound with Ghazghkull's Strength of 5. A model that suffers a wound from the head butt is stunned for the rest of the turn and may not attack in close combat.

Power of the Waaagh!: Ghazghkull has always been a mighty prophet of the Waaagh! and is capable of rousing entire planetary populations of Orks into a frenzy of conquest and bloodshed. Once, during a battle, Ghazghkull can unleash the power of the Waaagh! the awesome unconscious psychic energy of Orks fighting. This can be summoned at any time including during an opponent's turn. For the remainder of that player's turn and all of the following player's turn Ghazghkull gains a 2+ Invulnerable save. In addition, for the duration of the Waaagh! all Orks pass their Leadership tests and Morale checks automatically and recover from pinning immediately. Orks fighting in close combat double their Initiative just as if they had charged and passed a mob size check this turn. Note that Grots never benefit from the power of the Waaagh! (they're just too weedy).

Goff Army: Ghazghkull is a member of the Goff clan and his army is shaped by his prejudices. An army including Ghazghkull must have at least one mob of Skarboyz but may not include more than one unit of each of the following troops or vehicles: *Kommandos, Burna Boyz, Wartraks/Buggies, Warbikes, Big Gunz, Lootas and Looted vehicles.*

Independent Character: Unless accompanied by a bodyguard, Ghazghkull is an independent character and follows all the independent character rules as given in the Warhammer 40,000 rulebook.

Bodyguard: Ghazghkull can be accompanied by a Ork Warboss bodyguard.

"I'm da hand of Gork and Mork, dey sent me to rouse up da boyz to crush and kill 'cos da boyz forgot what dere 'ere for. I woz one of da boyz till da godz smashed me in da 'ead an' I 'membered dat Orks is meant to conquer and make slaves of everyfing they don't kill.

I'm da profit of da Waaagh an' whole worlds burn in my boot prints. On Armour-Geddem I led da boyz through da fire deserts and smashed da humies' metal cities to scrap. I fought Yarik, old one-eye at Tartarus, an' he fought good but we smashed iz city too.

I'm death to anyfing dat walks or crawls, where I go nothin' stands in my way. We crushed da stunties on Golgotha, an' we caught old one-eye when da speed freeks blew da humies' big tanks ta bits. I let 'im go 'cause good enemies iz 'ard ta find, an Orks need good enemies ta fight like they need meat ta eat an' grog ta drink.

I iz more cunnin' than a Grot an' more killy dan a dread, da boyz dat follow me can't be beat. On Pissenah we jumped da marine-boyz an' our bosspoles was covered in da helmets we took from da dead 'uns. We burned dere port an' killed dere bosses an' left nothin' but ruins behind.

I'm Warlord Ghazghkull Mag Uruk Thraka an' I speak wiv da word of da gods. We iz gonna stomp da 'ooniverse flat an' kill anyfing that fights back. We iz gonna do this coz we're Orks an' we was made ta fight an' win."

Graffiti on Warlord Titan Wreckage found by Dark Angels at Westerisle, Piscina IV

WARLORD NAZDREG UG URDGRUB

WARLORD NAZDREG

	Points	WS	BS	S	T	W	I	A	Ld	Sv
Nazdreg	186	5	4	5	4	3	3	4	9	2+

An Ork army of at least 2,000 points may be led by Nazdreg. If you decide to include him then he counts as one of the HQ choices for the army. He must be used exactly as described below, and may not be given any additional equipment from the Ork Armoury.

Wargear: Bosspole, mega armour, mega boosta, stikkbomb chucka, *Kustom Blast-X*.

SPECIAL RULES

Kustom Blasta-X: Nazdreg 'persuaded' a Mekboy to build a special kustom blasta onto his mega armour. This has the following characteristics:

Rng: 36"   Str: 7   AP: 2   Type: Assault 1, Blast*

*Gets hot as per plasma weapons.

Kunnin' plans: Nazdreg is renowned for his low cunning and sneaky plans. To represent this one Elites or Troops mob in Nazdreg's army can use either the *Infiltrators* or *Deep Strike* rules. If the option to Deep Strike is chosen, this may be used regardless of whether the scenario normally uses these rules. The mob chosen must be on foot and may not number more than twenty models.

Bad Moon Army: Nazdreg is a member of the Bad Moon clan and his well-equipped army will reflect this. If Nazdreg leads an army it may include up to one extra Heavy Support unit over and above the number shown on the force organisation chart. It may not include more than one unit of each of the following troops or vehicles: *Skarboyz, Stormboyz, Kommandos, Slugga Boyz, Stikk Bommas.*

Independent Character: Unless accompanied by a bodyguard, Nazdreg is an independent character and follows all the independent character rules as given in the Warhammer 40,000 rulebook.

Bodyguard: Nazdreg may be accompanied by an Ork Warboss bodyguard.

Commit to: Imperial Record RTS 05/1103
Inquisitoria 39011/4270
Crossfile To: Piracy SO/SS   Scylla ASHulks HI
Warlords OR/BM
Input Date: 5037998M41
Input Clearance: Inquisitor Tobias
Author: Inquisitor Nastor   Transmitted: Kaballas
Transmitter: Astropath Primus Tien'Szar
Thought For The Day: Ruthlessness is the kindness of the wise.

My investigations into the recent events within the Abiaus Sector have confirmed the reports that the Ork Warlord Nazdreg is operating in this area of space. Certain numbers of the citizens liberated from the Ork slave-world of Charakis eleven months ago reported seeing a huge and well-fleshed Ork leader in black and yellow armour directing the Orks there. By their account this leader spoke good Imperial Gothic and used reward as well as punishment to ensure increased production of munitions and armaments. The citizens involved have subsequently been placed into penal servitude for their betrayal of the Emperor in allowing themselves to be captured. I also asked a number of officers and soldiers at Hellaspont and I believe that Nazdreg's warband participated in the sacking of that planet, bringing the number of Imperial worlds which this beast has assailed to eighteen.

Evidently despite the destruction of Nazdreg's hulk, codenamed Scylla, in orbital battles around the fourth planet of the Piscina system it would now appear that he escaped, presumably on a surviving Ork vessel and left the system. I must confess to no small disappointment that the considerable forces directed to Piscina have failed to destroy either Nazdreg or Ghazghkull once and for all. However with the Emperor's blessing their schemes have been frustrated and given well known Ork rivalries I find it unlikely that they will act in concert again.

Given Nazdreg's past history of raiding and piracy I suspect he will remain as elusive as ever. The loss of the Scylla seems to have limited the scope of his ventures somewhat and it may be the case that he is seeking another space hulk as a replacement. If this is the case I can only pray that this thorn in our sides falls prey to Genestealers, renegades or something worse.

Your Ob'dt Servant: Brother Nastor

BOSS ZAGSTRUK AND DA VULCHA BOYZ

BOSS ZAGSTRUK										
	Points	WS	BS	S	T	W	I	A	Ld	Sv
Zagstruck	55	4	2	4	4	2	3	3	8	6+

Any Ork army of at least 1,000 points may be joined by Zagstruk and his Vulchas and they count as an Elites choice for the army. He must be used exactly as described below, and may not be given any additional equipment from the Ork Armoury.

Wargear: Jump pack, choppa, tankbusta bombz, frag stikkbombz, kustom slugga (S5 Assault 2).

SPECIAL RULES

Da Vulchas: Zagstruk always leads a mob of hand-picked Stormboyz into battle. These are chosen from the army list in the normal fashion and cost the same number of points. The Vulchas all use Zagstruk's *Turbo Swoop* ability on any turn that he does.

Turbo Swoop: Zagstruk and his Vulchas are prepared to push their jump packs beyond sane limits and swoop down upon their foes at full speed. When they make an assault the Vulchas may move up to 12". The increased velocity also means that Zagstruk and the Vulchas add +1 to their Strength when they charge. However, there is always a chance that the Vulchas have pushed things too far so they must always make a Difficult Terrain test for landing. Roll a D6 for each model in the unit (including Zagstruk): on a 2-6 the model landed alright, on a 1 the model crashes horribly and is removed as a casualty (no armour saves allowed). Make tests for landing after all attacks have been resolved (even a crashing Vulcha can take some of the enemy with them!) but any crash casualties count towards the close combat results.

> "If ya wanna be big an' mean,
> If ya wanna be best an' green,
> If ya wanna get da job done fast,
> Da Vulcha skwad iz where it's at!"
>
> Lift-off chant of the Vulcha Skwad

MAD DOK GROTSNIK

MAD DOK GROTSNIK										
	Points	WS	BS	S	T	W	I	A	Ld	Sv
Grotsnik	96	4	2	4	4(5)	2	3	3	7	3+

Any Ork army of at least 1,000 points may joined by Mad Dok Grotsnik. He counts as an HQ choice for the army and must be used as described here. He may not be given any additional equipment from the Ork Armoury.

Wargear: Power claw, slugga, 'eavy armour, Cybork body, bionik bonce, bionik arm, Dok's tools.

"Operate! Operate! Still time to operate!"

SPECIAL RULES

Mad!: Nutso, two slices short of a loaf, not playing with a full deck – you get the picture! Because of this Grotsnik is completely immune to the effects of morale and pinning. During the Ork turn Grotsnik will always move straight towards the nearest enemy and assault it if he is within range.

Bad Influence: If Grotsnik is part of a mob his crazed enthusiasm for mayhem infects the Boyz as well. Not only do they become immune to the effects of morale and pinning but they also move straight towards the nearest enemy and assault it if they can – they follow their Mad Dok in his headlong charge to glory!

More Machine than Ork: The extensive rebuilding Mad Dok Grotsnik has undertaken increases his Toughness characteristic by 1.

Independent Character: Mad Dok Grotsnik is an independent character and follows all the special rules as given in the Warhammer 40,000 rulebook.

BOSS SNIKROT AND DA REDSKULL KOMMANDOS

BOSS SNIKROT

	Points	WS	BS	S	T	W	I	A	Ld	Sv
Snikrot	45	4	2	4	4	2	4	3	7	6+

Any Ork army of at least 1,000 points may joined by Snikrot and his Kommandos and they count as an Elites choice for the army. He must be used exactly as described below, and may not be given any additional equipment from the Ork Armoury.

Wargear: Choppa, slugga, tankbusta bombz, frag stikkbombz.

SPECIAL RULES

Da Redskull Kommando: Snikrot leads a mob of expert kommandos who have fought on a dozen worlds. These are chosen from the army list in the normal fashion and cost the same number of points.

Unseen, Unheard: Snikrot and the Redskull Kommandos are such experts at sneaking that any enemy unit which wants to fire at them must check to see if they can spot them first using the scenario special rules for Night Fighting. Roll 2D6 and multiply the result by three: if Snikrot and his Kommandos are not within this distance in inches the enemy unit's firing is wasted – they blast away at half-seen shapes to no effect. If Snikrot and the Kommandos are within range resolve the enemy unit's firing as normal. If the battle is actually taking place at night then the normal spotting distance is halved (after it has been multiplied by three).

Backstabbers: Being expert Kommandos, Snikrot and the Boyz are especially good at eliminating sentries. Sentries halve their Initiative value when attempting to spot Snikrot and the Boyz and a sentry killed in close combat will only raise the alarm on a roll of 6 instead of 4+.

Provost-Major: You claim that the Orks took you by surprise attack? A race, I might add, not noted for their subtlety of tactics.

Lieutenant Gordo: I swear by the Emperor's immortal benevolence! We had pickets at fifty-pace intervals with regular half-hour contacts. There were no reports of enemy activity in our segment. The first we knew, the gate was blown and there were greenskins running all over the fort. Some of them must have sneaked in and killed the sentries before the others attacked.

P-M: You are asking us to believe that an Ork unit infiltrated your position, eliminating the sentries, and then set charges to detonate the main gate?

LG: I did not believe myself, sirs. We saw them for a moment, in the darkness, when the gate was first blown. They were wiry and sinewy, for Orks, wearing hardly any clothing. The cunning savages had painted camouflage over their skins and their heads were painted with red warpaint, and all we could clearly see were their red eyes glaring at us from the shadows. My platoon opened fire on them, but they must have slipped into the darkness before our salvo, none of them fell.

P-M: Half-glimpsed shadows? Orks wearing camouflage? Do you take us for imbeciles? Orks are barbaric and entirely single-minded. Army dogma, which has served us well for ten thousand years, teaches us this. Orks come on in a great horde, they do not slink and sneak in the shade. Are you saying that our ancestors, the illustrious commanders of the past, are fools?

LG: I'm not saying anything of the sort, sirs! All I'm saying is they never fought these Orks. And I pray I never have to fight them again...

P-M: Your prayers are answered, Lieutenant. Guards! Take the prisoner to the holding cells to await execution for cowardice and incompetence.

Extract from transcript of Courts Martial investigating the fall of Lathir Outpost.

WAZZDAKKA GUTZMEK

A hush fell amongst the Yoofs that had gathered around the old and gnarled Mekaniak. "Let me tellz ya about Wazzdakka Gutzmek," he began "da greatest bad Ork bikeboy ov dem all!"

"I was a pale-skinned yoof like yerselves da the first time I met 'im. 'E weren't much olda den meself, and 'e was a Mek too, but yer see, 'e liked riding da bikez and buggiez wot he made more dan 'e liked making dem. In no time at all 'e went and joined da Kult of Speed, and den he started to get really outa hand. Even so, 'e might have got away wiv it for a bit longer, 'cause he was as tough 'n 'ard a fighta as I've ever seen – and I've seen a few, I tell ya! – if 'e adun't gone an' smashed up da Warboss's fleet o' brand new wagons wid his warbike. But dat was Gutzmek for ya; 'e never could resist a dare…

Anywayz, 'e went and got 'imself banished, and went off to lead the life of a bad Ork bikeboy. Now 'e didn't want to ride round wid no pack of da ladz ('e always was a bit strange like dat), and so 'e rode off on 'is own after 'e was banished, an' disappeared into da wilderness for a time… and den he came back on dis 'uge great warbike! He rampaged all round our camp – to get 'is own back on da Boss, for banishing 'im like – and then rode off. HA! It was a laff I'll tell you, wot wiv da Boss jumping up an' down wiv rage, bashing all an' sundry on the noggin if they came too close. Happy dayz…

Wot's dat?!? Oh yeah, what happened to ole Gutzmek next. Well since den he's appeared all over da place. Dere's some wot even say dat 'e only getz offa 'is bike when 'es gotta do some fixin on it, and dat da rest ov da time he just lives in da saddle, kept awake wiv some brew wot's given to him by a Bad Dok wot he knows, and some ovva's say dat Mork an' Gork magik 'im from planet to planet so 'e can fight wiv da Boyz wot need 'im da most. I don't know if any of dat's true, but I do know 'e'll fight for any Boss what'll pay 'im in da spare parts and teef he needs to keep dat great warbike running, and 'e's still da toughest, meanest, greenest, most fightinest bad Ork bikeboy dere is. I should know, ya see, cause I knew 'im when 'e was a yoof…"

WAZZDAKKA GUTZMEK										
	Points	WS	BS	S	T	W	I	A	Ld	Sv
Wazzdakka	75	4	2	4	4(5)	2	3	3	7	5+

Any Ork army of at least 1,000 points may joined by Wazzdakka and he counts as an HQ choice for the army. He must be used exactly as described below, and may not be given any additional equipment from the Ork Armoury.

Wargear: Twin-linked autocannon, kustom blasta, power claw.

SPECIAL RULES

Warbiker: Wazzdakka is mounted on a warbike and follows all the normal rules for warbikes. He can fire the autocannons during the first round of close combat if he charges just like warbikers firing their big shootas, however he may not fire the kustom blasta in close combat.

Too Many (Big) Gunz: Wazzdakka's bike has been upgraded with captured twin-linked autocannon and a kustom blasta built by Wazzdakka himself. These may all be fired at the same time at the same target. As for warbikes the guns are all limited to a maximum range of 18".

Speed Freek: The Ork player must make a Leadership test for Wazzdakka at the start of each of his turns. If the test is passed all is well and the Ork player can move Wazzdakka normally. If the test is failed Wazzdakka feels a sudden need for speed! Move Wazzdakka 12+D6" forward in a straight line in whichever direction he is pointing. If Wazzdakka is in close combat or accompanying a unit at the time, he leaves it with no further effects on either side. If he moves into difficult ground make tests as necessary, if he moves off the table then it's bye bye! Wazzdakka (though he doesn't count as a casualty for victory point purposes).

Scrabbla: Wazzdakka's warbike is kept clean and shiny by his Gretchin assistant Fixit. In combat Fixit hangs on for grim death and helps to keep the bike going by hanging off it as a counterbalance or even jumping off and pushing occasionally. To represent this Wazzdakka may re-roll Difficult Terrain tests.

Independent Character: Wazzdakka is an independent character and follows all the special rules as given in the Warhammer 40,000 rulebook. He may only join a mob of warbikes.

ORK TRIBES AND HIERARCHY

The basic Ork fighting unit is the Warband, an organisation roughly equivalent to a Company in human military terms.

A warband can comprise anywhere between thirty and twenty thousand warriors plus their associated war machines and is commanded by a large and aggressive Ork chieftain, called the Warboss.

The Warband is split into a number of mobs, with each mob usually led by an Ork noble, referred to as a 'Boss' or 'Nob' (pronounced knob, not nobe).

Warbands are usually part of a tribe but can be independent. The tribe is ruled over by a powerful Warlord, the most dangerous and ambitious Warboss who has fought his way to dominance over his kind.

A tribe can comprise anything from several hundred to tens of thousands of Orks and will claim control of an entire continent or world. More commonly a vaguely habitable Ork world will sustain several Ork tribes in a more-or-less perpetual state of war with each other until they join in a Waaagh! against non Orks.

During a Waaagh! especially potent Ork Warlords sometimes succeed in forging an empire from their conquests (though their organisation is more feudalistic than imperial). The largest and most stable of these is undoubtedly the Ork empire of Charadon, which has survived for several thousand years under a succession of Warlords. Warlords commanding empires usually select their own title (after all who's going to argue!). Hence the empire of Charadon is ruled over by the Arch-Arsonist, Octarius by an Over-Fiend, Jagga by a Great Tyrant and so forth.

Cutting across warband and tribal boundaries are the Ork clans. The Clans embody a philosophy (for want of a better term) among Orks, each clan emphasising particular elements of Ork culture above others. For example, the Goff clan embraces aggression, hardiness and hand-to-hand combat as true Orky virtues while the Evil Sunz clan is dedicated to speed, lightning attack and having the snazziest vehicles.

Typically a tribe and its component warbands will exhibit the characteristics of a single clan. Some Orks become obsessed with clan ideals and it becomes something akin to a religion for them. Where this is the case the Ork will seek out like-minded individuals and join with them to create a warband which completely exemplifies the purest traits of their clan [See notes below]. However most tribes are less dominated by the clan ideal, and clan values merely serve to instill a sense of unity and make a common enemy of tribes which are part of other clans.

During an Ork Waaagh! warbands are destroyed and reformed from whatever survivors are available. In these times warbands or even whole tribes may emerge which comprise members of many different clans thrown together by the fortunes of war. In spite of their normal antipathy Orks will fight alongside each other for the duration of the Waaagh! as they become caught up in the tide of Orkish aggression.

At the conclusion of the Waaagh! a mixed warband or tribe will usually break up under the pressure of inter-clan rivalry. However warbands commanded by an especially determined leader will stubbornly hang together, abandoning their previous clan and tribe affiliations to become Freebooters, Orks who fight for profit and glory.

CLANS	DOMINANT CLAN CHARACTERISTICS
GOFFS	Ferocity, obsession with hand-to-hand combat.
BAD MOONS	Wealth, expensive weaponry and armour.
BLOOD AXES	Cunning, treachery.
DEATH SKULLS	Expert looters and scavengers.
SNAKE BITES	Nomadic, preference for 'simple' weaponry and a mistrust of vehicles and mechanisms.
EVIL SUNZ	Obsession with vehicles and speed.

TRIBES WITH A DOMINANT CLAN CHARACTER

GOFFS: Skull Cleavers, White Fangs, Black Slayers

BAD MOONS: Crooked Moon, Yellow Skulls, Krushers

BLOOD AXES: Red Knives, Blades, Stabbers

DEATH SKULLS: Wreckers, Killers, Red Eyes

SNAKE BITES: White Spiders, Skorpions, Kobras, Chargers

EVIL SUNZ: Death Wheelz, Blitzers, Sharks

FREEBOOTER TRIBES & WARBANDS

Blood Handz (tribe), Green Death (tribe), Red Skulls, Arsonists, Jolly Ork (pirates).

"You know not the valour of the Orks; they believe that the more enemy there are the more glory they will win and the more plunder they will secure."

Inquisitor Yuan, of the Ordo Xenos addressing the regimental commanders at Gundastol

"The Orks are the pinnacle of creation. For them, the great struggle is won. They have evolved a society which knows no stress or angst. Who are we to judge them? We Eldar who have failed, or the Humans, on the road to ruin in their turn. And why? Because we sought answers to questions that an Ork wouldn't even bother to ask! We see a culture that is strong and despise it as crude."

Uthan the Perverse.

*S*irs, what follows is a report filed by Genetor-Major Lukas Anzion, based upon observations conducted in the Appelor system. I have taken the liberty of abridging this report down to its fundamental facts – in some areas Anzion has indulged himself in such a degree of speculation in the original as to render it highly suspect.

...To understand the Orkoid species, one must first be aware of their, so far, unique xenological traits. When I refer to the Orkoid species, I refer to all aspects of the green-skinned society, from the dominant "Orks", through the smaller "Gretchin", "Snotlings" and the sub-animal "Squigs". Although physically and anatomically diverse, these different species all share a common genetic base.

Every Orkoid is a symbiosis of two biologies within a single structure. As well as a standard gene-spiral [See fig 453/b] every Orkoid also possesses a spiral of an algal/fungal base. The standard genetic structure of an Orkoid remains essentially the same as that of Man, in that it dictates the majority of the creature's form and biological processes. However, it is the plant-like secondary structure, which gives Orks their resilience to damage and is the key to understanding their procreative cycle.

The algal cellular sub-system is comparable in many ways to the human bloodstream. It is bound within their anatomical structure at a molecular level and works

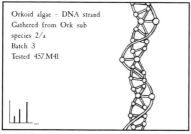

Orkoid algae – DNA strand
Gathered from Ork sub
species 2/a
Batch 3
Tested 457.M41

fig 453/b

alongside the standard genetic and biological processes. The Orkoid algal structure responds to damage in combination with blood clotting and so forth. This means that even large wounds will be covered with a hard, skin-like layer within a few hours of the injury occurring, as the algal cells rapidly replicate to repair the damage.

We found that however serious the injury, if the Orkoid did not die immediately from shock it was unlikely to die from loss of blood or organ trauma. This regenerative process is aided by the Orks' crude medical knowledge – whole limbs can be grafted on, organs freely swapped,

wounds stapled shut and so forth with only 0.0023% chance of tissue rejection. The Orkoid's ability to withstand such usually mortal wounds makes them such a fearsome prospect.

[Note to Fabricator-General: Please have our Imperial Commanders examine the dedication with which we conduct battlefield cleansing techniques. No matter how mortal a wound looks, a live Ork must be dispatched in a conclusively lethal manner such as beheading and disembowelling. Ferire Cum Ultio.]

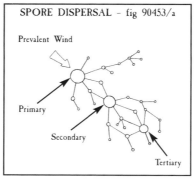

SPORE DISPERSAL – fig 90453/a

Prevalent Wind

Primary

Secondary

Tertiary

Despite the symbiosis of the two cell structures, each has its own unique gene-strand [See fig 90453/a]. The Orkoids' standard strand defines what type it is [Ork, Gretchin etc] while the algal gene-strand remains consistent, whatever sub-species of Orkoid. This common heritage is remarkable and leaves me with no other conclusion than that of genetic manipulation and re-structuring some time in the Orkoids' distant past.

Anzion goes on to elucidate at some length regarding his theory of Orkoids being a genetically engineered "survivor race", something I find hard to credit in light of Mankind's manifest destiny to rule the galaxy.

We have long known Orkoids to be tougher than humans, we now have the evidence to explain the nature and

source of this increased resilience. However, the algal sub-strand is a much more dangerous threat, due to the strange manner in which Orkoids procreate.

The algal matter within an Orkoid contains the genetic make-up of all the Orkoid species, not just the codes of life for the species carrying it. Throughout an Orkoid's life it sheds spore-like cells containing the entire genetic code of the Orkoid races. These are shed in an unconscious manner much as a human replicates skin cells and sheds the dead tissue them without realising it. These spores are microscopic in nature and fulfil a number of functions. Firstly, they can be detected by the highly sensitive nasal organs of the Orkoids, conveying a variety of information such as status, age and so on. It also enables an Orkoid to locate other Orkoids over quite a wide distance [several miles, given wind strength, direction and so on].

The spores are also the reproductive mechanism of an Orkoid. When they settle in the correct conditions, the spore will evolve into the species whose genetic structure it contains. Orkoid spores require dank, dark locations to activate, much like other algaes and fungi. Caves and forests are the most successful spawning sites for Orkoid spores, but even in the most arid conditions, a proportionate number of spores will still land within a site suitable for development. The spore grows downwards first, with tiny rootlets that seek out nutrition and moisture just like any other plant. However, once the algal stage is established, Orkoid cells are generated in tandem development, and the

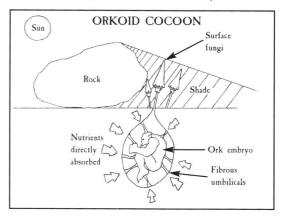

ORKOID COCOON

Sun

Rock

Surface fungi

Shade

Nutrients directly absorbed

Ork embryo

Fibrous umbilicals

Orkoid literally grows like any vegetative tumour. It's an amazing process to observe! It takes quite a long time for an Ork to grow, while the smaller Squigs, Snotlings and so forth take a proportionately shorter length of time to develop.

Orkoids do not emerge singly once they have reached the required degree of maturity. Due to the nature of the spore process, dozens or even hundreds of Orkoids will emerge within a short space of time. The Orkoid algal cells contain the gene-strands for the diverse Orkoid species, and so a single type of Orkoid can still propagate an entire community on its own. Gretchin, Orks, Snotlings and Squigs can all be generated from the same source, settle in the same area and grow proportionately. The Squigs emerge first and breed faster, creating a substantial food source, followed quickly by Snotlings who can start to prepare the area. Then the Gretchin arrive and pave the way for the emerging Orks to establish a whole thriving Community. Perhaps within a year of the spores landing the Orkoids will be thriving quite easily. Unus Creare Omnis.

Laboratory tests show that lone spores, even if they land within an agreeable environment, generally will only evolve into a simple fungus. The rare few that evolve into one of the higher Orkoid forms and manages to hatch generally wither and die within a very short period of time [a matter of hours rather than days] and show much regressed development compared with a newly emerging Orkoid amongst its own kind. Our studies of Orkoid growth and migration also prove that spores which land close to an existing settlement also suffer this fate.

We can find no decisive physical reason for this pattern. Together with some of my colleagues, I have formulated the Anzion Theorem of Psychic-Physical Growth of Orkoids...

...In essence Anzion speculates that some sort of psychic resonance limits spore growth in proximity to established Ork settlements, ensuring an even spread of colonisation. While Anzion's observations may lead him to conclude this he is the first to admit this is baseless conjecture, Anzion goes on to discuss the generation of spores, concluding that Orkoids generate a greater number of spores in the latter stages of their life span, with a final mass release after death. If correct this

observation means that old battlefields and worlds liberated from the Orks are exceedingly vulnerable to re-infestation at a later stage. It is also possible that ships could unwittingly transport spores from world to world. Anzion gets rather carried away with this concept and contemplates the dangers of infestation of Mars or Holy Terra by Orkoid spores – a farcical idea, although I have always been puzzled by reports of Orks killed in the lower reaches of Hive cities on Necromunda and Tarsulas....

[Note to Fabricator General: Please inform our Imperial Commanders that Orkoid bodies must be thoroughly burnt, disintegrated or dumped into the ether.]

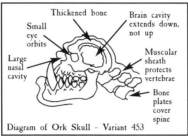

Diagram of Ork Skull – Variant 453

To make matters worse, the dormant Orkoids are almost undetectable with only a patch of common fungus or algal growth to indicate something is amiss. Emerging Orkoids are almost at their most mature state, almost fully grown, much like a human adolescent. Within a short period, the Orkoid will have all the characteristics of a full adult, including the facility of speech as well as understanding fairly complex mechanics and automotive processes. Skills seem to be genetically engineered into Orkoids. Their physicians, scientists and other specialists have their knowledge inherent in them. Think of the possibilities for training our own fighting forces if we could alter their genetic make-up so that they instinctively knew how to strip and clean a weapon, fight in close melee and had a rudimentary knowledge of strategy and tactics. Even with the genetically engineered Adeptus Astartes, it takes almost ten years of intensive therapy and physical alteration to perfect what an Ork knows instinctively! Bellator Natus.

Lastly, by fighting Orks we make them stronger. As insane as it may sound, the Orkoids [Orks more than other sub-species] literally thrive on warfare. Most Orks have similar physical dimensions when they have fully matured. However,

the more belligerent and aggressive the Ork is, the larger it grows. Due to the way the Orks' hierarchy is structured, with fighting to determine ranking, the most highly ranking Orks are the largest. This is not because they are better at fighting but that a belligerent, aggressive Ork – one who has beaten his opponent – will put on several pounds of additional muscle tissue over the next two to three weeks. Orks preparing to challenge a superior will also put on weight as their psyche develops the necessary aggression, and so the higher ranking Ork will be able to detect this and fight the usurper before it has reached full development. Over extended fighting, the average size of fighting Orks has been known to increase by several inches in height and almost a stone in solid muscular tissue.

It is not within my purpose to speculate on ways to combat these beasts, but to provide information to those who must. I myself am most alarmed by these findings, and never again will I mock our green-skinned adversaries no matter how crude and seemingly stupid they are [note, there is no evidence to suggest an Ork possesses an intelligence any less than a human – cultural styles merely dictate a more straightforward approach to problem-solving and a lack of theoretical aspect and conceptualising until completion].

Your obd't servant Genetor-Major Anzion

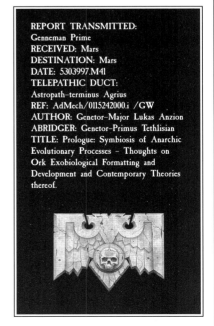

REPORT TRANSMITTED:
Genneman Prime
RECEIVED: Mars
DESTINATION: Mars
DATE: 5303997.M41
TELEPATHIC DUCT:
Astropath-terminus Agrius
REF: AdMech/0115242000.i /GW
AUTHOR: Genetor-Major Lukas Anzion
ABRIDGER: Genetor-Primus Tethlisian
TITLE: Prologue: Symbiosis of Anarchic Evolutionary Processes – Thoughts on Ork Exobiological Formatting and Development and Contemporary Theories thereof.

Ref: AdMech/0115242004/GW
Author: Genetor Lukas Anzion
Title: Chapter XVII: Genetic predetermination – Hereditary skill acquisition within the Ork caste and professional social structure.

It has long been known that the psychological aspects of a human is, in part, determined by their genetic heritage. Certain geno-types are disposed towards pre-determined personality traits which, in turn, informs the process of learning and aptitude. In Orks this genetic predetermination is also present, though in a different and even more pronounced fashion. It appears that not only is aptitude towards certain aspects of the culture present in the gene-structure, actual skills and knowledge are also encoded into the genetic strand.

The best analogy one can think of is to compare this knowledge with the basic motor skills present in a human child. A human child does not have to be taught how to breathe, how to make its heart beat or how to employ the many thousands of other biological functions that are already operating at the time of birth. In a similar way, an Ork predisposed towards science and mechanics [Meks] has an encoded knowledge of basic physics and mechanical engineering theory. However, this knowledge is as subconscious as the baby's ability to breathe; it is an unconscious competence in whatever field the individual is created for. In the same way that a child can learn to alter their breathing, hold their breath or, through exercise, improve the capacity of their lungs and vascular system, so too can an Ork build upon these innate skills through the normal process of learning. The two major skill groups created in this fashion are the castes known as Doks and Meks.

Doks are the Orkoid medical experts, who have a rough and ready knowledge of Orkoid xenological composition. Due to the hardiness of Ork physiognomy, Ork surgical and medical techniques are as crude but effective as the rest of their technology. Wounds can be easily stitched tight with wire or stapled, while broken bones need little in the way of setting to speed the healing process. Internal injuries are similarly treated, and the multiple redundancy of many Ork organs also provides plenty of transplant donors for those in need of such measures [although the donation is not always made voluntarily, particularly where the casualty is an important member of the society]. Orks are generally loathe to undergo medical treatment.

This is for two reasons. Firstly, many Orks consider such an activity as a sign of weakness, and there is a strong compulsion throughout Ork society for natural selection to take its course – the weak must die out so that the spores of the stronger may thrive and grow into stronger Orks. Secondly, the gene-determination of Doks imbues them with a highly active curiosity, coupled with a callous disregard for the well-being of those they treat. Many Doks see surgery and treatment as a means for experimentation upon their patient, and often Orks undergo horrendous and entirely unnecessary surgical procedures to satisfy the Dok's inquisitiveness or as a trial for a new procedure of prosthetic. Such treatments are not tested in any scientific manner before their employment and horribly disabling injuries can result from such procedures.

Meks are similarly driven to experimentation, although in the field of mechanical rather than medical science. Much of the weaponry and wargear used by the Orks, as well as more mundane artefacts, are designed and built by the Meks. As much of their knowledge is subconscious, the vast majority of Meks never truly understand what they are creating, or the exact functions of how they work. As Orks are poor rationalists, this can lead to rather unlikely conventions.

For example, it is widely believed by Orks that machines painted in a red colour operate faster. This could have come about by the following situation. A Mek builds two vehicles which, as far as it is aware of, are exactly the same except for the fact that one is painted red and the other yellow. However, due to some unseen variation in fuel, lubrication, or some other factor, the red vehicle in fact travels faster. To the Ork, the only conceivable explanation for this is that the vehicle travels faster because it is red.

However, as disturbing as it sounds, these 'facts' become true. Red Ork vehicles do travel perceptibly faster than those of other colours, even when all other design aspects are nominally the same. Similarly, many captured Ork weapons and items of equipment should not work, and indeed do not work unless wielded by an Ork. I believe this is linked to the strong psychic aura surrounding all Orkoids and have developed the Anzion Theorem of Orkoid Mechamorphic Resonant Kinetics. I theorise that many Ork inventions work because the Orks themselves think that they should work. The strong telekinetic abilities of the Orks' subconscious somehow ensure that the machinery or weaponry functions as desired.

As astounding as it may be, we cannot make any other conclusion based on the evidence to hand.

> Orkses is never beaten in battle. If we win we win, if we die we die so it don't count as beat. If we runs for it we don't die neither, so we can always come back for anuvver go, see!
>
> **Anon**